Palgrave Studies in Cybercrime and Cybersecurity

Series Editors
Marie-Helen Maras
John Jay College of Criminal Justice CUN
New York, NY, USA

Thomas J. Holt
Michigan State University
East Lansing, MI, USA

This book series addresses the urgent need to advance knowledge in the fields of cybercrime and cybersecurity. Because the exponential expansion of computer technologies and use of the Internet have greatly increased the access by criminals to people, institutions, and businesses around the globe, the series will be international in scope. It provides a home for cutting-edge long-form research. Further, the series seeks to spur conversation about how traditional criminological theories apply to the online environment. The series welcomes contributions from early career researchers as well as established scholars on a range of topics in the cybercrime and cybersecurity fields.

More information about this series at
http://www.palgrave.com/gp/series/14637

Anna Costanza Baldry
Catherine Blaya
David P. Farrington
Editors

International Perspectives on Cyberbullying

Prevalence, Risk Factors and
Interventions

palgrave
macmillan

Editors
Anna Costanza Baldry
Department of Psychology
Università degli Studi della Campania
Luigi Vanvitelli
Caserta, Italy

Catherine Blaya
UER Pédagogie Spécialisée
HEP du Canton de Vaud
Lausanne, Switzerland

David P. Farrington
Institute of Criminology
University of Cambridge
Cambridge, UK

Palgrave Studies in Cybercrime and Cybersecurity
ISBN 978-3-030-10342-2   ISBN 978-3-319-73263-3   (eBook)
https://doi.org/10.1007/978-3-319-73263-3

Cover illustration: Oleksandr Haisonok / Alamy Stock Vector
Inside image: Original design by Allesandro Vincenti, 12 years old

Printed on acid-free paper

This Palgrave Macmillan imprint is published by the registered company Springer International Publishing AG part of Springer Nature.
The registered company address is: Gewerbestrasse 11, 6330 Cham, Switzerland

Foreword

Cyberbullying, together with other kinds of risks on social media and the internet, is an emergent problem of this century. Even if the phenomenon itself was reported in the 1990s (sometimes called by other names such as 'electronic aggression'), public awareness of the issue, and research on the topic, only really emerged in the early 2000s. Surveys of publications on cyberbullying (Zych et al. 2015; Smith and Berkkun 2017) demonstrate an exponential increase over the last 15 years. Smith and Berkkun (2017), analyzing Web of Science publications from 2000 to 2015, found an average number of 33.6 articles per year; but this built up from a very slow start during the first 7 years of this century, then increased rapidly: from 2000 to 2006, a small trickle of articles (range 0 to 5 per year); from 2007 to 2011, a substantial but still modest number of articles (range 14 to 38 per year); but from 2012 on, a very large number of articles (range 85 to 131 per year). The year 2015 saw 131 articles, or about 2.5 new articles every week. Most articles (454 in all) reported empirical data, with 30 of these (9%) providing information on resources and interventions.

Although a life-span phenomenon, most of the research and attention on cyberbullying has been on children and young people, where it appears most prevalent. We know that involvement in cyberbullying, notably as a victim but also as a bystander or perpetrator, has negative consequences for all those involved, and also for the school climate (Kowalski et al.

2014; Astor and Benbenishty in press; and many chapters in this book). So what has the increased public awareness and the increased research effort achieved? There are certainly now more resources for young people, teachers and parents, mainly on websites or in the form of leaflets and advice packs. Are these helping to reduce the problem?

Some media hype about an increasing epidemic of cyberbullying is overstated. Obviously, the prevalence of cyberbullying has increased in this century, as penetration of the internet has increased, and smartphones became readily available from 2007. However, the evidence about changes in prevalence from recent years is mixed (see also Chap. 3). A partial follow-up of the EU Kids Online study, which assessed cyberbullying rates in 25 European countries in 2010, was reported by Mascheroni and Cuman (2014). In all seven countries in the follow-up, cyber victimization rates were somewhat higher in 2013 than in 2010, the average increasing from 9% to 12%. In contrast, a 10-year longitudinal study in 109 schools in Maryland, USA, found some increase in cyber victimization scores from 2005/06 to 2009/10 (from around 6% to 8%) but then a decline to 2013/14 (to around 5%) (Waasdorp et al. 2017).

While much has been done to understand and prevent cyberbullying, much more remains to be done. This book makes a significant contribution to such ongoing efforts. The Tabby online project described in Chap. 2 (and with findings reported in another six chapters), plus the reviews of the situation in Canada, the USA, and the UK and Ireland, are valuable resources in this endeavor. Cyberbullying is obviously an international problem and, despite national and cultural differences, there is much that we can learn from knowledge and experiences gained in different countries. Similar endeavors are also underway in drawing evidence on cyberbullying (as well as offline bullying) in Eastern countries such as Japan, South Korea, Mainland China and Hong Kong (Smith et al. 2016), and India and Australia (Smith et al. 2018). Especially useful in this book are the practical conclusions and policy recommendations in Chap. 12. Although unfortunately there is no one silver bullet to stop cyberbullying, the 10 silver bullet recommendations in this final chapter are succinct and sensible. They deserve to be widely discussed and implemented. The editors are to be congratulated in bringing together this valuable collection and in drawing out such important policy recommendations for the future.

Goldsmiths, University of London   Peter K. Smith
London, UK

References

Astor, R. A., & Benbenishty, R. (in press). *Bullying, school violence, and climate in evolving contexts: Culture, organization, and time.* New York: Oxford University Press.

Kowalski, R. M., Giumetti, G. W., Schroeder, A. N., & Lattanner, M. R. (2014). Bullying in the digital age: A critical review and meta-analysis of cyberbullying research among youth. *Psychological Bulletin, 140*(4), 1073–1137. https://doi.org/10.1037/a0035618.

Mascheroni, G., & Cuman, A. (2014). *Net Children Go Mobile: Final report* (with country fact sheets). Deliverables D6.4 and D5.2. Milano: Educatt. Retrieved from netchildrengomobile.eu/ncgm/wp-content/uploads/2013/07/NCGM_FinalReport_Country_DEF.pdf

Smith, P. K., & Berkkun, F. (2017). How research on cyberbullying has developed. In C. McGuckin & L. Corcoran (Eds.), *Bullying and cyberbullying: Prevalence, psychological impacts and intervention strategies* (pp. 11–27). Hauppauge: Nova Science.

Smith, P. K., Kwak, K., & Toda, Y. (Eds.). (2016). *School bullying in different cultures: Eastern and western perspectives.* Cambridge: Cambridge University Press.

Smith, P. K., Sundaram, S., Spears, B., Blaya, C., Schafer, M., & Sandhu, D. (Eds.). (2018). *Bullying, cyberbullying and pupil well-being in schools: Comparing European, Australian and Indian perspectives.* Cambridge: Cambridge University Press.

Waasdorp, T. E., Pas, E. T., Zablotsky, B., & Bradshaw, C. P. (2017). Ten-year trends in bullying and related attitudes among 4th-to 12th-graders. *Pediatrics, 139*(6), 1–8. https://doi.org/10.1542/peds.2016-2615.

Zych, I., Ortega-Ruiz, R., & del Rey, R. (2015). Scientific research on bullying and cyberbullying: Where have we been and where are we going. *Aggression and Violent Behavior, 24*, 188–198. https://doi.org/10.1016/j.avb.2015.05.015

Preface

We have written and edited this book to share our knowledge and experience on the topic of cyberbullying and cybervictimization in 10 different countries. We present some results from an innovative project and program addressing threat assessment as a new approach to early intervention to make students aware of the risks they run online either as victims, bullies, or both.

The threat assessment approach is based on the extensive knowledge in the criminology and social sciences fields on risk assessment. The assessment of the severity of threats and what they may lead to is based on risk assessment principles. To prevent future antisocial actions, it is important to identify static (stable) and dynamic (changeable) risk factors to establish the role they play in cyberbullying. It is also relevant to develop tailored intervention programs that target some of the risk factors and aim to strengthen the protective factors.

During the over five years of implementation of the TABBY *(Threat Assessment of Bullying Behaviour among Youngsters)* project, we have worked with thousands of children of many countries, cultures, languages, and ages. They all gave us joy in what we are doing: on one hand to make them more able to understand that going online and saying stupid things about a schoolmate does not mean that you are a bad person but that you need to understand about one's own and others' feelings, roles of social skills, social norms or group pressure. On the other to help those who suffer from cyberbullying to acknowledge they have no responsibility nor fault.

Sadly, it is often true that nobody really has taken the time to explain to children about the Internet and its risks and how and to whom to ask for help in cases of annoying things happening.

This project was developed thanks to the contribution of the European Commission Justice Department, JUST/2011/DAP/AG/3259, that put together a team of experts, most of whom contributed to this book.

We would like to thank the publisher for supporting our work; the teachers, students, and heads of schools who enthusiastically took part in the implementation of the project. They gave us the opportunity to address the risks associated with the Internet, and to address online risks and encourage concerned and educated youngsters.

In the first two chapters of the book, we give a general overview of cyberbullying and cybervictimization, looking at the problem according to the risk and needs assessment approach. We then present and explain the TABBY intervention program and how it was delivered.

In the following three chapters, excellent contributors from Canada, the USA, the UK, and Ireland provide an updated overview of the situation in their own countries with regard to prevalence rates and programs implemented regarding cyberbullying.

In the next part of the book, contributors from six different European countries present the situation in their country and some significant results and information about cyberbullying.

In the conclusion of the book, we try to draw some general and country-specific recommendations. What we realized, by working with different languages and different cultures, is that the Internet is indeed the same all over and children need to be instructed but also protected.

We are very grateful to our publisher and to all our contributors for helping to make this volume a comprehensive, up-to-date, and authoritative source of information about cyberbullying in many different countries.

Department of Psychology   Anna Costanza Baldry
Caserta, Italy
UER Pédagogie Spécialisée   Catherine Blaya
Lausanne, Switzerland
Institute of Criminology   David P. Farrington
Cambridge, UK

Contents

List of Authors

Christina Athanasiades is Assistant Professor of Counselling Psychology in the Department of Psychology of Aristotle University of Thessaloniki.

Anna Costanza Baldry is Full Professor at the Department of Psychology of the University of Campania "Luigi Vanvitelli" in Forensic and Social Psychology.

Catherine Blaya is Full Professor at University of Teacher Education of State of Vaud (Lausanne, Switzerland).

Sonya Cacace is a psychologist, who graduated with honors in Psychology Applied to Institutional Contexts at the University of Campania "Luigi Vanvitelli".

Juan Calmaestra is Reader at the Department of Psychology of the Universidad de Córdoba in Developmental and Educational Psychology

Wendy Craig is Professor and Head of Psychology, Queen's University Canada, Scientific Co-Director of PREVNet.

Dorothy L. Espelage is Professor of Psychology, Department of Psychology of University of Florida, USA.

David P. Farrington is Emeritus Professor of Psychological Criminology in the Institute of Criminology, University of Cambridge

Hannah Gaffney is a Ph.D. candidate at the Institute of Criminology, University of Cambridge.

Tatiana García-Vélez is Lecturer at the Department of Developmental and Educational Psychology of the Universidad Autónoma de Madrid.

Jun Sung Hong is Assistant Professor of Social Work, School of Social Work, Wayne State University, USA, and Assistant Professor, Department of Social Welfare, Sungkyunkwan University, South Korea.

Andreas Kapardis is Full Professor of Legal Psychology in the Department of Law, University of Cyprus.

Antonio Maldonado is Associate Professor at the Department of Developmental and Educational Psychology of the Universidad Autónoma de Madrid.

Bálint Néray Ph.D., is a postdoctoral fellow with the Science Networks in Communities research group at Northwestern University, Chicago.

Katalin Parti Ph.D., is a senior research fellow with the National Institute of Criminology Hungary, and Lecturer at the Doctoral School of Police Sciences and Law Enforcement at National University of Public Service Budapest.

Debra Pepler is Distinguished Research Professor of Psychology, YORK University CANADA, and Scientific Co-Director of PREVNet.

George Poyiadjis is a school psychologist in private practice in Cyprus.

Julia Riddell is a Ph.D. candidate in Clinical-Developmental Psychology, York University, Canada

Andrea Schmidt is Assistant Professor at the Department of Science of Society and Economy at Moholy-Nagy University of Art and Design Budapest and a research fellow with the Institute of Sociology, Research Center of Social Sciences at Hungarian Academy of Sciences.

Peter K. Smith is Emeritus Professor of Psychology, Goldsmiths College, University of London, U.K. His most extensive research has been on bullying and violence in schools, and recent publications include the edited collection (with Keumjoo Kwak and Yuichi Toda) *School Bullying in Different Cultures: Eastern and Western Perspectives* (2016). In 2015 he was awarded the William Thierry Preyer award for Excellence in Research on Human Development by the European Society for Developmental Psychology.

Anna Sorrentino Ph.D., is a clinical and developmental psychologist and a researcher at the Department of Psychology of the University of Campania "Luigi Vanvitelli".

Alberto Valido is Project Coordinator in Espelage Violence Prevention Laboratory, University of Florida, USA.

List of Tables

Part I

Cyberbullying, Cybervictimization and Risk Factors

1

Cyberbullying and Cybervictimization

Anna Costanza Baldry, David P. Farrington,
Anna Sorrentino, and Catherine Blaya

Definition, Nature, and Prevalence

In its first stage, research on cyberbullying focused on trying to define the phenomenon and check on the possible similarities or discrepancies between offline school bullying and online bullying. The very first studies (Smith et al. 2008; Kowalski et al. 2008) adapted the Olweus definition of bullying (Olweus 1995) to the online world, simply adding the precision that bullying was performed via electronic means of communication within the cyberspace:

A. C. Baldry (✉) • A. Sorrentino
Department of Psychology, Università degli Studi della Campania Luigi
Vanvitelli, Caserta, Italy

D. P. Farrington
Institute of Criminology, University of Cambridge, Cambridge, UK

C. Blaya
UER Pédagogie Spécialisée - HEP du Canton de Vaud, Lausanne, Switzerland

© The Author(s) 2018
A. C. Baldry et al. (eds.), *International Perspectives on Cyberbullying*, Palgrave Studies in
Cybercrime and Cybersecurity, https://doi.org/10.1007/978-3-319-73263-3_1

an aggressive intentional act carried out by a group or individual, using electronic forms of contact, repeatedly and over time against a victim who cannot easily defend him or herself. (Smith et al. 2008, p. 376)

The authors resort to the same mechanism as for bullying, that is repetition, intentionality, and imbalance of power, and stress that offline bullying was more common within the school environment while cyberbullying happened often off the school grounds (Smith et al. 2008).

If to start with, researchers argued that cyberbullying was the 'same wine' in a new bottle (Li 2007), further investigations showed there were some important differences between traditional school bullying and cyberbullying and overcame the first restrictive definition to focus on the characteristics of online communication. As a matter of fact, the cyberspace facilitates anonymity through the use of pseudonyms (Steffgen and Konig 2009) that contribute to increasing the feeling of insecurity of the victims and that can disinhibit individuals who would have never engaged in bullying in the face-to-face world. The distance between the perpetrators and their victims reduces the feelings of empathy towards the targets (O'Brien and Moules 2010). Moreover, the dissemination capacities offered online are huge, with a wide audience and an unlimited number of potential supporters who could contribute to the dissemination of the humiliation or degrading messages/pictures in a snowball effect, and cyberbullying can be ongoing (7 days a week, 24 hours a day). As a consequence, victims have no respite.

Within the COST (European Cooperation in Science and Technology) project IS0801 '*Cyberbullying: coping with negative and enhancing positive uses of new technologies, in relationships in educational settings*', research was conducted to get a more accurate definition and understanding of what was cyberbullying within Europe (Smith and Steffgen 2013). It focused on the students' perception and definition of cyberbullying and showed that there were some differences between the participating countries: 'Cybermobbing' was more used in Germany, while in Spain the students would refer to 'harassment via Internet or mobile phone' and in Italy the terms used were virtual or cyberbullying. Further investigation on the characteristics of cyberbullying (repetition, intentionality, anonymity, imbalance of power, and private vs. public) was conducted within six European countries. The findings showed that the imbalance of power, intentionality, and anonymity were core common characteristics for the participants in the survey, whatever the country, although intentionality and anonymity were less important in Italy and Germany than in Sweden, Spain, Estonia, and France (Menesini et al. 2012).

As stressed by Berne and colleagues (2013) as well as by Corcoran et al. (2015), although 'cyberbullying' is the most used terminology, there is a great variety of concepts and measuring tools to evaluate online aggression. The validity and reliability of all of these terms has not been investigated and the prevalence of cyberbullying varies much from one study to the other, including within the same country. While some researchers use the term 'cyberbullying' (Smith et al. 2008; Calvete et al. 2010), others refer to more specific terms such as electronic bullying, cyberaggression, cyberviolence, cyberstalking, or cyber harassment (Grigg 2010; Vance 2010; Wachs 2012; Blaya 2013; Sticca et al. 2013), which influences the quality of responses. For instance, findings from research by Corcoran and Mc Guckin (2014) show that studies that use a more restrictive definition of cyberbullying find a lower prevalence of online victimization.

At the time of writing this chapter, the authors can only stress that there is still a lack of consensus regarding the terminology and concepts as well as the criteria to be included in the definition of cyberbullying (repetition, power imbalance, intention to harm, etc.) and there is a clear need for further research on these topics (Kowalski et al. 2014; Bauman and Bellmore 2015). These issues might never be resolved and represent a real impediment to performing genuine comparative research. Up to now very few cross-national research studies have been conducted using the same measurement tools and methods apart from the ones by Menesini et al. (2012) and Livingstone et al. (2011a, b). The TABBY project is one of them.

An International Perspective

By bearing in mind the above mentioned difficulties in comparing cyberbullying and cybervictimization prevalence rates across studies, we have also to consider that, to date, few studies have been carried out adopting a cross-cultural or a cross-national perspective. Furthermore, very few cross-national or cross-cultural research studies have been conducted using the same measurement tools and methods. Adopting such a common methodology could be necessary in order to consider the role that culture could have in influencing youngsters' involvement in cyberbullying and cybervictimization (Barlett et al. 2014) and to compare cyberbullying and cybervictimization prevalence rates across countries. To this aim, in this chapter, we will report the main cross-national and cross-cultural studies adopting the same methodology to compare cyberbullying and cybervictimization rates across countries (see Table 1.1 for details).

As far as we know, the EU Kids Online is the largest European cross-national study, which involved 25,142 students from 25 European countries. Results showed that about one in five or six children in Europe were cybervictimized, underlining the presence of high-risk countries such as Poland and low-risk countries such as Belgium. This first study contributed to our understanding of EU kids' online habits and online risky behaviours (Hasebrink et al. 2008). Afterwards, Lobe et al. (2011) reported that respectively 6% and 3% of students of the total sample were cybervictims and cyberbullies, with Romanian and Estonian youngsters reporting the highest cyberbullying involvement prevalence rates. These studies overcame one of the previous study limitations (Hasebrink et al. 2008), that is the lack of country comparisons with regard to youth involvement in cyberbullying.

In 2008, Li carried out the first study comparing Western (Canadian) and non-Western (Chinese) students aimed at analysing and comparing cyberbullying diffusion between these two samples. Results showed that more Canadian students than Chinese reported they had cyberbullied others, while no significant differences were found with regard to cybervictimization. Although this was the first cross-cultural study carried out, one of its most important limitations was to not consider the role that other cultural, individual, familial, and school-level variables could have in explaining these differences.

Mura et al. (2011) completed a cross-cultural study comparing Italian and Turkish university students' experiences of cyberbullying and cybervictimization. Even if some differences were found between the two samples, cyberbullying and cybervictimization experiences across these two

Table 1.1 Cyberbullying and cybervictimization cross-national/cross-cultural comparisons

Study	Nation	Sample size, age, method, time frame	Instrument	Criteria CB/CV	Main results	
Del Rey et al. (2015)	Poland, Spain, Italy, England, Germany, and Greece	5,679 11–23 years Self-report questionnaire Not reported	The European Cyberbullying Intervention Project Questionnaire (Brighi et al. 2012) 11 for CB and 11 for CV on a 5-point Likert scale (from 'Never' to 'several times a week')	At least once a month	Cybervictimization rates: 10.14% (GR), 8.04% (IT), 6.37% (U.K.), 6.11% (PL), 4.65% (E), and 4.13% (D)	Cyberbullying rates: 7.82% (GR), 6.85% (D), 6.77% (PL), 5.52% (IT), 5.12% (E), and 0.94% (UK)
Jaghoory et al. (2015)	Iran and Finland	1,250 M age = 12.7 (SD = 2.1) Self-reported questionnaire Not reported	The Mini-Direct & Indirect Aggression Scales (Österman 2008) 6 for CB and 6 for CV on a 5-point Likert scale (from 'Never' to 'several times a week')	Not reported	All types of cybervictimization behaviours were significantly higher among Iranian students. The same applies for cyberbullying; Iranian adolescents performed more cyberbullying, of all kinds, than Finnish adolescents did	With regard to cybervictimization in both countries, girls were more exposed to nasty telephone communications and nasty e-mails, while boys were more exposed to being filmed while someone else was evil against them

(continued)

Table 1.1 (continued)

Study	Nation	Sample size, age, method, time frame	Instrument	Criteria CB/CV	Main results
Tsitsika et al. (2015)	Spain, Poland, the Netherlands, Romania, Iceland, and Greece	10,930 14–17 years Self-reported questionnaire Past 12 months	Questionnaire developed by the EU NET ADB consortium (Tsitsika et al. 2012) 1 for CV with 3 response options: 'no', 'yes', and 'do not know/prefer not to say'	Not reported	21.4% of the students reported cybervictimization in the past 12 months	Cybervictimization prevalence is the highest in Romania (37.3%) and Greece (26.8%) and the lowest in Iceland (13.5%) and Spain (13.3%)
Wright et al. (2015)	China, India, and Japan	1,637 11–15 years Self-reported questionnaire During the school years	Cyber Aggression Involvement 9 for CB and 9 for CV on a 5-point Likert scale (from 'Never' to 'several times a week')	At least once or twice	Indian adolescents reported greater cyberbullying (M = 1.86; SD = 0.74) and cyber victimization (M = 1.79; SD = 0.86) than adolescents from China and Japan

(continued)

Table 1.1 (continued)

Study	Nation	Sample size, age, method, time frame	Instrument	Criteria CB/CV	Main results	
Barlett et al. (2014)	Japan and USA	980 M age = 20.51 Self-reported questionnaire The past year	Cyber behaviour questionnaire (Ybarra et al. 2007) 3 for CB	At least once or twice	US students reported higher involvement in cyberbullying than Japanese ones	Both US and Japanese male students scored higher on cyberbullying involvement than females did
Ang et al. (2013)	USA and Singapore	757 11–17 years Self-reported questionnaire The current school term	Cyberbullying Questionnaire (Ang and Goh 2010) 9 for CB on a 5-point Likert scale (from 'Never' to 'A few times every week')	At least once or twice	Respectively 17.9% and 16.4% of US and Singapore students were involved in cyberbullying	
Ortega et al. (2012)	England, Italy, and Spain	5,862 8–10–12 grades Self-reported questionnaire Past 2 months	DAPHNE Questionnaire (Genta et al. 2012) 12 for mobile phones CV and 12 for Internet CV on a 5-point Likert scale (from 'Never' to 'Several times a week')	At least once or twice	Mobile phone frequent victimization: 2.0% (UK) 2.2% (IT), 0.5% (ES)	Internet frequent victimization: 2.6% (UK), 1.9% (IT), 1.3% (ES)

(continued)

Table 1.1 (continued)

Study	Nation	Sample size, age, method, time frame	Instrument	Criteria CB/CV	Main results
Lobe et al. (2011)	Austria, Belgium, Bulgaria, Cyprus, Czech Republic, Denmark, Estonia, France, Finland, Germany, Greece, Hungary, Ireland, Italy, Lithuania, the Netherlands, Norway, Poland, Portugal, Romania, Spain, Slovenia, Sweden, Turkey, and United Kingdom,	25,142 9–16 years Face to face interview In the last 12 months	EU Kids Online Survey 2 for CB and CV with 3 response options: 'no', or 'yes', and 'do not know/prefer not to say'	Not reported	In Romania (14.0%) and Estonia (13.0%), cyberbullying is more than twice the average. Cyberbullying rates are lower in some Southern European countries such as Portugal, Italy, Turkey, and Greece, and the Netherlands	With regard to the total sample, 6% of participants were cybervictimized while 3% were cyberbullies

(continued)

Table 1.1 (continued)

Study	Nation	Sample size, age, method, time frame	Instrument	Criteria CB/CV	Main results	
	Italy, and Turkey	337 IT = 18–33 years TR = 18–36 years Self-reported questionnaire Past 6 months	Items were based on the Revised CyberBullying Inventory (RCBI; Topcu and Erdur-Baker 2010) 8 for CB and 8 for CV on a 3-point scale (from 'Never' to '3 times or more')	At least once	The most common types of cybervictimization were gossip for Italian students (30.5%) and prank calls (42.9%) for Turkish students	With regard to cyberbullying, Italian students reported higher rates of gossiping (27.8%) publication of private messages (19.0%), and embarrassing photo (7.0%). Turkish students reported higher levels of prank calls (21.7%) and mean threatening email/ text (13.7%)
	Canada and China	354 7th grade Self-reported questionnaire Not reported	Survey 3 for CB and 4 for CV from 'Less than 4 times' to 'Over 10 times'	At least 1–3 times	Respectively 25.0% and 33.0% of Canadian and Chinese students reported cybervictimization	Respectively 15.0% and 7.0% of Canadian and Chinese students reported cyberbullying

Note: CV cybervictimization, CB cyberbullying

cultures were explained referring to students' frequency of Information Communication Technology (ICT), rather than to possible cultural factors.

Ortega et al. (2012) compared cybervictimization rates between English, Italian, and Spanish students and found that Italian and English students reported the highest frequency of mobile phone cybervictimization compared to Spanish students, while English students reported the highest frequency of Internet cybervictimization compared to Italian and Spanish students.

Ang et al. (2013) compared US and Singaporean youth experiences of involvement in cyberbullying and found no significant differences across nationalities. Respectively, 17.9% and 16.4% of US and Singaporean students were involved in cyberbullying at least once or twice in the current school year, respectively.

Barlett et al. (2014) completed a cross-cultural research (comparing US and Japanese students) with the aim of addressing the limitations of some previous studies, such as the lack of a theoretical framework and the need for a longitudinal design, in order to assess cross-cultural changes in cyberbullying. The study provided very interesting results showing that cultural differences (Japan vs United States) moderate the relationship between positive attitudes towards cyberbullying, in interdependent self-construal, and cyberbullying frequency.

In their work on the validation at a cross-national level of the European Cyberbullying Intervention Project Questionnaire (ECIPQ; Brighi et al. 2012), Del Rey et al. (2015) gathered data from students from six European countries (Spain, Germany, Italy, Poland, United Kingdom, and Greece). The cross-national comparisons highlighted that Greek, Italian, and Polish students reported higher prevalence rates in both cyberbullying and cybervictimization.

Jaghoory et al. (2015) surveyed 630 Iranian and 620 Finnish adolescents in order to investigate the existence of differences in youth involvement in cyberbullying and cybervictimization and found that Iranian students scored higher in both cyberbullying and cybervictimization. To explain these results, authors hypothesized that Iranian students could be characterized by higher levels of aggressiveness as a result of the psychological challenges they are exposed to in their society. However, the study did not provide support for this hypothesis since students' aggressiveness was not measured.

Tsitsika et al. (2015), in their cross-sectional study involving students from Spain, Poland, the Netherlands, Romania, Iceland, and Greece, obtained similar results to Del Rey et al. (2015) and Lobe et al. (2011), namely that cybervictimization rates were the highest in Romania (37.3%) and Greece (26.8%).

Wright et al. (2015) compared data on cyberbullying and cybervictimization gathered from 1,637 Indian, Chinese, and Japanese students. The results revealed that Indian students had the highest levels of cyberbullies compared to Chinese and Japanese adolescents. The same was found with regard to students' experience of being cybervictimized, with Indian students reporting higher rates of cybervictimization.

By reviewing the existing literature, it emerges that studies adopting a cross-national or a cross-cultural perspective are rare and often do not adopt a methodology (including cultural-free surveys, materials, and standardized procedures to collect data) aimed at comparing cyberbullying and cybervictimization rates across different countries. This stresses the need to have more cross-national studies (Walrave and Heirman 2011) in order to better understand, compare, and generalize cyberbullying and cybervictimization diffusion and experience among different countries. The majority of the existing studies do not provide explanations of the differences found across counties, and/or do not include measures that might be able to explain such differences in terms of cultural influences. Furthermore, one of the main problems when carrying out cross-national or cross-cultural studies lies in the fact that both participants' countries and students participating in these researches are often selected according to convenience, and this could hinder generalizability and the possible impact that cross-national or cross-cultural differences can have on studies' findings (Ortega et al. 2012).

Despite the possible methodological and sampling difficulties, consistent with Hasebrink et al. (2008), we stress the importance of adopting a cross-national perspective as developed in the TABBY project. Adopting such a perspective could be crucial not only to investigate children's and teens' use of new technologies, as well as the risks they face online, such as cyberbullying and cybervictimization, but also to make possible comparisons and generalize cyberbullying prevention and intervention policies at an European level.

Risk and Protective Factors for Cyberbullying

Research on cyberbullying has for a long time investigated the role that risk and protective factors have in predicting youngsters' involvement in this phenomenon (Ortega- Ruiz and Núñez 2012).

With regard to risk factors for cyberbullying, being male, Internet use frequency, and risky online habits are significant risk factors for youth involvement as cyberbullies (Chen et al. 2017; Gámez-Guadix et al. 2016; Kowalski et al. 2014; Casas et al. 2013; Sticca et al. 2013; Mishna et al. 2012; Walrave and Heirman 2011; Erdur-Baker 2010; Hinduja and Patchin 2008; Ybarra and Mitchell 2004). Also, previous involvement in school bullying (Chen et al. 2017; Hemphill and Heerde 2014; Modecki et al. 2013, 2014; Kowalski et al. 2014; Cappadocia et al. 2013; Kowalski and Limber 2013; Sticca et al. 2013; Del Rey et al. 2012; Mishna et al. 2012; Gradinger et al. 2009; Vandebosch and Van Cleemput 2009; Hinduja and Patchin 2008; Smith et al. 2008; Raskauskas and Stoltz 2007), high levels of peer rejection (Bayraktar et al. 2014; Wright and Li 2013), poor parental involvement in the Internet use of their children (Zhou et al. 2013; Mesch 2009; Vandebosch and Van Cleemput 2009), and perceived negative school climate are all factors associated with cyberbullying.

On the other hand, being female (Sampasa-Kanyinga and Hamilton 2015; Payne and Hutzell 2017; Bayraktar et al. 2014; Holt et al. 2014), spending more time on the Internet, and being involved in so-called online risky behaviours (Chen et al. 2017; Álvarez-García et al. 2015; Peluchette et al. 2015; Kowalski et al. 2014; Zhou et al. 2013; Mishna et al. 2012; Walrave and Heirman 2011; Erdur-Baker 2010; Katzer et al. 2009; Mesch 2009; Vandebosch and Van Cleemput 2009; Hinduja and Patchin 2008; Ybarra and Mitchell 2004), and school victimization (Chen et al. 2017; Álvarez-García et al. 2015; Holt et al. 2014; Hemphill and Heerde 2014; Kowalski et al. 2014; Cappadocia et al. 2013; Del Rey et al. 2012; Mishna et al. 2012; Gradinger et al. 2009; Vandebosch and

Van Cleemput 2009; Hinduja and Patchin 2008; Smith et al. 2008; Raskauskas and Stoltz 2007) are all risk factors associated with youngsters' cybervictimization. Several studies also highlighted the role that peers could play in influencing students' involvement in cybervictimization. In particular, it seems that cybervictimization is associated with having antisocial friends (Hemphill and Heerde 2014) and peers (Bayraktar et al. 2014; Katzer et al. 2009). In addition, poor parental mediation and low levels of control of their children's online activities (Chen et al. 2017; Khurana et al. 2015; Kowalski et al. 2014; Aoyama et al. 2012; Mesch 2009) and youngsters' perception of a negative school climate (Kowalski et al. 2014; Wang et al. 2014) are significant risk factors for cybervictimization.

Even if several studies exist, and the role of some risk and protective factors for youngsters' involvement in cyberbullying and/or cybervictimization have been investigated and identified, what characterizes the majority of these studies is the lack of a conceptual and theoretical framework (Tokunaga 2010; Slonje et al. 2013).

Assessing Threats

Risk/needs assessment is the procedure to identify the personal, social, and contextual variables that are related to juveniles' antisocial and delinquent behaviour. It deals with the identification and evaluation of factors, characteristics related to the individual, and his/her social and familial context that are or might be associated with criminal behaviour and the risk of recurrence. In the field of criminology and forensic psychology, risk assessment has been adopted for the last 20 years, identifying a set of dimensions that are precursors of concurrent crime (Baldry and Sorrentino 2017). The *threat assessment approach* described below (Borum et al. 1999; Fein and Vossekuil 1998, 1999; Fein et al. 1995) was adopted as the theoretical framework for the implementation of the TABBY project and for the development of all its' materials, in order to overcome the limitations of some previous studies regarding risk factors for cyberbullying and cybervictimization.

A Risk and Needs Assessment Approach

The *threat assessment approach* (Borum et al. 1999; Fein and Vossekuil 1998, 1999; Fein et al. 1995) was adopted for the implementation of the TABBY project. This is a theoretical and scientific-based framework for the identification, assessment, and management of people considered at risk for involvement in criminal violent behaviour, and it has been used mainly with juvenile offenders (Baldry and Sorrentino 2017).

The term 'threat assessment' refers here to a strategy useful to identify, assess, and manage the risks of targeted violence and its potential perpetrators (Fein et al. 1995) even before the actual violence has taken place or the threat posed becomes a fact. The main aims of the threat assessment approach are identification of the perpetrator of the threat, assessment of the risks of violence posed by the perpetrator at a given time, and subsequently efficient management of the perpetrator and protection of the victim.

The threat assessment approach is guided by several operational principles, and it is based on some key questions that research suggests should be investigated for the purpose of assessing the risk of the involvement of individuals in violent behaviour (Borum et al. 1999; Fein and Vossekuil 1998, 1999; Fein et al. 1995).

According to the main principles of this approach, juvenile involvement in violent and antisocial behaviours is a process, and the product of an interaction among three factors: (a) the individual, (b) the stimulus or conditions that lead the subject to see violence as a solution, and (c) a setting that facilitates or permits the violence (Fein et al. 1995).

This approach had been successfully applied to other forms of violence (Borum et al. 1999) such as school violence (Fein et al. 2002). For these reasons, it could be a useful framework for studying and assessing the risk of aggressive behaviours among children and youth such as cyberbullying and cybervictimization. Applying this method to investigate these issues requires the evaluation of those risk factors that the international literature suggests as being significant for students' involvement in cyberbullying. This assessment is relevant in the sense that it is the conjunction and combination of these factors that might increase the credibility of the threat: that is, a student's likelihood of being involved in cyberbullying and cybervictimization.

References

Álvarez-García, D., Núñez Pérez, J. C., Dobarro González, A., & Pérez, C. R. (2015). Risk factors associated with cybervictimization in adolescence. *International Journal of Clinical and Health Psychology, 15*(3), 226–235. https://doi.org/10.1016/j.ijchp.2015.03.002

Ang, R. P., & Goh, D. H. (2010). Cyberbullying among adolescents: The role of affective and cognitive empathy, and gender. *Child Psychiatry and Human Development, 41*(4), 387–397. https://doi.org/10.1007/s10578-010-0176-3

Ang, R. P., Huan, V. S., & Florell, D. (2013). Understanding the relationship between proactive and reactive aggression, and cyberbullying across United States and Singapore adolescent samples. *Journal of Interpersonal Violence, 29*(2), 237–254. https://doi.org/10.1177/0886260513505149

Aoyama, I., Utsumi, S., & Hasegawa, M. (2012). Cyberbullying in Japan: Cases, government reports, adolescent relational aggression and parental monitoring roles. In Q. Li, D. Cross, & P. K. Smith (Eds.), *Cyberbullying in the global playground: Research from international perspectives* (pp. 183–201). Malden: Blackwell.

Baldry, A. C., & Sorrentino, A. (2017). Risk and needs assessment. In C. J. Schreck, M. Leiber, H. L. Miller, & K. Welch (Eds.), *The encyclopedia of juvenile delinquency and justice*. Wiley-Blackwell. https://doi.org/10.1002/9781118524275.ejdj0110.

Barlett, C. P., Gentile, D. A., Anderson, C. A., Suzuki, K., Sakamoto, A., Yamaoka, A., & Katsura, R. (2014). Cross-cultural differences in cyberbullying behavior a short-term longitudinal study. *Journal of Cross-Cultural Psychology, 45*(2), 300–313. https://doi.org/10.1177/0022022113504622

Bauman, S., & Bellmore, A. (2015). New directions in cyberbullying research. *Journal of School Violence, 14*(1), 1–10. https://doi.org/10.1080/15388220.2014.968281

Bayraktar, F., Machackova, H., Dedkova, L., Cerna, A., & Sevcíková, A. (2014). Cyberbullying: The discriminant factors among cyberbullies, cybervictims, and cyberbully-victims in a Czech adolescent sample. *Journal of Interpersonal Violence, 18*, 1–25. https://doi.org/10.1177/0886260514555006

Blaya, C. (2013). *Les ados dans le cyberespace – prises de risqué et cyberviolence.* Bruxelles: De Boeck.

Borum, R., Fein, R., Vossekuil, B., & Berglund, J. (1999). Threat assessment: Defining an approach for evaluating risk of targeted violence. *Behavioral Sciences & the Law, 17,* 323–337. https://doi.org/10.1002/(SICI)1099-0798(199907/09)17:3<323::AID-BSL349>3.0.CO;2-G

Brighi, A., Ortega, R., Pyzalski, J., Scheithauer, H., Smith, P. K., Tsormpatzoudis, C., & Barkoukis, V., et al. (2012). *European Cyberbullying Intervention Project Questionnaire (ECIPQ).* Unpublished Manuscript, University of Bologna. Retrieved from bullyingandcyber.net

Calvete, E., Orue, I., Estévez, A., Villardón, L., & Padilla, P. (2010). Cyberbullying in adolescents: Modalities and aggressors' profile. *Computers in Human Behavior, 26*(5), 1128–1135. https://doi.org/10.1016/j.chb.2010.03.017

Cappadocia, M. C., Craig, W. M., & Pepler, D. (2013). Cyberbullying prevalence, stability, and risk factors during adolescence. *Canadian Journal of School Psychology, 28*(2), 171–192. https://doi.org/10.1177/0829573513491212

Casas, J. A., Del Rey, R., & Ortega-Ruiz, R. (2013). Bullying and cyberbullying: Convergent and divergent predictor variables. *Computers in Human Behavior, 29*(3), 580–587. https://doi.org/10.1016/j.chb.2012.11.015

Chen, L., Ho, S. S., & Lwin, M. O. (2017). A meta-analysis of factors predicting cyberbullying perpetration and victimization: From the social cognitive and media effects approach. *New Media & Society, 19*(8), 1194–1213. https://doi.org/10.1177/1461444816634037

Corcoran, L., & Mc Guckin, C. (2014). Addressing bullying problems in Irish schools and in cyberspace: A challenge for school management. *Educational Research, 56*(1), 48–64. https://doi.org/10.1080/00131881.2013.874150

Corcoran, L., Mc Guckin, C., & Prentice, G. (2015). Cyberbullying or cyber aggression? A review of existing definitions of cyber-based peer-to-peer aggression. *Societies, 5,* 245–255. https://doi.org/10.3390/soc5020245

Del Rey, R., Elipe, P., & Ortega-Ruiz, R. (2012). Bullying and cyberbullying: Overlapping and predictive value of the co-occurrence. *Psicothema, 24*(4), 608–613.

Del Rey, R., Casas, J. A., Ortega-Ruiz, R., Schultze-Krumbholz, A., Scheithauer, H., Smith, P., Thompson, F., Barkoukis, V., Tsorbatzoudis, H., Brighi, A., Guarini, A., Pyżalski, J., & Plichta, P. (2015). Structural validation and cross-cultural robustness of the European Cyberbullying Intervention Project Questionnaire. *Computers in Human Behavior, 50,* 141–147. https://doi.org/10.1016/j.chb.2015.03.065

Erdur-Baker, Ö. (2010). Cyberbullying and its correlation to traditional bullying, gender and frequent and risky usage of internet-mediated communication tools. *New Media & Society, 12*(1), 109–125. https://doi. org/10.1177/1461444809341260

Fein, R. A., & Vossekuil, B. (1998). *Protective intelligence & threat assessment investigations: A guide for state and local law enforcement officials* (NIROJP/ DOJ Publication No. 170612). Washington, DC: U.S. Department of Justice.

Fein, R. A., & Vossekuil, B. V. (1999). Assassination in the United States: An operational study of recent assassins, attackers, and near-lethal approachers. *Journal of Forensic Sciences, 44*, 321–333.

Fein, R. A., Vossekuil, B., & Holden, G. A. (1995). *Threat assessment: An approach to prevent targeted violence* (Vol. 2). Washington, DC: US Department of Justice, Office of Justice Programs, National Institute of Justice.

Fein, R. A., Vossekuil, B., Pollack, W. S., Borum, R., Modzeleski, W., & Reddy, M. (2002). *Threat assessment in schools. A guide to managing threatening situations and to creating safe school climates.* Washington, DC: United States Secret Service and United States Department of Education.

Gámez-Guadix, M., Borrajo, E., & Almendros, C. (2016). Risky online behaviors among adolescents: Longitudinal relations among problematic internet use, cyberbullying perpetration, and meeting strangers online. *Journal of Behavioral Addictions, 5*(1), 100–107. https://doi.org/10.1556/2006.5. 2016.013

Genta, M. L., Smith, P. K., Ortega, R., Brighi, A., Guarini, A., Thompson, F., Tippett, N., Mora-Merchán, J. A., & Calmaestra, J. (2012). Comparative aspects of cyberbullying in Italy, England, and Spain: Findings from a DAPHNE project. In Q. Li, D. Cross, & P. K. Smith (Eds.), *Cyberbullying in the global playground: Research from international perspectives* (pp. 15–31). West Sussex: Wiley-Blackwell.

Gradinger, P., Strohmeier, D., & Spiel, C. (2009). Traditional bullying and cyberbullying: Identification of risk groups for adjustment problems. *Zeitschrift für Psychologie/Journal of Psychology, 217*(4), 205–213. https://doi. org/10.1027/0044-3409.217.4.205

Grigg, D. W. (2010). Cyber-aggression: Definition and concept of cyberbullying. *Journal of Psychologists and Counsellors in Schools, 20*(2), 143–156. https://doi.org/10.1375/ajgc.20.2.143

Hasebrink, U., Livingstone, S., & Haddon, L. (2008). *Comparing children's online opportunities and risks across Europe: Cross-national comparisons for EU Kids Online.* London: EU Kids Online. Retrived from http://eprints.lse.ac. uk/21656/1/D3.2_Report-Cross_national_ comparisons.pdf

Hemphill, S. A., & Heerde, J. A. (2014). Adolescent predictors of young adult cyberbullying perpetration and victimization among Australian youth. *Journal of Adolescent Health, 55*(4), 580–587. https://doi.org/10.1016/j. jadohealth.2014.04.014

Hinduja, S., & Patchin, J. W. (2008). Cyberbullying: An exploratory analysis of factors related to offending and victimization. *Deviant Behavior, 29*(2), 129–156. https://doi.org/10.1080/01639620701457816

Holt, T. J., Fitzgerald, S., Bossler, A. M., Chee, G., & Ng, E. (2014). Assessing the risk factors of cyber and mobile phone bullying victimization in a nationally representative sample of Singapore youth. *International Journal of Offender Therapy and Comparative Criminology*, 1–18. https://doi.org/10.11 77/0306624X14554852

Jaghoory, H., Björkqvist, K., & Österman, K. (2015). Cyberbullying among adolescents: A comparison between Iran and Finland. *Journal of Child and Adolescent Behaviour, 3*(6), 265–272. https://doi.org/10.4172/2375-4494.1000265.

Katzer, C., Fetchenhauer, D., & Belschak, F. (2009). Cyberbullying: Who are the victims?: A comparison of victimization in internet chatrooms and victimization in school. *Journal of Media Psychology: Theories, Methods, and Applications, 21*(1), 25–36. https://doi.org/10.1027/1864-1105.21.1.25

Khurana, A., Bleakley, A., Jordan, A. B., & Romer, D. (2015). The protective effects of parental monitoring and internet restriction on adolescents' risk of online harassment. *Journal of Youth and Adolescence, 44*(5), 1039–1047. https://doi.org/10.1007/s10964-014-0242-4

Kowalski, R. M., & Limber, S. P. (2013). Psychological, physical, and academic correlates of cyberbullying and traditional bullying. *Journal of Adolescent Health, 53*(1), S13–S20. https://doi.org/10.1016/j.jadohealth.2012.09.018

Kowalski, R. M., Limber, S. P., & Agatston, P. W. (2008). *Cyber bullying: Bullying in the digital age*. Malden: Blackwell Publishing.

Kowalski, R. M., Giumetti, G. W., Schroeder, A. N., & Lattanner, M. R. (2014). Bullying in the digital age: A critical review and meta-analysis of cyberbullying research among youth. *Psychological Bulletin, 140*(4), 1073–1137. https:// doi.org/10.1037/a0035618

Li, Q. (2007). New bottle but old wine: A research of cyberbullying in schools. *Computer in Human Behavior, 23*(4), 1777–1791. https://doi.org/10.1016/j. chb.2005.10.005

Livingstone, S., Haddon, L., Gorzig, A., & Ölafsson, K. (2011a). *Risks and safety on the internet: The perspective of European children. Full findings*. London: EU Kids Online.

Livingstone, S., Haddon, L., Görzig, A., & Ólafsson, K. (2011b). *EU Kids Online: Final report*. London: EU Kids online, London School of Economics and Political Science.

Lobe, B., Livingstone, S., Ólafsson, K., & Vodeb, H. (2011). *Cross-national comparison of risks and safety on the internet: Initial analysis from the EU Kids Online survey of European children*. London: EU Kids Online.

Menesini, E., Nocentini, A., Palladino, B. E., Frisén, A., Berne, S., Ortega-Ruiz, R., Calmaestra, J., Scheithauer, H., Schultze-Krumbholz, A., Karin, P. L., Naruskov, K., Blaya, C., Berthaud, J., & Smith, P. K. (2012). Cyberbullying definition among adolescents: A comparison across six European countries. *Cyberpsychology, Behavior, and Social Networking, 15*(9), 455–463. https://doi.org/10.1089/cyber.2012.0040

Mesch, G. S. (2009). Parental mediation, online activities, and cyberbullying. *CyberPsychology & Behavior, 12*(4), 387–393. https://doi.org/10.1089/cpb.2009.0068

Mishna, F., Khoury-Kassabri, M., Gadalla, T., & Daciuk, J. (2012). Risk factors for involvement in cyberbullying: Victims, bullies and bully-victims. *Children & Youth Services Review, 34*(1), 63–70. https://doi.org/10.1016/j.childyouth.2011.08.032

Modecki, K. L., Barber, B. L., & Vernon, L. (2013). Mapping developmental precursors of cyber-aggression: Trajectories of risk predict perpetration and victimization. *Journal of Youth and Adolescence, 42*(5), 651–661. https://doi.org/10.1007/s10964-013-9938-0

Modecki, K. L., Minchin, J., Harbaugh, A. G., Guerra, N. G., & Runions, K. C. (2014). Bullying prevalence across contexts: A meta-analysis measuring cyber and traditional bullying. *Journal of Adolescent Health, 55*(5), 602–611. https://doi.org/10.1016/j.jadohealth.2014.06.007

Mura, G., Topcu, C., Erdur-Baker, O., & Diamantini, D. (2011). An international study of cyber bullying perception and diffusion among adolescents. *Procedia-Social and Behavioral Sciences, 15*, 3805–3809. https://doi.org/10.1016/j.sbspro.2011.04.377

Olweus, D. (1995). Bullying or peer abuse at school: Facts and intervention. *Current Directions in Psychological Science, 4*(6), 196–200. https://doi.org/10.1111/1467-8721.ep10772640

Ortega, R., Elipe, P., Mora-Merchán, J. A., Genta, M. L., Brighi, A., Guarini, A., Smith, P. K., Thompson, F., & Tippett, N. (2012). The emotional impact of bullying and cyberbullying on victims: A European cross-national study. *Aggressive Behavior, 38*(5), 342–356. https://doi.org/10.1002/ab.21440

Ortega-Ruiz, R., & Nùnez, J. C. (2012). Bullying and cyberbullying: Research and intervention at school and social contexts. *Psicothema, 24*(4), 603–607.

Payne, A. A., & Hutzell, K. L. (2017). Old wine, new bottle? Comparing interpersonal bullying and cyberbullying victimization. *Youth & Society, 49*(8), 1149–1178. https://doi.org/10.1177/0044118X15617401

Peluchette, J. V., Karl, K., Wood, C., & Williams, J. (2015). Cyberbullying victimization: Do victims' personality and risky social network behaviors contribute to the problem? *Computers in Human Behavior, 52*, 424–435. https://doi.org/10.1016/j.chb.2015.06.028

Raskauskas, J., & Stoltz, A. D. (2007). Involvement in traditional and electronic bullying among adolescents. *Developmental Psychology, 43*(3), 564. https://doi.org/10.1037/0012-1649.43.3.564

Sampasa-Kanyinga, H., & Hamilton, H. A. (2015). Use of social networking sites and risk of cyberbullying victimization: A population-level study of adolescents. *Cyberpsychology, Behavior, and Social Networking, 18*(12), 704–710. https://doi.org/10.1089/cyber.2015.0145

Smith, P. K., Mahdavi, J., Carvalho, M., Fisher, S., Russell, S., & Tippett, N. (2008). Cyberbullying: Its nature and impact in secondary school pupils. *Journal of Child Psychology and Psychiatry, 49*, 376–385. https://doi.org/10.1111/j.1469-7610.2007.01846.x

Steffgen, G., & König, A. (2009). Cyber bullying: The role of traditional bullying and empathy. In B. Sapio, L. Haddon, E. Mante-Meijer, L. Fortunati, T. Turk, & E. Loos (Eds.), *The good, the bad and the challenging. Conference proceedings* (Vol. II, pp. 1041–1047). Brussels: Cost Office.

Sticca, F., Ruggieri, S., Alsaker, F., & Perren, S. (2013). Longitudinal risk factors for cyberbullying in adolescence. *Journal of Community and Applied Social Psychology, 23*(1), 52–67. https://doi.org/10.1002/casp.2136

Tokunaga, R. S. (2010). Following you home from school: A critical review and synthesis of research on cyberbullying victimization. *Computers in Human Behavior, 26*(3), 277–287. https://doi.org/10.1016/j.chb.2009.11.014

Topcu, C., & Erdur-Baker, O. (2010). The Revised Cyberbullying Inventory (RCBI): Validity and reliability studies. *Procedia: Social and Behavioral Sciences, 5*, 660–664. https://doi.org/10.1016/j.sbspro.2010.07.161

Tsitsika, A., Janikian, M., Wójcik, S., Makaruk, K., Tzavela, E., Tzavara, C., Greydanus, D., Merrick, J., & Richardson, C. (2015). Cyberbullying victimization prevalence and associations with internalizing and externalizing problems among adolescents in six European countries. *Computers in Human Behavior, 51*, 1–7. https://doi.org/10.1016/j.chb.2015.04.048

Vance, J. W. (2010). *Cyber-harassment in higher education: Online learning environments* (Doctoral dissertation). University of Southern California. Retrieved from http://digitallibrary.usc.edu/cdm/compoundobject/collection/p15799coll127/id/309077/rec/19

Vandebosch, H., & Van Cleemput, K. (2009). Cyberbullying among youngsters: Profiles of bullies and victims. *New Media & Society, 11*(8), 1349–1371. https://doi.org/10.1177/1461444809341263

Wachs, S. (2012). Moral disengagement and emotional and social difficulties in bullying and cyberbullying: Differences by participant role. *Emotional and Behavioural Difficulties, 17*(3–4), 347–360. https://doi.org/10.1080/13632752.2012.704318

Walrave, M., & Heirman, W. (2011). Cyberbullying: Predicting victimisation and perpetration. *Children & Society, 25*(1), 59–72. https://doi.org/10.1111/j.1099-0860.2009.00260.x

Wang, W., Vaillancourt, T., Brittain, H. L., McDougall, P., Krygsman, A., Smith, D., Cunningham, C. E., Haltigan, J. D., & Hymel, S. (2014). School climate, peer victimization, and academic achievement: Results from a multi-informant study. *School Psychology Quarterly, 29*(3), 360–377. https://doi.org/10.1037/spq0000084

Wright, M. F., & Li, Y. (2013). The association between cyber victimization and subsequent cyber aggression: The moderating effect of peer rejection. *Journal of Youth and Adolescence, 42*(5), 662–674. https://doi.org/10.1007/s10964-012-9903-3

Wright, M. F., Aoyama, I., Kamble, S. V., Li, Z., Soudi, S., Lei, L., & Shu, C. (2015). Peer attachment and cyber aggression involvement among Chinese, Indian, and Japanese adolescents. *Societies, 5*(2), 339–353. https://doi.org/10.3390/soc5020339

Ybarra, M. L., & Mitchell, K. J. (2004). Youth engaging in online harassment: Associations with caregiver-child relationships, Internet use, and personal characteristics. *Journal of Adolescence, 27*, 319–336. https://doi.org/10.1016/j.adolescence.2004.03.007

Ybarra, M. L., Espelage, D. L., & Mitchell, K. J. (2007). The co-occurrence of Internet harassment and unwanted sexual solicitation victimization and perpetration: Associations with psychosocial indicators. *Journal of Adolescent Health, 41*(6), S31–S41. https://doi.org/10.1016/j.jadohealth.2007.09.010

Zhou, Z., Tang, H., Tian, Y., Wei, H., Zhang, F., & Morrison, C. M. (2013). Cyberbullying and its risk factors among Chinese high school students. *School Psychology International, 34*(6), 630–647. https://doi.org/10.1177/0143034313479692

2

The TABBY Online Project: The Threat Assessment of Bullying Behaviours Online Approach

Anna Costanza Baldry, David P. Farrington,
Catherine Blaya, and Anna Sorrentino

The TABBY Project: Aims and Rationale

The Threat Assessment of Bullying Behaviours among Youngsters (TABBY) Internet program was developed initially in 2010 and implemented in 2011–2013 in Italy and further four EU countries (Bulgaria, Greece, Cyprus, and Hungary) and was then undertaken in three additional EU countries (Spain, France, and Poland) with new components. The program was developed on the basis of what was known in the scientific community with regard to the reduction of cyberbullying and increased awareness of cyber risks. The program has been developed and

A. C. Baldry (✉) • A. Sorrentino
Department of Psychology, Università degli Studi della Campania Luigi
Vanvitelli, Caserta, Italy

D. P. Farrington
Institute of Criminology, University of Cambridge, Cambridge, UK

C. Blaya
UER Pédagogie Spécialisée - HEP du Canton de Vaud, Lausanne, Switzerland

© The Author(s) 2018   **25**
A. C. Baldry et al. (eds.), *International Perspectives on Cyberbullying*, Palgrave Studies in
Cybercrime and Cybersecurity, https://doi.org/10.1007/978-3-319-73263-3_2

implemented thanks to the support of the European Union Daphne Security and Justice Program for the reduction of violence against women and children, and in some of the original countries (Italy, Spain, France, Hungary) it is still used as one of the existing intervention programs.[1]

The TABBY program aims to reduce cyberbullying (and cybervictimization) by increasing awareness about the risks related to an individual's own use of cyber communication and reducing the risk of falling into the most common "online traps" (Willard 2007). In order to achieve this goal, we developed a multicomponent program based on the theoretical assumption of what cyberbullying is and why youngsters are at risk of cyberbullying others and of being cyberbullied themselves. In developing the TABBY in Internet program, we referred to the *perspective-taking cognitive approach* (Winkel and Baldry 1997), according to which antisocial behaviour can be considered as the consequence of a lack of awareness of the negative impact of one's own behaviour. This lack of empathy (cognitive and emotional; Jolliffe and Farrington 2006) and of awareness of the consequences of one's own actions might be even more enhanced in the cyber world, where there is usually a lack of direct contact with the victim (i.e., the person towards whom the action or threat is addressed) (Menesini et al. 2012c).

Social psychological research also documents a strong relationship between aggressive behaviour and the inability to place oneself in another's position (Ellis 1982; Luengo et al. 1994; Richardson et al. 1994). Several studies suggest that these kinds of skills can be influenced through specific training programs. For example, for quite some time (Chandler 1973) it has been proved that it is possible to influence perspective taking. Training to reduce aggression, including bullying, provides exposure to the impact of an individual's own actions from the point of view of the other person and uses role-playing to improve perspective-taking skills (the training effect) and decrease the delinquent behaviour of juveniles (the generalization of the carry-over effect). This model can be applied by directly involving students by showing them videos depicting possible negative consequences arising from their own actions and by explaining the meaning and consequences of those actions.

Chalmers and Townsend (1990) found a similar training effect on delinquent girls. Winkel and Baldry (1997) adopted and confirmed this approach when assessing an intervention program to increase awareness among young Italian and Dutch students about the negative impact of antisocial behaviours, often manifested as bullying in schools. To our knowledge, this approach in the cyberbullying domain has only been used to assess the role of bystanders (Van Cleemput et al. 2014) and not been developed prior to the Tabby project to impact cyberbullying by increasing the understanding of the effects of one's own behaviour, and the need to make different choices, that is, safer use of the Internet that can reduce cyberbullying.

We therefore wanted to develop a program based on the understanding of the risk and protective factors related to cyberbullying and cyber-victimization and to help to understand young people when the threats they pose or receive online can be of low, middle, or high risk for cyberbullying. With the TABBY intervention program:

(1) Students are made aware of the risks of certain online behaviours, in terms of increased awareness of their possible consequences.
(2) Significant adults (e.g., teachers who interact with students) are themselves prepared to provide students with information about the risks associated with the Web world and how to avoid them.
(3) Students are confronted with their own risk of involvement in cyber behaviour related to the (mis)use of online/cyber devices to communicate.

According to the TABBY program approach, online communication lacks any direct cognitive and emotional response that regulates the intention of harming because of the mediation of the cyberspace. With this program, we identify the risk and protective factors that students report and establish their relationship with cyberbullying and cyber-victimization, which is useful for the intervention part of the program that addresses the (dynamic) risk factors.

The TABBY project was therefore designed to sensitize and increase students' awareness about the negative consequences of their cyber activities. Also, the program addressed school personnel by training teachers in order to assist them to be able to talk with students about cyber risks, recognize risk factors, and manage and solve cyberbullying accidents. The program trained teachers who interact with students on a daily basis.

Components of the TABBY Program

The TABBY program is based on two components: (1) the material available for students and teachers and (2) the activities with teachers and students. (For a summary of the components, see Table 2.1.) The first component constitutes the TABBY "toolkit" and includes the following elements: (a) an online self-report questionnaire and the TABBY checklist, which is also used to obtain a "risk of cyberbullying" profile; (b) four short videos (available online and on DVD); and (c) a teacher manual booklet (digital and paper version) with which teachers are trained. In order to make the program usable, applicable, and useful, (a), (b), and (c) are used as materials for the second component of the program to train teachers who then work with this material with students. The program foresees also (d) training for teachers on cyberbullying and (e) working with students. The working language for the production of the materials was English. Currently, the TABBY program and all of its materials have been translated into other languages by native speakers, senior researchers, and partners in the project. The TABBY program is now available in eight languages (English, Italian, French, Spanish, Bulgarian, Polish, Hungarian, and Greek). These components of the program are further analysed in this chapter.

(a) The TABBY online checklist is used to measure traditional bullying and cyberbullying and other online-related behaviours and the sociodemographic characteristics of students. It can also be considered as part of the intervention because it has been developed as a self-threat assessment tool on its own. After completing the questionnaire, students can obtain the so-called TABBY Profile, which is useful in assessing the level of risk related to being involved in cyberbullying as victims and/or as bullies. According to the answers they provide, students obtain one of four possible levels of risk: green, yellow, orange,

Table 2.1 Modules of the TABBY in Internet Project

Module and length	Activities	Goals
1. Students filled in the TABBY checklist online in their schools (about 15–20 min/student)	Sessions with students have been conducted in their schools' computer laboratory. The researchers with the school teacher introduced the students to the checklist and read the checklist and personal code instructions. A definition of cyberbullying was provided. Students were given the opportunity to raise questions. After filling in the checklist, students obtained a risk profile (the so-called TABBY profiles)	The Tabby online checklist is used to measure traditional bullying and cyberbullying and other online-related dimensions and the socio-demographic characteristics of the respondent. Data obtained during this first checklist data collection constitute the baseline data, which have to be compared with the post-test administration (four months after the intervention) to evaluate if the TABBY program has been effective in terms of prevention and reduction of the cyberbullying accidents and to compare these results with the ones of the Control Group
2. Teachers' training (four meetings of 180 min each)	Training group of 15–20 teachers for each group/school on different aspects: cyberbullying, nature, prevalence, risk, and protective factors for youngsters' involvement; The TABBY toolkit: how to use the checklist, the teacher manual, and the videos. How to recognize, prevent, and manage cyberbullying accidents. Legal issues related to cyberbullying	The main aim is to train and to sensitize teachers about the cyberbullying phenomenon. The training is focused on the use of the TABBY toolkit: TABBY checklist Booklet for teachers TABBY videos

(continued)

Table 2.1 (continued)

Module and length	Activities	Goals
3. Students' intervention: video and discussion (two to three class group meetings of 60 min each and ongoing)	Trained teachers organize class groups in order to show students the TABBY videos Students think about their own experiences online and of cyberbullying and discuss actions that can be "rewind", or change to avoid the risk of becoming a cyberbully or cybervictim Videos' contents are discussed via interactive methods such as role-playing, group discussions, and focus groups	The four TABBY videos are useful stimuli to make youngsters think about the cyberbullying phenomenon and its consequences both for bullies and victims. Based on the perspective-taking skills, to increase approach and change behavior via understanding of risk, each video takes the form of an interactive lesson, where trained teachers can discuss and make adolescents think about the safety and conscious use of the new communication technologies
4. Monitoring students' online and school experience (about 15–20 min per student)	After four months, students are conducted to the school's computer laboratory The researchers and their assistants read the checklist instructions, and a definition of cyberbullying and meaning of the online questionnaire were provided After filling in the checklist, students obtained a risk profile ("TABBY profiles") based on their answers	The conclusive data collection at T2 enables testing whether there are changes after the intervention between T1 and T2 and also whether these changes are only in the experiment group or they are also in the control group so that the TABBY online questionnaire is also affecting cyberbullying behaviour

red. The risk and protective factors are weighted according to a formula based on risk and protective factors and scores derived from previous studies (Baldry et al. 2015) and now the final validated version or self-threat assessment is available on the website (www. tabby.eu).

(b) The four online videos (see Table 2.2. for a summary of content and description) are didactical, instructive, can be watched online, have been developed as self-explanatory tools, and can be used as a stimulus to get youngsters thinking about cyberbullying and its consequences. The videos constitute the *core* part of the intervention; they are theoretically driven to increase perspective-taking skills and understand consequences of action as a basis for changing behaviour and to increase awareness of the possible consequences of one's own behaviour. Each video addresses one form of possible cyberbullying, and all are based on the idea that, if youngsters make different online decisions, they might avoid either getting into trouble or becoming a cyberbully. At the end of each video, after each cyber scenario is presented, there is a "rewind" regarding cyber actions taken that have led to distress and sadness for a victim. The "rewind" shows what would or could have happened if the characters in the video had acted differently (*cyber action*), stressing the possible alternative (positive) outcome. The videos are tailored to help youngsters to avoid being victimized online or via other digital communication, but primarily they address cyberbullying others. At the end of the rewind scene, some recommendations are provided on the safe use of the Web based on the specific type of cyber problems presented in the video (see Table 2.2). The videos are soundless and make use of cartoon characters that interact as in a "silent movie", with the use of only significant sounds (e.g., crying, laughing, slamming doors, ringing bells). This is done to override possible language and cultural barriers so that TABBY videos can be used in different cultural contexts and in different countries and are easy to interpret and to use for different school grades. As in silent movies, some written explanatory text is presented throughout the videos, and these are written in the language of use in that country.

(c) The teacher's manual is a booklet developed for teachers available both in a printed form and as a downloadable pdf file. It consists of several short chapters with definitions and some scientific information on cyberbullying and its differences and similarities with school bullying, on the legal aspects (this part of the booklet differs from country to country, according to national legislation). At the end of

Table 2.2 Content of the four TABBY videos

Video title	Area of cyberbullying addressed: Content of videos	Recommendations for youngsters provided at the end of the video related to the topic addressed
1. *"Everyone can be everyone"*	The new communication technologies' features This video aims to make youngsters think about the risk they face when they accept a friendship request from someone they don't know, and the importance of protecting their privacy; the anonymity made possible by the Internet allows everyone to be anyone	*Check carefully their privacy settings. Choose a password that is difficult to guess Do not accept the friendship of those you do not know and do not trust appearances since anyone can be anyone! Never share personal information, especially do not provide online your cell phone number, address, or other information that can make a person physically traceable. If you agree to personally meet someone you met online, tell someone you trust. Do not go alone, and choose a public and crowded place. Be aware*
2. *"Internet, all forever"*	Videos and photos diffusion on the Internet The video shows how devastating it could be for the victims to post or to share embarrassing photos or videos (even as a joke). The focus is to make youngsters understand that once such materials are published online they will remain online forever	*When you put something on the Web, remember that everyone can see it and forward it to others making it virtually impossible to delete the tracks from the Web. Think before you click! Before sharing a friend's information, photos, or videos ask them for permission: you may commit a crime! Everyone is capable of teasing others: to be popular among friends it is better to engage in something positive that harms no one*

(continued)

Table 2.2 (continued)

Video title	Area of cyberbullying addressed: Content of videos	Recommendations for youngsters provided at the end of the video related to the topic addressed
3. "Virtual actions, but real consequences"	The new communication technologies' improper use The video underlines how it could be harmful for youngsters to not protect their privacy on the Internet or to leave their mobile phones unattended. Some materials, such as one's own photos, can be used, as this video shows, to create fake social network profiles with the aim of damaging that person's reputation or friendships	*Pay attention to your phone, do not leave it unattended; it contains data and valuable information about you.* *Learn how to set it properly: using it all the time does not mean you know how to use it. Never leave your personal accounts or digital device unattended. Think ahead. Remember that what may seem like a joke to you can cause pain and discomfort to others* *Talk to an adult you trust if something happens to you that worries you or makes you sick*
4. "Joke or crime?"	Videos and/or photos sharing that seriously damage other people's reputations This video deals with the sexting phenomenon and with the negative consequences, for both the victim and the perpetrator, associated with the diffusion of materials such as personal photos or videos as a means of taking revenge against the victim. The focus is to make youngsters understand that to spread such materials could constitute a crime	*To post friends' photos without their permission is a crime; think about it first* *To damage someone's reputation is a crime* *If you're angry with someone, tell him/her rather than trying to take revenge*

Source: www.tabby.eu

the manual, there is also a tutorial on the meaning and use of the videos with students and the meaning of the risk profiles of the TABBY checklist. The manual can be used by any adult, and therefore also by parents.

The full on-site TABBY program has two additional components directly conducted with the school taking part in the experimentation. The videos and the booklet are part of the teacher training conducted by an expert on the use of the TABBY method.

1. A training that lasts three days (approx. three hours each session, once a week for three weeks, plus an additional day on the possible legal implications of cyberbullying, age of responsibility, and civil and criminal and administrative aspects). The training schedule is organized as follows: (a) the cyberbullying phenomenon, its forms and features, and risk factors for youngsters' involvement in this type of aggression; (b) the TABBY toolkit: how to use the checklist, the booklet, and the videos; (c) how to recognize, prevent, and manage cyberbullying accidents; (d) legal issues related to cyberbullying.
2. Once teachers are trained, they work with students and organize two or three class group meetings to show the videos and to discuss their content via interactive methods such as role-playing, group discussions, and focus groups. Follow-ups also take place.

This activity with students focuses on the importance of making good choices when using Web 2.0 communication technologies and electronic communication in general. During this interaction stage with students, the TABBY risk profiles that emerged from the data collection are discussed to identify possible strategies to reduce any risk.

The TABBY program, after its initial experimental stage and the data analyses, partly presented in this book, has reached numerous youngsters and increased awareness in them and in teachers. It is now available online for the part of the self-risk assessment by students, as well as most of the material. A part of the program to have it all implemented at its full efficacy consisting in the training of teachers can now also be done online (www.sara-cesvis.org), but only in Italian.

In the other countries it is used with all or some of its components, showing a high impact in terms of interest by students and adults, and as an efficient tool to enable addressing not only cyberbullying in terms of its knowledge, but through the innovative approach of the risk and needs assessment procedure. It is a program that will need additional testing for its efficacy. Here we present how it is structured; elsewhere we present data on its efficacy (Athanasiades et al. 2016).

Notes

1. JLS/2009/DAP/AG/1340 & JUST/2011/DAP/AG/3259.

References

Baldry, A. C., Farrington, D. P., & Sorrentino, A. (2015). "Am I at risk of cyber-bullying"? A narrative review and conceptual framework for research on risk of cyberbullying and cybervictimization: The risk and needs assessment approach. *Aggression and Violent Behavior, 23*, 36–51. https://doi.org/10.1016/j.avb.2015.05.014

Chalmers, J. B., & Townsend, M. A. (1990). The effects of training in social perspective taking on socially maladjusted girls. *Child Development, 61*(1), 178–190. https://doi.org/10.1111/j.1467-8624.1990.tb02770.x

Chandler, M. J. (1973). Egocentrism and antisocial behavior: The assessment and training of social perspective-taking skills. *Developmental Psychology, 9*(3), 326. https://doi.org/10.1037/h0034974.

Ellis, P. L. (1982). Empathy: A factor in antisocial behavior. *Journal of Abnormal Child Psychology, 10*(1), 123–133. https://doi.org/10.1007/BF00915957.

Jolliffe, D., & Farrington, D. P. (2006). Development and validation of the Basic Empathy Scale. *Journal of Adolescence, 29*(4), 589–611. https://doi.org/10.1016/j.adolescence.2005.08.010

Luengo, M. A., Carrillo-de-la-Peña, M. T., Otero, J. M., & Romero, E. (1994). A short-term longitudinal study of impulsivity and antisocial behavior. *Journal of Personality and Social Psychology, 66*(3), 542–548. https://doi.org/10.1037/0022-3514.66.3.542

Richardson, D. R., Hammock, G. S., Smith, S. M., Gardner, W., & Signo, M. (1994). Empathy as a cognitive inhibitor of interpersonal aggression. *Aggressive Behavior, 20*(4), 275–289. https://doi.org/10.1002/1098-2337(1994)20: 4<275::AID-AB2480200402>3.0.CO;2-4

Van Cleemput, K., Vandebosch, H., & Pabian, S. (2014). Personal characteristics and contextual factors that determine "helping", "joining in" and "doing nothing" when witnessing cyberbullying. *Aggressive Behavior, 40*(5), 383–396. https://doi.org/10.1002/ab.21534

Willard, N. E. (2007). *Cyberbullying and cyberthreats: Responding to the challenge of online social aggression, threats, and distress.* Champaign: Research Press.

Winkel, F. W., & Baldry, A. C. (1997). An application of the Scared Straight principle in early intervention programming: Three studies on activating the other's perspective in pre-adolescents' perceptions of a stepping-stone behaviour. *Issues in Criminological and Legal Psychology, 26,* 3–15.

Part II

International Perspectives on Cyberbullying

3

Cyberbullying in Canada

Julia Riddell, Debra Pepler, and Wendy Craig

Cyberbullying in Canada

Cyberbullying is a significant problem in Canada, with high prevalence rates that have remained stable over the past decade (Boak et al. 2016; Craig et al. 2016). A number of highly publicized Canadian cases have underscored the significant implications of involvement in cyberbullying. For example, Amanda Todd, a 15-year-old from western Canada, was lured by a man who manipulated her to share intimate pictures of herself with him (BBC News 2014). When these pictures were posted to Facebook, Amanda was severely bullied by peers at school, causing her to change schools a number of times. She posted a video on YouTube that detailed her struggles with cyberbullying before taking her own life (BBC News 2014). Another young woman, Rehtaeh Parsons, had a photo of her sexual assault shared with peers via text messages (Gillis 2013). After

J. Riddell (✉) • D. Pepler
York University, Keele Campus, Toronto, ON, Canada

W. Craig
Queen's University, Kingston, ON, Canada

© The Author(s) 2018
A. C. Baldry et al. (eds.), *International Perspectives on Cyberbullying*, Palgrave Studies in Cybercrime and Cybersecurity, https://doi.org/10.1007/978-3-319-73263-3_3

this picture was shared, she was severely bullied both online and in person, leading her to commit suicide at age 17 (Gillis 2013).

Canada is currently developing policies at both the provincial and school levels to address cyberbullying and prevent tragedies such as the ones described above. Cyberbullying legislation was first developed in the province of Ontario through an amendment to the Education Act in 2012 called Bill 13 (PREVNet 2015). This bill (entitled the Accepting Schools Act) outlines the rights and responsibilities of principals, teachers, schools, school boards, and the Ministry of Education when preventing or dealing with bullying incidents. This law specifies that the rights and responsibilities apply to all incidents of bullying that affect the school's learning climate, whether on or off school property, face-to-face or electronically (PREVNet 2015). Similarly, the western Canadian province of Alberta amended its Education Act in 2012 to include bullying behaviors that occur both within the school building and by electronic means (Education Act 2012). Other provinces, such as Manitoba, state in their revised Education Act that parents are responsible for their children's cyberbullying if they were aware of this problem behavior, could have reasonably predicted the effect, and did nothing (The Public Schools Act 2015). Efforts to prevent cyberbullying, however, are not consistent across Canada, partly due to the fact that there is still much to learn about this important social problem. In order to develop effective prevention and intervention programs for cyberbullying, and to continue developing effective legislation, more information on cyberbullying is needed. In this chapter, we describe the prevalence of cyberbullying and cybervictimization in Canada, as well as known risk and protective factors. We also describe the state of evidence on cyberbullying prevention and intervention programs in Canada, closing with recommendations for advancing this important work.

The Prevalence of Cyberbullying and Cybervictimization in Canada

The national rate of cyberbullying in Canada ranges from 4.5% of university-aged youth engaging in cyberbullying at any time (Cunningham et al. 2015) to 33.7% of adolescents in the past three months (Mishna et al. 2010). Estimates of cybervictimization prevalence in university range from 5.7% of youth being cybervictimized at any time (Cunningham et al. 2015) to 49.5% of adolescents reporting cybervictimization in the past three months (Mishna et al. 2010). These prevalence rates vary greatly due to sample characteristics, including the age, gender, and geographic location of the individuals sampled (e.g., province, language spoken, urban or rural location). Canada is a large country with provincial jurisdiction that has both urban and rural areas within each province. Therefore, cultural differences between urban and rural areas may partly explain the large differences in prevalence rates of cyberbullying and cybervictimization across studies. Further, there are methodological differences in the studies such as the time period of reporting, response rate, method of sampling, and whether or not a definition of cyberbullying was provided. Each of these key features will be explored in detail to explain differences in rates of cyberbullying and cybervictimization in Canada. Table 3.1 presents a summary of the studies in Canada examining the prevalence of cyberbullying and cybervictimization.

Differences in Prevalence Due to Sample Characteristics

Age

Most studies of the prevalence of cyberbullying and cybervictimization in Canada have been conducted with adolescents. The estimated prevalence of cyberbullying in adolescence ranges from 7% to 33.7% over the past few months, and the estimated prevalence of cybervictimization ranges from 5.1% to 49.5% over the past few months. When Boak et al. (2016) sampled 10,426 students aged 12 to 18, they found that the prevalence of cybervictimization ranged from 19.0% to 21.3% over the past year. The highest rate of cybervictimization occurred when youth were about 15 years old (21.3%), although the differences in age were not statistically significant. A recent systematic review of the prevalence of cyberbullying in Canada indicated that prevalence rates tended to increase over childhood, with the highest rates of victimization reported when youth

Table 3.1 Prevalence of cyberbullying and cybervictimization in Canada

Source	Sample N	Ages	Prevalence of cyberbullying	Prevalence of cybervictimization	Time period of reporting
Boak et al. (2016) using OSDUHS	10,426	12 to 18	Not reported	25.8% for girls; 14.0% for boys	Past year
Craig et al. (2016) HBSC 2014 data	29,784	11 to 15	7% (as calculated by the authors of this chapter)	8% to 12% for boys; 14% to 22% for girls; 14.4% overall	Past couple of months
Cunningham et al. (2015)	1,004	~18	4.5%	5.7%	During university
Holfeld and Leadbeater (2015)	714	10 to 12	10.2% at Time 1; 13% at Time 2	22.0% at Time 1; 26.8% at Time 2	Past 30 days
Li and Craig (2015)	800	12 to 18	17% of boys; 12% of girls	42% overall; 45% of boys; 38% of girls	Past 4 weeks
Cénat et al. (2014) using QYRRS	8,194	14 to 20	Not reported	26.4% for girls; 18.1% for boys	Past 12 months
Cappadocia et al. (2013) using HBSC 2006 and 2007 data	1,972	14 to 18	4.9% at Time 1 only; 4.7% at Time 2 only; 1.9% at both times	5.1% at Time 1 only; 6.5% at Time 2 only; 1.9% at both times	Past 2 months
Perreault (2011) using 2009 Statistics Canada data	25,000	15 to 17, 18 to 24, 25 and up	Not reported	12% to 19% for ages 15 to 17; 17% for ages 18 to 24; 5% for ages 25 and up	Ever (lifetime prevalence)
Mishna et al. (2010)	2,186	11 to 16	33.7% overall	49.5% overall	Past 3 months
Vaillancourt et al. (2010)	16,799	9 to 18	9.7%	12.4%	Past 3 months

(continued)

Table 3.1 (continued)

Source	Sample		Prevalence of cyberbullying	Prevalence of cybervictimization	Time period of reporting
	N	Ages			
Estimated national prevalence	*96,879*	*9 to adult*	*4.5% to 33.7%*	*5.1% to 49.5%*	*Past 30 days to ever*

begin high school around age 14 (Bilsbury 2015). This finding is consistent with the results of the 2014 Health Behavior in School-aged Children (HBSC) survey, which indicated that the highest rate of cybervictimization occurred during the first year of high school (Craig et al. 2016). Averaged across genders, the HBSC data revealed that the rate of cybervictimization increased from 15% at age 13 to 17% at age 14, and then decreased back to 15% by age 15 (Craig et al. 2016).

Other Canadian studies, however, have found the opposite trend with respect to age. Li and Craig (2015) conducted a study with a representative sample of 800 youth aged 12 to 18 who completed an online survey. They found that older youth were significantly more likely than younger youth to be cybervictimized in the past four weeks (47% of youth aged 17 to 18, compared to 36% of youth aged 12 to 14). These differences may be due to methodological differences between the studies, which will be discussed in detail in the section below.

Holfeld and Leadbeater (2015) conducted a study with a sample of pre-adolescent children aged 10 to 12. They asked these children to complete measures at two time points, corresponding with the beginning and end of the school year. At the beginning of the school year, 10.2% of children reported engaging in one or more cyberbullying behaviors, compared to 13% of children at the end of the year. About twice this number of children (22.0%) reported being cybervictimized at the beginning of the school year and 26.8% reported being cybervictimized at the end of the year. These prevalence rates of cyberbullying and cybervictimization in children appear to be consistent with the prevalence rates in adolescents.

Based on the two Canadian studies measuring cyberbullying and cybervictimization in adults, the prevalence appears to be lower for emerging adults (aged 18 to 24) and adults (over age 25) compared to children and adolescents. Cunningham et al. (2015) conducted a survey with 1,004 students in a first-year university class. In this study, 5.7% of the students reported that they had experienced cybervictimization at some point in university, 4.5% had engaged in cyberbullying, and 4.9% had both cyberbullied others and been cybervictimized. Higher prevalence rates for this age group were reported by Perreault (2011) using a large nationally representative survey with a sample of 25,000 participants. Results indicated that 17% of young adults (aged 18 to 24) had been cybervictimized in their lifetime. This study provided the only prevalence rate for cybervictimization in adults over the age of 25 (5% lifetime prevalence), which is much lower than the prevalence rates reported for adolescents (Perreault 2011). This may be related to increased use of social media over time. In conclusion, the rates of cybervictimization in Canada are the highest in adolescence and drop significantly during young adulthood and adulthood.

Gender

Most Canadian studies suggest that the rates of cybervictimization are higher for girls than for boys. In her systematic review, Bilsbury (2015) determined that there were small but significant sex differences such that girls were more likely to be cybervictimized than boys. Craig et al. (2016) found that girls reported much higher rates of cybervictimization (18.8% over the past few months) compared to boys (10% over the past few months). Two other studies indicated a significantly higher proportion of girls compared to boys reporting cybervictimization over the past year. Boak et al. (2016) found that 25.8% of girls compared to 14.0% of boys reported being cybervictimized in the past year. Similarly, Cénat et al. (2014) found that 26.4% of girls and 18.1% of boys reported being cybervictimized.

Much less is known about gender differences in perpetrating cyberbullying. Li and Craig (2015) found that boys were significantly more likely to report engaging in cyberbullying in the past four weeks (17% of boys compared to 12% of girls). Further, Cunningham et al. (2015) found that young men in their first year of university were more likely than young women to report that they both cyberbullied others and were cybervictimized.

Urban or Rural Location

Holfeld and Leadbeater (2015) conducted a study of cyberbullying and cybervictimization with 714 children from predominately rural areas across Canada. At the beginning and end of the school year, these children were asked how many times they engaged in four cyberbullying behaviors. Averaged across the two time points, 11.6% of students reported engaging in one or more cyberbullying behaviors, and 24.4% reported being cybervictimized in the past 30 days. Mishna et al. (2010) used an urban sample of youth and found that 49.5% of students had experienced behaviors that the researchers identified as cybervictimization in the past three months. Further, 33.7% of participants indicated that they had cyberbullied others in the past three months. The differences in the reporting period make it difficult to compare across these two studies, as discussed in detail below.

Differences in Prevalence Due to Study Methodology

Time Period of Reporting

As shown in Table 3.1, the studies reviewed in this chapter vary greatly in their reporting period, with some youth being asked to report experiences of cyberbullying/cybervictimization over the past 30 days and others reporting a lifetime prevalence. These differences in the reporting period present challenges in comparing the prevalence rates across studies. Recently, a systematic review of the prevalence of cyberbullying in Canada was completed based on 45 studies (Bilsbury 2015). An overall estimate of prevalence could not be calculated due to heterogeneity in the definition of cyberbullying used, sample characteristics, and length of the reporting period. Instead, a summary of each study was provided, with studies divided into two categories based on the length of the reporting period (3 months or less, and 4 to 12 months). For studies that reported cyberbullying over the past 3 months, estimates ranged from 2% to 28% of youth engaging in cyberbullying and between 4% and 38% of students being cybervictimized. For studies reporting cyberbullying over the past 12 months, estimates ranged from 2% to 34% of youth engaging in

cyberbullying and between 4% and 39% of students being cybervictimized. Adopting a standardized reporting period for all cyberbullying studies in Canada would be helpful to calculate a national prevalence rate and
compare across studies with different sample characteristics.

Response Rate and Method of Sampling

One study with particularly high prevalence rates was conducted by
Mishna et al. (2010). They found that 49.5% of students reported being
cybervictimized in the past three months and 33.7% of participants
reported having cyberbullied others. The response rate on this survey was
low (35% in Grades 6 and 7 and 17% in Grades 10 and 11); therefore, it
is possible that students involved in cyberbullying were more likely to
participate than those not involved. The prevalence rates reported by
Mishna et al. (2010) are notably higher than those reported by Perreault
(2011), in which the response rate was 61.6%, and by Craig et al. (2016),
in which the response rate was 77%. Therefore, the response rate and
method of selection may greatly impact the prevalence rates reported.

Providing a Definition of Cyberbullying

The studies presented in Table 3.1 vary in terms of whether or not they
provided a definition of cyberbullying as part of the questionnaire.
Vaillancourt et al. (2010) provided students with a definition of bullying
and then asked about their experiences of bullying using two questions
from the Olweus Bully/Victim Questionnaire (1996). Li and Craig
(2015) defined cyberbullying as being threatened, embarrassed, gossiped
about, or made to look bad online. Cunningham et al. (2015) asked
young adults to read a definition of cyberbullying before rating their
involvement in ten randomly presented electronic formats (Facebook,
YouTube, Twitter, text messages, etc.) as a witness, perpetrator, or victim.
As part of the HBSC survey used by Cappadocia et al. (2013) and Craig
et al. (2016), participants were provided with a standard definition of
bullying including three main components: intention to harm, repetition, and power differential (Cappadocia et al. 2013; Craig et al. 2016).
Prevalence rates across these studies varied widely, as can be seen in

Table 3.1. Of note, Mishna et al. (2012) used a questionnaire that contained a number of questions about perpetrating or being victimized by different types of online behaviors, without explicitly defining the behaviors as bullying. In this study, 49.5% of students indicated that they had experienced behaviors that the researchers identified as cybervictimization in the past three months, and 33.7% of participants indicated that they had engaging in cyberbullying. The overall prevalence rates of cyberbullying and cybervictimization reported in this study were higher than most other studies. It is possible that since the behaviors were not labeled as bullying, students were more likely to endorse them.

Other Considerations Related to Cyberbullying Prevalence

Stability Over Time

Cappadocia et al. (2013) examined the stability of prevalence estimates using two waves of data collected one year apart. In terms of engaging in cyberbullying, 4.9% reported cyberbullying others at Time 1 only, 4.7% at Time 2 only, and 1.9% at both time points. In terms of experiencing cybervictimization, 5.1% reported being victimized at Time 1 only, 6.5% at Time 2 only, and 1.9% at both time points. Although the rates of cyberbullying and cybervictimization between the two time points were similar, less than half of the youth involved at one time point were involved at both time points, suggesting that short-term estimates of cyberbullying are not completely stable over the school year.

Another consideration is how stable the Canadian rates of cyberbullying have been over the past few years. A report by Boak and colleagues examined the well-being of students in Ontario using The Centre for Addiction and Mental Health's Ontario Student Drug Use and Health Survey (OSDUHS), which has been conducted every two years since 1977 (Boak et al. 2016). The authors noted that the overall percentage of students who reported being cybervictimized in 2015 (19.8%) was not significantly different than the percentages in 2013 (19%) and in 2011 (21.6%; Boak et al. 2016). One of the most representative sources of information on cyberbullying among youth across Canada is the HBSC survey, which is conducted in collaboration with the World Health Organization every four years. In the 2006 edition of this survey, students aged 11 to 15 were asked how often they cyberbullied another student using a computer, email messages or pictures, or a mobile phone in the past couple of months. In this survey, 4.8% of Canadian youth reported engaging in cyberbullying and 5.8% of youth reported being cybervictimized over the past two months (Cappadocia et al. 2013). These prevalence rates are slightly lower than those found in the 2014 edition of the HBSC survey, which indicated that across grades and gender 14.4% of youth reported having been cybervictimized in the past few months (Craig et al. 2016). More information is needed on changes in cyberbullying and cybervictimization over time.

Involvement in Both Cyberbullying and Cybervictimization

Most research suggests that youth who engage in cyberbullying have also been involved in cybervictimization. Using a nationally representative sample, Craig et al. (2016) found that 4.8% of youth reported that they had both cyberbullied others and been cybervictimized in the past two months (compared to 7% of students who reported only cyberbullying others). Similarly, Cappadocia et al. (2013) found that some students were both cybervictimized and engaged in cyberbullying over the past two months: 1.4% at Time 1 only, 2.7% at Time 2 only, and 0.5% at both time points (Cappadocia et al. 2013). A nationally representative study with a smaller sample found that youth who reported that they had been cybervictimized at least once were also significantly more likely to report they had cyberbullied others (32%) compared to youth who had not been cybervictimized (2%; Li and Craig 2015).

Type of Cyberbullying

Studies have shown that some types of cyberbullying are more prevalent than others. Holfeld and Leadbeater (2015) found that the most common types of cybervictimization were "*received a text message that made you upset or uncomfortable*" and "*someone posted something on your online page or wall that made you upset or uncomfortable.*" Mishna et al. (2010)

identified the most common cyberbullying experiences as being called names (27%), having rumors spread about the participant (22%), having someone pretend to be the participant (18%), being threatened (11%), and receiving unwelcome sexual photos or text messages (10%). The main cyberbullying behaviors that students endorsed were calling someone names (22%), pretending to be someone else (14%), and spreading rumors about someone (11%). The majority of this cyberbullying took place through instant messages or email, with less cyberbullying occurring over Internet games (12%) or on social networking sites (10%). Understanding the type of cyberbullying and where it occurs is helpful in designing interventions to support those who engage in cyberbullying and those experiencing cybervictimization. Knowledge about the nature of cyberbullying behaviors over particular platforms will need to be continually updated to keep pace with ongoing changes in technology and user preferences.

Risk and Protective Factors

Six Canadian studies have examined the risk and protective factors associated with cyberbullying and cybervictimization. These risk and protective factors have been organized using a social ecological framework, with a discussion of factors at the individual, family, school, and neighborhood level. Table 3.2 contains a summary of the risk and protective factors associated with cyberbullying and cybervictimization in Canadian children, organized by participant age.

Individual-Level Risk and Protective Factors

Internet-Use Characteristics

Three studies investigated whether particular Internet-use characteristics were related to cyberbullying and cybervictimization (Cappadocia et al. 2013; Mishna et al. 2012; Perreault 2011). Mishna et al. (2012) found that compared to a reference group of uninvolved children, children involved in cyberbullying were more likely to use the computer for more

Table 3.2 Risk and protective factors associated with cyberbullying and cybervictimization in Canada

| Source | Sample | | Risk factors for cybervictimization | Risk factors for cyberbullying | Protective factors for being cybervictimized |
	N	Ages			
Dafoe (2016)	193	~12 to 13	Having more friends; Poor self-awareness	–	–
Schumann et al. (2014) using 2010 HBSC data	17,777	11 to 15	Individual-level social capital; Low SES	–	Being male, South Asian, and older; Higher collective efficacy; Community-based opportunities for recreation
Cappadocia et al. (2013) using 2006 HBSC data	1,972	14 to 16	Higher levels of traditional victimization; Higher levels of depression; Being in the transition year for high school (Grade 9)	Involvement in traditional bullying; Alcohol use; Fewer prosocial peers	–
Dittrick et al. (2013)	492 children 397 parents	10 to 17	–	Playing highly violent and mature video games	–

(continued)

Table 3.2 (continued)

Source	Sample		Risk factors for cybervictimization	Risk factors for cyberbullying	Protective factors for being cybervictimized
	N	Ages			
Mishna et al. (2012)	2,186	~11 to 16	More time on computer per day; Giving passwords to friends; Violence toward peers at school; Having parents who speak English at home	More time on computer per day; Giving passwords to friends; Violence toward peers at school; Greater age	—
Perreault (2011) using 2009 Statistics Canada data	25,000	15 to 17, 18 to 24, 25 and up	Using chat sites or social networking sites; Being single, separated, or divorced; Younger age (ages 18 to 24); Identifying as bisexual or homosexual; Having an activity limitation	—	Being Francophone; Trusting family relationships

hours a day and more likely to give their passwords to friends. These findings were consistent across three groups: those who had been cybervictimized, those engaged in cyberbullying, and those who were involved with both cyberbullying and cybervictimization. Perreault (2011) found that adolescents and adults who used chat sites or social networking sites were almost three times more likely than non-users to report being cybervictimized. Conversely, Cappadocia et al. (2013) did not find the total amount of time spent online to be a significant predictor of cyberbullying or cybervictimization.

Demographic Variables

A number of demographic characteristics were associated with a higher risk of experiencing cybervictimization. In one study, these risk factors included being single, being homosexual or bisexual, and having a long-term physical or mental health condition (Perreault 2011). Specifically, individuals who were single, separated, or divorced were more likely than married or common-law individuals to have been cybervictimized. Among Internet users, 24% of those who identified as bisexual and 18% of those who identified as homosexual were cybervictimized compared with only 7% of individuals who identified as heterosexual. Lastly, people who were limited in the amount or type of activity they could do because of a long-term physical or mental health problem were more likely than those with no condition to report having been cybervictimized (22% of those with a condition compared to 10% of those with no condition).

A few Canadian studies have explored risk factors associated with ethnicity, language use, and immigrant status. In one study, being South Asian was identified as a protective factor against cybervictimization (Schumann et al. 2014). Mishna et al. (2012) found that compared to a reference group of uninvolved children, children involved in cyberbullying were more likely to have parents who speak English at home. Further, English-speaking adolescents and adults were more likely to report being cybervictimized than French-speaking individuals (Perreault 2011). The reasons why English-speaking individuals are at greater risk for involvement in cyberbullying and cybervictimization is unclear.

Consistent with the gender-based prevalence rates discussed above, young women are more likely to be involved in cyberbullying and cybervictimization compared to young men. Schumann et al. (2014) identified being male as a protective factor against cybervictimization, and Mishna et al. (2012) identified being female as a risk factor for cyberbullying others and being cybervictimized.

As reported in the prevalence section above, being an adolescent is linked to the highest levels of cybervictimization. Two studies illustrated that youth aged 14 to 16 were more likely to cyberbully others and be cybervictimized compared to youth aged 11 and 12 (Mishna et al. 2012; Cappadocia et al. 2013). Further, Perreault (2011) found that young adults between 18 and 24 years of age were about three times more likely than those aged 25 and over to report having been cybervictimized. Within adolescence, however, it is unclear when the rates of cybervictimization are the highest. Cappadocia et al. (2013) found that students in a lower grade (i.e., Grade 9) at Time 1 were more likely to be involved in cybervictimization at Time 2, suggesting that the rates of cybervictimization increase over the first year of high school. Another study using the 2010 HBSC dataset found the opposite—being older (ages 14 to 15) was a protective factor against cybervictimization (Schumann et al. 2014). More information on the role of age in cybervictimization is needed.

Socio-emotional and Behavioral Variables

Cappadocia et al. (2013) analyzed one-year longitudinal data from the 2006 HBSC survey to examine risk factors associated with cyberbullying among Canadian children. The main individual-level risk factor they identified for engaging in cyberbullying was alcohol use, and the main individual-level risk factor for cybervictimization was depression. In a recent doctoral dissertation, Dafoe (2016) asked 193 students aged 12 and 13 from a large urban area to complete questionnaires related to social-emotional learning (i.e., self-awareness, self-management, social awareness, relationship skills, and responsible decision-making) and a range of bullying behaviors (i.e., physical, verbal, social, sexual, and cyber). Results of this study suggested that having poor self-awareness was associated with a higher level of cybervictimization (Dafoe 2016).

Other Individual-Level Factors

Dittrick and colleagues examined the association between cyberbullying and violent video games using a stratified random sample of 492 Canadian children aged 10 to 17 years, as well as 397 of their parents (Dittrick et al. 2013). Parents and children completed an online survey of children's bullying behaviors and listed their three favorite video games. Dittrick and colleagues determined that playing highly violent and mature video games was associated with cyberbullying according to both parent and child reports.

Schumann and colleagues used the 2010 edition of the HBSC to examine individual-level variables associated with both traditional bullying and cyberbullying (Schumann et al. 2014). The two individual-level variables that predicted cybervictimization were individual-level social capital (involvement in clubs, groups, sports or volunteering) and low socioeconomic status (i.e. poverty). This study also replicated the high overlap between children involved in cyberbullying and cybervictimization (e.g., Cappadocia et al. 2013; Craig et al. 2016; Li and Craig 2015).

Risk and Protective Factors Associated with the Family

A few Canadian studies have investigated family-level factors associated with a reduced risk of cyberbullying and cybervictimization. In particular, trusting family relationships have been identified as a protective factor against cybervictimization (Perreault 2011). Internet users who indicated that they can trust people in their family "a lot" were less likely to be cybervictimized than those who indicated that they could "more or less" trust them (6% compared to 13%; Perreault 2011). Further, child-reported frequency of parent involvement in school activities was identified as an important protective factor for cybervictimization (Leadbeater et al. 2015). Conversely, Cappadocia et al. (2013) tested whether parental trust and communication, parental support, and parental involvement with school were related to cyberbullying and cybervictimization, and did not find significant results. Mishna et al. (2012) found that compared to a reference group of uninvolved children, children involved in cyberbullying were more likely to have parents who supervised their Internet use and had blocking programs for the Internet. The direction of effect for parent behavior is not clear: parents of youth engaged in cyberbullying may have been stricter with monitoring Internet activity prior to involvement in cyberbullying, or parents may have used this software as a result of youths' involvement in cyberbullying. Overall, there are few studies examining family factors associated with cybervictimization, and those that have been conducted have demonstrated inconsistent results with respect to the association between cybervictimization and the quality of relationships in the family.

Risk and Protective Factors Associated with Peers and School

The role of relationships with teachers has been investigated as a potential risk and protective factor for involvement in cyberbullying and cybervictimization. Positive student–teacher relationships were identified as a protective factor against cybervictimization (Leadbeater et al. 2015). Conversely, poor relationships with teachers were found to be both a risk factor and a consequence of peer cybervictimization. That is, parent ratings of student–teacher relationships were reciprocally related to their children's reports of peer victimization from the beginning to the end of the school year (Leadbeater et al. 2015). These findings illustrate the importance of relationships with teachers in protecting against cybervictimization.

Relationships with peers have also been linked with involvement in cyberbullying and cybervictimization. Mishna et al. (2012) found that compared to a reference group, children involved in cyberbullying were more likely to act violently toward peers at school. Similarly, Cappadocia et al. (2013) found that involvement in traditional bullying was a risk factor for involvement in both cyberbullying and cybervictimization. In terms of cybervictimization, the authors determined that students who reported higher levels of traditional victimization at Time 1 were more likely to be involved in cybervictimization at Time 2. Further, students who reported traditional victimization at Time 1 were almost four times more likely than peers who had not been victimized to report simultaneous cyberbullying and cybervictimization at Time 2 (Cappadocia et al. 2013). In this study, one of the main risk factors linked to higher levels of cyberbullying was having fewer prosocial peers (Cappadocia et al. 2013). Conversely, Dafoe (2016) found that having more close friends was associated with a higher level of cybervictimization. This discrepancy in findings may be due to the influence of other peer relationship factors, such as the quality of relationships, peer culture, and status within that peer group. This suggestion is consistent with the Canadian research on in-person bullying which found that low friendship quality was a significant predictor of subsequent in-person victimization, and having high-quality friendships was a protective factor against victimization (Goldbaum et al. 2003). Therefore, models of cybervictimization need to consider multiple peer relationship factors, including the number and quality of friendships, social status, peer culture, and wider school culture, as well as involvement in in-person or traditional forms of bullying.

Neighborhood and Societal-Level Risk and Protective Factors

Using the 2010 edition of the HBSC, Schumann and colleagues examined a number of community-level variables associated with both traditional bullying and cyberbullying (Schumann et al. 2014). They examined the following community-level variables: community socioeconomic status (SES), built social capital, built recreational opportunity, community stability, and population density. Only one community-level factor was significantly associated with cybervictimization: community recreation. In this study, high levels of community recreation were a protective factor associated with lower levels of cybervictimization. Further, Schumann et al. (2014) measured how students felt about the safety, cooperation, and trust that existed in their neighborhoods, which they termed collective efficacy. Results indicated that higher collective efficacy was associated with lower rates of cybervictimization. As there is only one known Canadian study exploring the impact of neighborhood and societal-level variables, more research is needed in order to effectively inform public policy.

Cyberbullying and Cybervictimization Intervention Programs

Many cyberbullying and digital citizenship resources and programs have been developed in Canada including The Canadian Red Cross Respect Education resources, MediaSmarts resources, Canadian government resources, and some provincial Ministries of Education programs. There are, however, no evaluations of these resources and programs available in the literature. The authors located two international systematic reviews on cyberbullying interventions that contained at least one Canadian intervention (Della Cioppa et al. 2015; Mishna et al. 2009a). Both of these systematic reviews contained one Canadian study, which is an evaluation of the Missing cyber safety program (Crombie and Trinneer 2003). Since this evaluation was summarized in a report submitted to a national funding agency and was not publicly available, the results discussed below are from the systematic review by Mishna and colleague (2009). The Missing cyber safety program included an interactive computer game designed to encourage youth to develop guidelines for safe Internet use. In this game, youth assumed the role of a police officer and solved a series of puzzles to find a missing teenager who was lured away from home by an Internet predator (Crombie and Trinneer 2003). The goal of the game was to highlight that revealing personal information about oneself on the Internet may lead to cybervictimization. The outcomes included the frequency of disclosing personal information online, attitudes regarding the safety of disclosing personal information online, and attitudes about trusting people met online. Crombie and Trinneer (2003) measured these behaviors and attitudes before and three weeks after the intervention.

As part of their systematic review, Mishna and colleagues (2009) calculated effect size measures for all 64 individual behaviors and attitudes measures; they then conducted z-tests to determine whether the effect sizes were significantly different between the intervention and control group. Only three variables were significant: disclosing one's gender to a stranger in a chat room or by email, disclosing one's age to a stranger in a chat room or by email, and posting one's school name on a web page. That is, youth who participated in the Missing program showed a greater reduction in these three specific behaviors compared to the control group. There was no significant change in the other 61 behaviors and attitudes measured in this study, leading the authors of the systematic review to conclude that the program did not result in significant change overall (Mishna et al. 2009a, b).

In summary, there are few documented cyber intervention programs in Canada, and those that do exist are old and/or have not been evaluated. This lack of evidence-based programming specifically for cyberbullying may be due to the fact that there is a strong link between involvement in traditional bullying and involvement in cyberbullying, as described in the prevalence and risk sections above. Therefore, it may not be necessary to develop interventions specifically targeting cyberbullying. Instead, the most effective strategy to address cyberbullying may be to focus on creating healthy relationships in general (Mishna et al. 2012; Pepler 2006; Craig and Pepler 2007). This approach includes promoting healthy relationships with peers, teachers, family members, and neighbors.

To design effective cyberbullying interventions, it is important to consider youths' voices in terms of the kinds of interventions they would find most helpful. A few recent studies have examined youths' preferences for cyberbullying programs using discrete choice conjoint experiments: one with university students (Cunningham et al. 2015) and another with younger children (Cunningham et al. 2011). In the study by Cunningham et al. (2015), the participants were 1,004 university students in an introductory psychology class. While the response rate for this study was excellent (95.7%), the sample is not representative of all young adults in Canada. More than 90% of the sample expressed a preference for a comprehensive approach that included teaching strategies to prevent cyberbullying, encouraging anonymous reporting, and imposing consequences when cyberbullying is detected. In particular, students preferred a policy that encourages but does not require students to report cyberbullying.

Students also expressed a preference for the university suspending Internet privileges of students who cyberbully. The preference for comprehensive programs combining prevention and consequences is consistent with the recommendations of younger students (Cunningham et al. 2011).

Conclusion

Estimates of the prevalence of cyberbullying and cybervictimization in Canada vary widely depending on a multitude of sample characteristics and methodological considerations. In particular, the differences in the reporting period used across studies make it impossible to calculate an overall estimate of cyberbullying prevalence in Canada. Adopting a standardized reporting period for all studies in Canada would make it possible to calculate a national prevalence rate and to compare across studies with different sample characteristics. Other methodological differences between studies are currently a barrier to developing a fulsome understanding of cyberbullying in Canada. Standardized assessment and regular monitoring of cyberbullying are needed to understand the extent of the problem, identify risk and protective factors, and guide the development of prevention and intervention strategies.

Regardless of the reporting period assessed, cyberbullying is a significant problem in Canada. There are common risk factors for cyberbullying and cybervictimization, most notably, involvement in traditional bullying. There have been limited studies on protective factors in Canada, and ones that have been conducted are not consistent in their findings. Therefore, more research on this important topic is needed. The few studies on protective factors that have been conducted in Canada have highlighted the importance of close relationships with teachers and parents, highlighting the need for education for adults on how to cultivate healthy relationships with youth. High levels of community recreation were shown to be a protective factor against cybervictimization. It may therefore be worthwhile to invest in community recreation programs for youth as a cyberbullying prevention strategy, particularly if these programs are run by supportive adults who can create safer spaces for youth. Collective efficacy (how students feel about the safety, cooperation, and trust in their neighborhoods) is a protective factor against cybervictimization. Each of us has a role in increasing neighborhood cooperation, and we can all play a part in reducing cyberbullying. Finally, lower individual social capital and low socioeconomic status predict cybervictimization. There is a need to address inequities and structural barriers that may contribute to cyberbullying and cybervictimization, such as poverty and classism.

Moving forward, there is a need to identify youth involved in cyberbullying and cybervictimization to provide support, as well as a need to teach strategies for online bystander intervention. Canada must develop and implement evidenced-based interventions to address the problem; however, given the dearth of research, we may need to rely on the research conducted in other countries to guide the development of these interventions. If we are to improve the lives of youth and reduce the risk of other tragedies due to cybervictimization, we need to start this work immediately. Currently, there is a lack of effective programming to identify vulnerable youth and ensure that they are stabilized and supported. Without these interventions, the rates of cyberbullying and cybervictimization are likely to remain stable over time.

We cannot truly address cyberbullying until we address racism, sexism, homophobia, ableism, and fat phobia. When we look carefully at the content of cyberbullying messages, they commonly fall along these societal lines of discrimination and marginalization. Students learn to use the word "gay" as an insult because they have heard adults do this. Children cyberbully each other by making comments about each other's physical appearance and weight because our culture has modeled this for them. Children learn to exclude and vilify those who are different because, as adults, we do this, usually in more subtle and insidious ways. As is the case with other forms of bullying, cyberbullying involves a power imbalance between individuals. To truly address cyberbullying, we need to think about the ways in which we use power over others as opposed to sharing power with others. These different ways of negotiating power between individuals shape the structures in our society and send powerful messages to children. To eradicate cyberbullying, we need more public education on how to have respectful relationships with each other—in the workplace, at the grocery store, at the dinner table, in our places of worship, and through digital media. If we truly want to end cyberbullying, we need a cultural shift in how we interact with each other each and every day.

References

BBC News. (2014). *Man charged in Netherlands in Amanda Todd suicide case.* Retrieved from http://www.bbc.com/news/world-europe-27076991

Bilsbury, T. (2015). *A systematic review of the prevalence of cyberbullying in Canada* (Master's thesis). Dalhousie University. Retrieved from http://hdl.handle.net/10222/58197

Boak, A., Hamilton, H. A., Adlaf, E. M., Henderson, J. L., & Mann, R. E. (2016). *The mental health and well-being of Ontario students, 1991– 2015: Detailed OSDUHS findings* (CAMH Research Document Series No. 43). Toronto: Centre for Addiction and Mental Health. Retrieved from https://www.camh.ca/en/research/news_and_publications/ontario-student-drug-use-and health-survey/Documents/2015%20OSDUHS%20Documents/2015OSDUHS_Detailed%20MentalHealthReport.pdf

Cappadocia, M. C., Craig, W. M., & Pepler, D. (2013). Cyberbullying prevalence, stability, and risk factors during adolescence. *Canadian Journal of School Psychology, 28*(2), 171–192. https://doi.org/10.1177/0829573513491212

Cénat, J. M., Hébert, M., Blais, M., Lavoie, F., Guerrier, M., & Derivois, D. (2014). Cyberbullying, psychological distress and self-esteem among youth in Quebec schools. *Journal of Affective Disorders, 169,* 7–9. https://doi.org/10.1016/j.jad.2014.07.019

Craig, W. M., & Pepler, D. J. (2007). Understanding bullying: From research to practice. *Canadian Psychology, 48*(2), 86–93. https://doi.org/10.1037/cp2007010

Craig, W., Lambe, L., & McIver, T. (2016). Bullying and fighting. In J.G. Freeman, M. A. King, & W. Pickett (Eds.), *Health Behaviour in School-aged Children (HBSC) in Canada: Focus on relationships* (pp. 167–182). Ottawa: Public Health Agency of Canada. Retrieved from http://healthycanadians.gc.ca/publications/science-research-sciences-recherches/health behaviour-children-canada-2015-comportements-sante-jeunes/index-eng.php

Crombie, G., & Trinneer, A. (2003). *Children and internet safety: An evaluation of the missing program. A report to the Research and Evaluation Section of the*

National Crime Prevention Centre of Justice Canada. Ottawa: University of Ottawa.

Cunningham, C. E., Vaillancourt, T., Cunningham, L. J., Chen, Y., & Ratcliffe, J. (2011). Modeling the bullying prevention program design recommendations of students from grades 5 to 8: A discrete choice conjoint experiment. *Aggressive Behavior, 37*(6), 521–537. https://doi.org/10.1002/ab.20408

Cunningham, C. E., Chen, Y., Vaillancourt, T., Rimas, H., Deal, K., Cunningham, L. J., & Ratcliffe, J. (2015). Modeling the anti-cyberbullying preferences of university students: Adaptive choice-based conjoint analysis. *Aggressive Behavior, 41*(4), 369–385. https://doi.org/10.1002/ab.21560

Dafoe, T. L. (2016). *The role of social-emotional learning skills in bullying behaviour* (Doctoral dissertation). University of Toronto.

Della Cioppa, V., O'Neil, A., & Craig, W. (2015). Learning from traditional bullying interventions: A review of research on cyberbullying and best practice. *Aggression and Violent Behavior, 23*, 61–68. https://doi.org/10.1016/j.avb.2015.05.009

Dittrick, C. J., Beran, T. N., Mishna, F., Hetherington, R., & Shariff, S. (2013). Do children who bully their peers also play violent video games? A Canadian national study. *Journal of School Violence, 12*(4), 297–318. https://doi.org/10.1080/15388220.2013.803244

Education Act, Revised Statutes of Alberta. (2012, Chapter E-0.3). Retrieved from the Province of Alberta website: http://www.qp.alberta.ca/documents/Acts/e00p3.pdf

Gillis, W. (2013, April 12). Rehtaeh Parsons: A family's tragedy and a town's shame. *The Star.* Retrieved from https://www.thestar.com/news/canada/2013/04/12/rehtaeh_parsons_a_ family s_ tragedy_ and_a_towns_ shame.html

Goldbaum, S., Craig, W. M., Pepler, D., & Connolly, J. (2003). Developmental trajectories of victimization: Identifying risk and protective factors. *Journal of Applied School Psychology, 19*(2), 139–156. https://doi.org/10.1080/1538822 0.2013.803244

Holfeld, B., & Leadbeater, B. J. (2015). The nature and frequency of cyber bullying behaviors and victimization experiences in young Canadian children. *Canadian Journal of School Psychology, 30*(2), 116–135. https://doi.org/10.1177/0829573514556853

Leadbeater, B., Sukhawathanakul, P., Smith, D., & Bowen, F. (2015). Reciprocal associations between interpersonal and values dimensions of school climate and peer victimization in elementary school children. *Journal of Clinical*

Child and Adolescent Psychology, 44(3), 480–493. https://doi.org/10.1080/15 374416.2013.873985

Li, J., & Craig, W. (2015). *Young Canadians' experiences with electronic bullying.* Retrieved from http://mediasmarts.ca/sites/mediasmarts/files/publication-report/full/young-canadians-electronic- bullying.pdf

Mishna, F., Cook, C., Saini, M., Wu, M., & MacFadden, R. (2009a). Interventions for children, youth, and parents to prevent and reduce cyber abuse. *Campbell Systematic Reviews, 2009*, 2.

Mishna, F., Saini, M., & Solomon, S. (2009b). Ongoing and online: Children and youth's perceptions of cyberbullying. *Children and Youth Services Review, 31*, 1222–1228. https://doi.org/10.1016/j.childyouth.2009.05.004

Mishna, F., Cook, C., Gadalla, T., Daciuk, J., & Solomon, S. (2010). Cyber bullying behaviors among middle and high school students. *American Journal of Orthopsychiatry, 80*(3), 362–374. https://doi.org/10.1111/j.1939-0025. 2010.01040.x

Mishna, F., Khoury-Kassabri, M., Gadalla, T., & Daciuk, J. (2012). Risk factors for involvement in cyberbullying: Victims, bullies and bully-victims. *Children &Youth Services Review, 34*(1), 63–70. https://doi.org/10.1016/j.childyouth. 2011.08.032

Olweus, D. (1996). *The revised bully/victim questionnaire for students.* Bergen: University of Bergen.

Pepler, D. J. (2006). Bullying interventions: A binocular perspective. *Journal of the Canadian Academy of Child and Adolescent Psychiatry, 15*(1), 16–20.

Perreault, S. (2011). *Self-reported Internet victimization in Canada, 2009* (Statistics Canada catalogue No. 85-002-X). Retrieved from http://www.stat-can.gc.ca/pub/85-002 x/2011001 /article/11530-eng.htm

PREVNet. (2015). *For Parents.* Retrieved from http://www.prevnet.ca/resources/ policy-and-legislation/ontario/for-parents

Schumann, L., Craig, W., & Rosu, A. (2014). Power differentials in bullying: Individuals in a community context. *Journal of Interpersonal Violence, 29*(5), 846–865. https://doi.org/10.1177/0886260513505708

The Public Schools Act, Revised Statutes of Canada. (2015, C.C.S.M c.P250). Retrieved from the Manitoba Law website: http://web2.gov.mb.ca/laws/stat-utes/ccsm/_pdf.php?cap=p250

Vaillancourt, T., Trinh, V., McDougall, P., Duku, E., Cunningham, L., Cunningham, C., Hymel, S., & Short, K. (2010). Optimizing population screening of bullying in school-aged children. *Journal of School Violence, 9*(3), 233–250. https://doi.org/10.1080/15388220.2010.483182

4

Cyberbullying in the United States

Dorothy L. Espelage, Jun Sung Hong,
and Alberto Valido

Introduction

Cyberbullying is recognized as a critical public health concern in the
United States (Centers for Disease Control and Prevention 2009a, b;
Srabstein et al. 2008; Ybarra and Mitchell 2004) and is broadly concep-
tualized as a digital version of peer-based aggression. Technological
advances have significantly increased adolescents' use of social media and
online communication platforms, such as Facebook and Twitter.
According to Hinduja and Patchin (2009), cyberbullying is defined as
*"willful and repeated harm inflicted through the use of computers, cell phone,
or other electronic devices"* (p. 5). Definitions and forms of cyberbullying
vary, but some common examples include flaming, harassment, stalking,
impersonation, outing, trickery/phishing, as well as exclusion. Utilizing

D. L. Espelage (✉) • A. Valido
University of Florida, Gainesville, FL, USA

J. S. Hong
Wayne State University, Detroit, MI, USA

Sungkyunkwan University, Seoul, South Korea

© The Author(s) 2018
A. C. Baldry et al. (eds.), *International Perspectives on Cyberbullying*, Palgrave Studies in
Cybercrime and Cybersecurity, https://doi.org/10.1007/978-3-319-73263-3_4

technology, the perpetrator can send or post humiliating or threatening messages or photos of the victim to a third party or to a public forum visited by many online participants (Hinduja and Patchin 2009).

Similar to face-to-face bullying and peer victimization (Patchin and Hinduja 2012; Kulig et al. 2008), cyberbullying is found to be associated with a variety of poor psychological and behavioral outcomes, including depressive symptoms, anxiety, risky behaviors, self-injury, and suicidal thoughts and behaviors (Bauman et al. 2013; Gámez-Guadix et al. 2013; Hinduja and Patchin 2010a, b; Hoff and Mitchell 2009; Patchin and Hinduja 2010a, b; Price and Dalgleish 2010; Schneider et al. 2012; Ybarra et al. 2007). One meta-analytic study (Van Geel et al. 2014) reported that both peer victimization and cybervictimization were associated with suicidal ideation and attempts. Interestingly, cyberbullying was found to be more strongly related to suicidal ideation relative to face-to-face peer victimization.

Prevalence of Cyberbullying and Cybervictimization in the United States

According to the Pew Research Center, 92% of U.S. children and adolescents report going online daily, and 71% use more than one type of social media (Lenhart 2015), which increases their exposure to cyberbullying. According to the US Department of Justice, approximately 7% of students in U.S. public schools nationwide reported being cyberbullied in 2013 (Zhang et al. 2016). Although the rate of cyberbullying is lower than the rate of face-to-face peer victimization (22%), the report also found that cyberbullied students were less likely to notify an adult than face-to-face bullying victims were (23% vs. 39%; Zhang et al. 2016). Further, an online survey among 1,501 young regular Internet users (aged 10–17 years) revealed that 19% of adolescents were involved in online aggression in the past year (Ybarra and Mitchell 2004). Twelve percent reported being perpetrators of online aggression, 4% reported being victims/targets, and 3% reported being both perpetrators and targets. A systematic review of cyberbullying prevalence among U.S. adolescents by Selkie et al. (2016) also summarized that the rates of cyberbullying perpetration range between 1% and 41% based on 32 studies; the rates of cyberbullying victimization range between 3% and 72% based on 55 studies; and the rates of being both a perpetrator and a victim of cyberbullying range between 2.3% and 16.7% respectively based on 10 studies.

Cyberbullying is also prevalent in many other countries, as estimated by a systematic review and meta-analysis of 166 cyberbullying research studies from different countries. The prevalence rates of cybervictimization around the world range approximately between 10% and 40% (Kowalski et al. 2014). In the United Kingdom, the National Children's Home (NCH 2005) surveyed 770 participants (aged 11–19 years) and found that 20% of the study participants had been cyberbullied or threatened online, and 11% of the study participants had perpetrated cyberbullying. In a study among 11,227 students (aged 11–15 years) in the United Kingdom, about 7% of students reported that they had "received any nasty or threatening text messages or emails" at least "once in a while" (Noret and Rivers 2006). In Sweden, Slonje and Smith (2008) surveyed 360 adolescents (aged 12–20 years) and found that 5.3% reported being cyberbullied inside school in the last couple of months. In Canada, utilizing one-year longitudinal data (two time points) among 1,972 adolescents from the Health Behavior in School-Aged Children Study, Cappadocia et al. (2013) found that 11.6% of the study participants had been involved in cyberbullying perpetration; 13.5% had been involved in cybervictimization; and 4.6% had been involved in cyberbullying perpetration and victimization. Thus, it appears that US rates of cyberbullying perpetration and victimization are more similar to U.K. statistics than Canada statistics.

Issues in Reporting the Prevalence Rate of Cyberbullying

The reported prevalence rates are different not only across countries, but also within countries. The variability in reported prevalence may result from several measurement issues in studies on cyberbullying. First, the definition of cyberbullying is not consistent across studies. When asked whether they have ever been bullied, harassed, threatened, or embarrassed by someone using the Internet, cell phone, and other technologies, the same participants responded differently from when they were asked about others "repeatedly [trying] to hurt you or make you feel bad by e-mailing/e-messaging you or posting a blog about you on the internet." The former question generated a prevalence rate of 31% (Pergolizzi et al. 2011), while the latter generated a prevalence rate of 9% (Bevans et al. 2013). Second, there are discrepancies in the time frame being assessed. For example, in a survey of middle school students, 9% of students reported having ever been cyberbullied in their lifetime, whereas 9% reported being cyberbullied in the last 30 days. Finally, in terms of response options, some studies provided binary responses while others used Likert-type scales. The cutoff points in studies with Likert scales to decide whether participants had experienced cyberbullying were often-times not validated (Selkie et al. 2016). Despite the issues related to differential methods to assess cyberbullying, the extant literature suggests that cyberbullying involvement is prevalent and should be considered a public health concern.

Theories Explaining Cyberbullying and Cybervictimization

Compared to face-to-face bullying, theories providing empirical support for cyberbullying and cybervictimization are sparse (Espelage et al. 2012). As stated by Tokunaga (2010), research on cyberbullying has largely been conducted in the absence of theoretical frameworks, although theory can foster cohesiveness to a body of literature by establishing an order to the variables that have already been tested (see also Dublin 1978). Tokunaga (2010) also argued that theories not only help to predict behaviors of bullies and victims, but can possibly shed light as to why the effects of cyberbullying would be amplified compared to those of face-to-face bullying. Nevertheless, several theories that can provide insights into our understanding of cyberbullying—social cognitive theory, routine activity theory, and general strain theory are next reviewed.

According to Bandura (2001), *social cognitive theory* argues that attitudes and behaviors are acquired directly through observing others in social interactions or other outside influences, such as the media. For learning to occur, individuals need to (a) attend to the observed behavior, (b) encode images of the observed behavior, (c) reproduce those images, and (d) be motivated to perform the behavior (Bandura 1978). Although the social cognitive theory is similar to Bandura's (1986) social learning theory, social cognitive theory places importance on cognitions in determining individual behavior (Bandura 1978). In addition, moral values, moral emotions, and moral justifications are important components of social cognitive theory (Perren and Gutzwiller-Helfenfinger 2012). Social cognitive theory has long been applied to examine aggressive behavior (Bandura 1978), and a limited number of studies have also applied this theory to understand cyberbullying (Bauman 2010; Perren and Gutzwiller-Helfenfinger 2012). Many study findings demonstrate an association between observing and experiencing bullying and cyberbullying (e.g., Jang et al. 2014; Sticca et al. 2013). Because the social cognitive perspectives involve learning, thinking, and reasoning, it is recognized as one of the most effective strategies in addressing bullying and cyberbullying (Boxer and Dubow 2002; Thorton et al. 2000).

Routine activity theory can also provide a perspective on why certain adolescents engage in cyberbullying. This theory does not attribute violence or crime to social causes, but rather argues that the prosperity of societies offers more opportunities for crime or violence. Routine activity theory is an ecological approach to exploring the antecedents of cyberbullying, as it considers the location, accessibility, and presence or absence of environmental characteristics and certain types of individuals who are at risk for cyberbullying and cybervictimization. Proposed by Cohen and Felson (1979), routine activities refer to generalized patterns of social activities, which can provide opportunities for situations to emerge where perpetrators target victims (Wikstrom 2009). For crime or cyberbullying to occur, spending time away from family or being unsupervised can increase opportunities for cyberbullying and cybervictimization (Groff 2007). Cyberbullying occurs as an end result of the convergence of a motivated offender (cyberbully), a suitable target (cybervictim), and a lack of guardianship or parental monitoring (control; e.g., parents or teachers; Wikstrom 2009). A cyberbully needs to be a motivated individual in order to perpetuate bullying online. The cybervictim is a suitable target that draws the motivated offender because the victim might be vulnerable for reasons such as having a limited social support network or low parental monitoring of their technology use (Felson and Boba 2010). Although this theory is highly criticized, it has been found to predict cyberbullying among adolescents and young adults (Marcum et al. 2010; Navarro and Jasinski 2011, 2013).

Robert Agnew's *general strain theory* has received significant empirical attention over the years. Although the strain theory dates back to early twentieth century through the work of Edwin Sutherland and Robert Merton, it was later modified by Robert Agnew, who developed the general strain theory. The general strain theory holds that individuals who experience strain and negative emotions are at a heightened risk for engaging in deviant behavior, such as cyberbullying (Hinduja and Patchin 2010a, b). According to the general strain theory, strain originates from (a) failure to achieve valued goals, (b) removal of stimuli with positive values, and (c) introduction of negative stimuli which results in negative emotional responses (Agnew 2001). Strain and stressors do not directly cause deviant behavior; rather, they can increase the risk of negative emotions, such as anger and frustration, which can lead to the development of negative or aggressive emotions (Agnew 2001). As a result, youth experiencing strain may release their frustration out on others through verbal abuse or by insulting (Agnew 2001)—both online and offline. As expected, the general strain theory has received wide empirical support for explaining why certain youth are predisposed to cyberbullying and cybervictimization (Hay et al. 2010; Paez 2016; Patchin and Hinduja 2010a, b). For instance, Paez's (2016) study, which utilized a nationally representative sample of children, explored whether individual and social factors associated with general strain theory were associated with cyberbullying. Supporting the general strain theory, their results showed that students who experienced strain were more likely to engage in cyberbullying.

Factors Associated with Cyberbullying Perpetration and Victimization

Risk Factors

The social-ecological model of human development serves as a conceptual framework to understand how bullying and cyberbullying can emerge. It focuses on understanding how individual characteristics of children interact with environmental contexts or systems to promote or prevent bullying victimization and perpetration (Bronfenbrenner 1977; Espelage 2012; Hong and Espelage 2012). These structures include peer groups, families, and schools among other settings.

Individual Factors Researchers are divided about whether boys or girls engage in higher level of cyberbullying (Kowalski et al. 2014). In some studies, boys were more often perpetrators of cyberbullying whereas girls were more frequently victimized (Kowalski et al. 2014; Sourander et al. 2010). Other studies have found no significant effect of gender on cyberbullying perpetration or victimization (Li 2006; Ybarra and Mitchell 2004). Studies also offer conflicting reports of age as a risk factor for cyberbullying perpetration or victimization (Slonje and Smith 2008). For example, Ybarra and Mitchell (2004) reported a higher incidence of cyberbullying in students 15 years or older, while Kowalski et al. (2012) reported higher prevalence among younger adolescents. Moreover, Smith et al. (2006) found no change of cyberbullying rates from early to late adolescence.

Other individual-level risk factors include low affective empathy, or an inability to feel other's emotions; low cognitive empathy, or an inability to understand other's emotions; and narcissistic personality traits (Kowalski et al. 2014). Moreover, depression, anxiety, and low self-esteem were also found to be associated with cyberbullying victimization in one study (Kowalski et al. 2014). Interestingly, permissive attitudes toward cyberbullying, a desire to control others, and a sense of superiority have been positively related to cyberbullying perpetration (Kowalski et al. 2014; Gradinger et al. 2011).

School Lower levels of school belonging, lower academic achievement, and higher unexcused absences were found to be linked to cyberbullying victimization in several studies (Hinduja and Patchin 2008; Ybarra and Mitchell 2004). Furthermore, a negative perception of school climate was associated with higher engagement in cyberbullying (Williams and Guerra 2007).

Peer Peer victimization in the forms of verbal, physical, or relational aggression exacerbate cyberbullying perpetration and victimization (Kowalski et al. 2014; Ybarra and Mitchell 2004). For example, Twyman et al. (2010) found that children who were involved in cyberbullying were more likely to have suffered from previous peer victimization. Additionally, lower peer support, substance use, and bullying perpetration were found to be related to higher cyberbullying victimization and perpetration (Espelage et al. 2012; Ybarra and Mitchell 2004).

Family Low parental support has been associated with cyberbullying perpetration and victimization in one study using a nationally representative sample of adolescents (Wang et al. 2009). Among the family-level predictors, those with higher cyberbullying perpetration and victimization also had higher socioeconomic status, and greater access to technology and higher Internet usage (Walrave and Heirman 2011; Ybarra and Mitchell 2004). Additionally, cyberbullying victims also report lower levels of connection with their parents and lower parental monitoring of Internet activities (Kowalski et al. 2014; Ybarra and Mitchell 2004).

Protective Factors

Relative to risk factors, protective factors have been less well studied in the field of adolescent behavior. More recently, however, scholars have begun to realize the importance of considering factors that operate in individual, peer, family, and school domains that may insulate youth from problem behavior or mitigate the effects of risks (Dekovic 1999). In their review and meta-analysis of cyberbullying studies, Kowalski et al. (2014) identified several protective factors. Protective factors associated with cyberbullying perpetration included empathy, parental monitoring, peer support, school climate, and school safety (Kowalski et al. 2014). For victims of cyberbullying, protective factors included social intelligence, school safety, parental monitoring, perceived support, empathy, school climate, and parental control of technology (Kowalski et al. 2014).

Certain psychological variables reportedly insulate adolescents from being involved in cyberbullying. One notable protective factor is empathy, which has been considered in research on bullying. *Empathy* is defined as an "*emotional response that stems from another's emotional state or condition*" (Eisenberg and Strayer 1987, p. 5). There is strong evidence that low levels of empathy are associated with greater cyberbullying perpetration (Renati et al. 2012; Steffgen et al. 2011). Also considering the developmental literature that females are more likely to display empathy than males (Rueckert and Naybar 2008), studies have examined whether empathy can explain gender differences in both offline and online bullying (Topcu and Erdur-Baker 2012). Topcu and Erdur-Baker (2012) found, for example, that boys tend to bully others more frequently as they are seen as less empathic than females. The study also found that both affective and cognitive empathy indirectly mediated the association between sex differences and cyberbullying. Interestingly, Ang and Goh's (2010) study, using a sample of 396 Singaporean adolescents, found that youth with low levels of cognitive empathy scored higher on cyberbullying than those with high levels of cognitive empathy, irrespective of gender.

Variables representing family-level protective factors may include parental monitoring and support, which have been implicated in research on cyberbullying. Although cyberbullying occurs primarily in the home, parents are often excluded from many of their children's online activities, and youth rarely tell their parents about their involvement in cyberbullying (Mishna et al. 2009; Subrahmanyam and Greenfield 2008). As a result, parents are often unaware of their children's involvement in cyberbullying (Dehue et al. 2008). However, parents are recognized as having a very strong influence on the behavior of their children, and a strong bond between parent and child can insulate youth from engaging in deviant activities (Hinduja and Patchin 2013). Given this, it is not surprising that parental monitoring and support have been a major focus of cyberbullying intervention and prevention efforts (Beale and Hall 2007). Numerous studies consistently demonstrate that children who are involved in cyberbullying as perpetrators and victims receive limited parental monitoring and support than those who are not (Low and Espelage 2013; Fanti et al. 2012; Mesch 2009; Wade and Beran 2011; Wang et al. 2009; Ybarra and Mitchell 2004). From a national representative sample of U.S. students in grades 6–10, Wang et al. (2009) reported that higher parental support was related to less involvement in online and offline bullying and peer victimization. Using a large U.S. sample of youth Internet users, Ybarra and Mitchell's (2004) study also revealed that youth engaging in Internet-based bullying reported experiencing poor parent–child relations in the home. A more recent study conducted by Low and Espelage (2013) found that lower levels of parental monitoring predicted higher levels of cyberbullying among a sample of racially diverse early adolescents in fifth through seventh grades in four U.S. Midwestern middle schools.

School districts have been challenged to develop ways to prevent and intervene in bullying and cyberbullying situations. Educators and schools have an important role in promoting positive youth development and preventing students from engaging in deviant behaviors (Torney-Purta 2002). This is particularly true when considering the amount of time students spend in their school (Hinduja and Patchin 2013). Students' positive perceptions of the school climate, teacher support, and teacher involvement are some examples of school-level protective factors that have been found to be related to not only less face-to-face bullying, but also cyberbullying in one study (Sourander et al. 2010). Casas et al. (2013) found that students who perceive their teachers as supportive are less likely to report cyberbullying. Smokowski et al. (2014) also reported from a rural adolescent sample that teacher support was inversely related to both face-to-face bullying and cyberbullying victimization. Likewise, according to Hinduja and Patchin's (2013) findings, students (6th–12th grades) who perceived that adults in their life (e.g., teachers) are involved and impose consequences on them for cyberbullying were less likely to participate in such behavior. Teachers are a potential source of social support and play a critical role in helping students make sense out of confusing and dangerous situations. Teachers can also serve as a role model and refuge for students who are confronted with situations that they perceive as beyond their understanding and control (Bowen et al. 1998).

Are the Factors Associated with Face-to-Face Bullying and Cyberbullying Similar?

As noted previously, compared to traditional bullying, the incidence of cyberbullying is generally less frequent (e.g., Espelage et al. 2012; Slonje and Smith 2008; Smith et al. 2008). Extant research has demonstrated a close relation between traditional bullying and cyberbullying. Experiencing traditional victimization increases the risk for being a victim of cyberbullying (e.g., Juvonen and Gross 2008; Nansel et al. 2001; Raskauskas and Stoltz 2007). But there is evidence that a small portion of adolescents who are perpetrators or victims of cyberbullying do not experience traditional forms of bullying (Olweus 2012; Raskauskas 2010).

Studies that have contrasted different forms of bullying perpetration (with individual and family correlates) suggest areas of both overlap and uniqueness. For example, David-Ferdon and Hertz (2009) posit that "*like perpetrators of other forms of aggression, perpetrators of electronic aggression were more likely to believe that bullying peers and encouraging others to bully peers are acceptable behaviors*" (p. 8). Findings from this study also suggested that cyberbullies were more likely to engage in other forms of aggression, implying shared underlying risk factors. Wang et al. (2009) found that cyberbullying (as well as physical, verbal, and relational bullying) was similarly related to low parental support; however, unlike other forms of bullying, cyberbullying was not related to having more friends. These authors assert that further research is needed to clarify shared and non-shared features across various forms of bullying in order to begin placing cyberbullying in a larger theoretical framework.

However, findings from a recent longitudinal study of U.S. middle school students revealed that cyberbullying is more distinct than other forms of aggression, as one study found a greater overlap between non-physical bullying and fighting perpetration than associations with cyber-bullying perpetration (Low and Espelage 2013). This study also found that predictors of cyberbullying varied as a function of gender and race. More specifically, cyberbullying was less stable than other forms of aggression, and continuity appeared to be limited to white youth and females. Differences in stability are noteworthy and warrant further investigation. The study data also implied that cyberbullying is a relatively low-frequency behavior and arguably more sporadic than other forms of bullying, though less so for females.

Prevention and Intervention Approaches and Programs

Legal and Policy Considerations in the United States

Given that bullying is a public health concern, schools need to take actions to reduce both cyberbullying and bullying inside and outside of school buildings. Schools that choose to seek legal action against students suspected of cyberbullying may face difficult legal battles. Vague court decisions and the changing environment of cyberbullying laws in different states often thwart schools' obligations toward students' safety (Hinduja and Patchin 2011).

One of the first cases questioning the ability of schools to govern students' actions came with Tinker v. Des Moines Independent Community School District in 1969. Des Moines School district pressed charges against a student protesting against the Vietnam War on school grounds (Tinker et al. v. Des Moines Independent Community School District et al. 1969). The court decided that the student's freedom of expression had to be respected and not subjected to disciplinary actions unless the school could prove significant disruption to educational activities (Hinduja and Patchin 2011). In other words, if school officials could not prove that the incident was sufficiently disruptive, they were unable to limit students' communication. Later court cases also decided that students were free to act if it happened away from school.

Although well intentioned, the Tinker standard limited the ability of schools to deter students from cyberbullying. Cyberbullying can deprive the victim of an environment conducive to learning. But if the cyberbullying occurred outside of the school, most likely, school officials were unable to follow any type of legal action against students. Later court cases created further precedents limiting schools' authority to follow legal actions against students (Hinduja and Patchin 2011). For example, in Klein v. Smith (1986) the court decided in favor of a student who showed the middle finger to a teacher outside of school, despite claims from the school that the action was specifically directed at a school official. These rulings complicate intervention and prevention efforts because schools have traditionally been focused on behavior within school. Cyberbullying by definition can happen anywhere outside the jurisdiction of the school.

More recently, many states have enacted laws that address cyberbullying specifically. Notar and colleagues recommend that schools consult with trained lawyers to handle these cases given students' First Amendment rights in the United States (Notar et al. 2013a, b). Administrators are advised to proceed with caution when disciplining students for behavior that may have occurred outside of class (Wong-Lo 2009). Tragic incidents have occurred where children who are cyberbullied have committed suicide and schools have been in legal battles with the families. (Notar et al. 2013a, b). Given this complexity, it is ideal to develop and implement clear preemptive policies and programs that aim at reducing cyberbullying (Willard 2011).

The dynamic nature of digital media and inexperience of school officials offer another complication in addressing cyberbullying. That is, it is unreasonable to monitor several, often changing, social media platforms in an attempt to manage cyberbullying behavior (Lane 2011). This is especially true given the autonomy or privacy offered by numerous platforms. Schools cannot fully control behavior that happens via digital devices, but school-based programs that educate and advise children could be beneficial. The report offers guidelines and implications for school personnel who work on developing programs (Twyman et al. 2010).

Schools have been advised to incorporate some of the previously mentioned factors into their programs designed to eliminate cyberbullying.

Schools should define cyberbullying, have strong policies, and solid training as well implementation. Kowalski et al. (2012) offered nine intervention tips: save the evidence, ignore minor offenses, report the offense to the digital platform, investigate further, communicate perpetration with school officials, get parents involved, seek legal advice, report to law enforcement, and get the students mental health care.

Online Resources/Guidance for Youth, Parents, Teachers, and Administrators

Although most agree that something should be done to change the culture of cyberbullying in schools, the research lacks empirical consensus regarding preventive strategies or intervention programs (Bauman 2013). Nevertheless, an approach that many programs do agree upon is the involvement of multiple stakeholders. Curriculum programs in the United States often involve students, parents, and school staff (Couvillon and Ilieva 2011; Notar et al. 2013a, b). Programs focus on definitions of cyberbullying and strategies to prevent children from becoming victims (Cassidy et al. 2013; Pearce et al. 2011).

Schools often employ websites, tip sheets, and other online resources to disseminate cyberbullying information and increase awareness (e.g., http://www.stopbullying.gov/cyberbullying/index.html) (Keith and Martin 2005). In a meta-analysis of 17 cyberbullying prevention websites, Ahlfors (2010) found that 14 were directed to parents, 7 were constructed for elementary age children (6–10 years old), 8 addressed tweens (11–12 years old), and 11 included information specifically created for adolescents (ages 13 to 18). Websites created for health-care providers who often have to treat victims of cyberbullying were absent from the list of resources. Some of the websites reported were based in a commercial intervention or curriculum and only ten offered citations to the research (Ahlfors 2010).

Many of these websites are directed to parents. Many researchers point to parents as an essential component of any productive cyberbullying campaign (Aboujaoude et al. 2015). It has been observed that parental involvement leads to considerable reduction in bullying victimization

(Farrington and Ttofi 2009). Although students may not go to their parents for help when they are cyberbullied, parents should be prepared to answer decisively any cyberbullying incident (Juvonen and Gross 2008). Additionally, youth should have access to online resources that offer them a way to protect themselves online without supervision from their parents. It is noteworthy that although many online resources are based on recommendations from the scientific literature, many commercial products that offer school prevention strategies may not be based on empirical findings.

Scholars have suggested several guidelines for youths who are being cyberbullied, and to support parents and school staff who deal with cyberbullying (Beale and Hall 2007; Couvillon and Ilieva 2011; Feinberg and Robey 2009). Some recommend that the victim not read the messages sent by the cyberbullies (Keith and Martin 2005); parents are encouraged to find information (Beale and Hall 2007), and schools are advised to demand adherence to Student Internet Policies, perform professional development training, and subscribe to school-wide interventions that address cyberbullying specifically (Pearce et al. 2011; Couvillon and Ilieva 2011).

Moreover, Ortega-Ruiz et al. (2012) recommend the following tactics to develop a successful prevention program: "(1) Proactive policies, procedures, and practices; (2) Raising school staff's and youth's individual awareness and online social competence; (3) Promoting protective school environment; and (4) School-family-community partnerships to promote cooperation between school staff, families, and local organizations."

Students' and Educators' Awareness, Attitudes, and Perceptions of Cyberbullying

Schools' preventive efforts have expanded to include assemblies, software programs, and student lead campaigns to increase awareness of the negative consequences of cyberbullying. The research is still in its infancy, since no more than a handful of studies have assessed the effectiveness of these programs. One of the studies exploring the effectiveness of assembly-style presentations was carried by Roberto et al. (2014) with "The *Arizona*

Attorney General's Social Networking Safety Promotion and Cyberbullying Prevention" presentation. The 45-minute long session tried to shift students' online safety attitudes (Roberto et al. 2014). Some of the topics covered during this training ranged from cyberbullying prevention to Internet safety (Roberto et al. 2014). An analysis of the effectiveness of the presentation revealed that students who received the training were more engaged in Internet safety activities than those in the control group (Roberto et al. 2014). The results also showed that they were more likely to keep their account information private, and stay away from people they didn't know online. However, the study had limited validity due to the short follow-up after the presentation. Therefore, further longitudinal research is needed to evaluate the effectiveness of these programs.

School-Based Programs

There have been a variety of programs implemented in the United States. The Seattle Public School District developed their own program that focused on debunking misperceptions about digital behavior, building empathy, teaching online safety, and empowering victims (Holladay 2011). This program also emphasized parental and teacher engagement. Other curriculum-based programs aimed at addressing cyberbullying have been designed: I-SAFE Internet Safety Program, Cyber Bullying: A Prevention Curriculum (Kowalski et al. 2012); Sticks and Stones: Cyberbullying (Wilson 2007); Lets Fight It Together: What We All Can Do to Prevent Cyberbullying (Juvonen and Gross 2008); and The Second Step Violence Prevention Program (Craig et al. 2000). Often these programs involve videos, websites, resources, and scripted lessons. There are also numerous online programs such as www.stopcyberbullying.gov which offer similar resources and curriculum. Although this list is not comprehensive, it illustrates the scope of programs available in the United States (see Notar et al. 2013a, b).

Table 4.1 also shows some of the leading prevention approaches and programs in the United States, their intended goals, and audience. Among the most prominent, we find the Olweus Bullying Prevention Program (OBPP), the Second Step Bullying Prevention Program, and the I-SAFE curriculum.

Table 4.1 Cyberbullying prevention programs and interventions in the United States

Program/Intervention	Type	Target population	Length	State	Program targets	Research evidence
Olweus Bullying Prevention Program (OBPP)[a] The OBPP is a school-wide intervention bringing together staff, parents, and the community. The training integrates multiple levels of prevention	Curriculum Professional development	K–12 Students, Teachers, community members	Long term	US-wide	Prosocial behaviors, school climate, social support	Research-based, efficacious[b] Nationally recognized
The Second Step Bullying Prevention Program The program is based on Social Emotional Learning skills and attitudes that help prevent cyberbullying. Encourages helpful bystander behavior	Curriculum Professional development	5–12 years Student, parents, teachers	13–15 lessons	US-wide	Empathy, emotion management, social problem-solving skills	Research-based, efficacious[c]

(continued)

Table 4.1 (continued)

Program/Intervention	Type	Target population	Length	State	Program targets	Research evidence
I-SAFE Prevention-oriented lessons based on peer networks and student leadership. Educates students in cyberbullying, social networking, cyber etiquette, and e-safety	Curriculum, Digital resources, professional development	5–8 years Students, school, staff, parents	5 lessons	US-wide	Cyber privacy, prevention, e-safety	Not research-based
Seattle curriculum School-sponsored cyberbullying prevention program. Four main areas: breaking myths about digital behavior, creating empathy and understanding, learning online safety skills, and strategies to reject abusive behavior online[d]	Curriculum, professional development	5–8 years Students, teachers, parents	9 lessons	Washington State	Awareness, parental involvement	Research-based

(continued)

Table 4.1 (continued)

Program/Intervention	Type	Target population	Length	State	Program targets	Research evidence
Help-Assert Yourself-Humor-Avoid-Self-Talk-Own it Offers students strategies to deal with cyberbullying on their own. The words in the title are steps to follow when bullied	Curriculum	10–12 years	5 lessons	US-wide	Social emotional learning	Moderate reductions in cyberbullying
Cyberbullying prevention engine Aims to protect children from cyberbullying and risky online behavior by filtering content delivered to mobile devices. Monitors communications by keywords	Monitoring software	Parents, school staff, adults	Not applicable	US-wide	Cyber security, privacy	Not research-based

(continued)

Table 4.1 (continued)

Program/Intervention	Type	Target population	Length	State	Program targets	Research evidence
Stop Bullying.gov A federal government website with information about cyberbullying prevention. Offers advice of what to do if someone is been cyberbullied	Website	Students, parents, school staff, adults	Not applicable	US-wide	Awareness, prevention, online resources	Not research-based
A thin line words/ wounds[e] MTV campaign to empower youth to stand up to cyberbullying, sexting, and textual harassment	Website, resource	Students and young adults	Not applicable	US-wide	Awareness, empowerment, empathy	Not research-based

(continued)

Table 4.1 (continued)

Program/Intervention	Type	Target population	Length	State	Program targets	Research evidence
The Cyberbullying: A Prevention Curriculum Educational materials to understand cyberbullying. Enrolls the help of peer leaders and parents	Curriculum, printouts, posters, etc.	Parents, students in grades 6–12, peer leaders	8 sessions	US-wide	Knowledge, education, awareness	Not research-based
The Anti-defamation League[f] Professional development workshops for educators, teachers, and administrators to combat cyberbullying	Professional development, Workshop, online lesson plans	Parents, school administrators, teachers (elementary, middle, and secondary students)	Varying lengths	US-wide	Awareness, knowledge, empowerment	Not research-based

(continued)

Table 4.1 (continued)

Program/Intervention	Type	Target population	Length	State	Program targets	Research evidence
ConRed Based on the Olweus Anti-bullying program. Combats the risks of using the Internet and social networks	Curriculum Professional development, community outreach	Students, teachers, and families	8 sessions	US-wide	Awareness, debate, interaction, knowledge	Evidence-based

[a]Olweus (1993)
[b]Bowllan (2011)
[c]Notar et al. (2013b)
[d]http://www.cfchildren.org/about-us/enewsletter/the-second-step-program-and-the-bullying-prevention-unit-a-powerful-combination
[e]http://www.athinline.org/about
[f]Snakenborg et al. (2011)

The OBPP was one of first anti-bullying programs in the world. In the United States, the intervention has been adopted across elementary, middle, and high school settings in virtually every state (Olweus and Limber 2010). The hallmark of the OBPP is the restructuring of the school environment to "shift bullying norms" with the help of parents, school staff, and teachers. Although the intervention has yielded significant reductions in bullying and peer victimization in many countries, studies in the United States have found mixed results (Olweus and Limber 2010). For example, the first randomized clinical trial conducted in South Carolina schools had such poor implementation that the data were never published (Olweus and Limber 2010). Also, Bauer et al. (2007) conducted a controlled trial of the OBPP and found that there were mixed effects varying by gender, ethnicity, and grade but no school-wide effect. These studies indicate that while transporting programs from other countries into the United States implementation issues must be considered more diligently.

The Second Step: Student Success through Prevention Program (Committee for Children 2008) uses a Social Emotional Learning Framework to decrease bullying and cyberbullying perpetration. In a clinical trial testing the efficacy of the Second Step Program, Espelage et al. (2015) found reductions of self-reported delinquency, bullying, and cyberbullying over a three-year period for schools following the program. Although The Second Step Program was not designed specifically to address cyberbullying, reductions in cyberbullying were found through the reduction of delinquency (Espelage et al. 2015). These findings lend some support to the general strain theory discussed earlier. The prevention curriculum capitalizes on current knowledge of risks and protective factors by targeting disruptive classroom behaviors, violence, and impulsivity (Espelage et al. 2015). The lessons are divided according to the grade level and include topics that teach students to control their own emotions, cope with stress, develop problem-solving skills, and substance use prevention (Espelage et al. 2015).

Another noteworthy prevention program is the I-SAFE curriculum. Mishna and colleagues (Mishna et al. 2009) studied the impact of the U.S.-developed I-SAFE curriculum (Chibnall et al. 2006). The program's main module includes five lessons (60 minutes) on Internet safety, cyberbullying, social networking, and cyber etiquette. The lessons of the I-SAFE program are taught by teachers during school hours. The target population were students ranging from 5 to 8 years old. Mishna and colleagues report improvements of students' knowledge on Internet safety following the intervention (Mishna et al. 2009).

The *Help-Assert Yourself-Humor-Avoid-Self-Talk-Own it* tactic addresses the needs of middle school students (aged 10–12) by developing social skills to navigate cyberbullying episodes (Mishna et al. 2009). The program improved the knowledge of e-safety issues, but did not have an effect on online behaviors (Salvatore 2006; Mishna et al. 2009). Moreover, Salvatore (2006) found that the program resulted in small improvements in the levels of cyberbullying victimization ($g = 0.32$).

Summary and Future Directions

Prevention programs are only now being developed and evaluated to address cyberbullying and cyber safety issues among youth and their families. Websites, tip sheets, and other online resources might be sources where parents and teachers are receiving information about how to best protect their children. However, it appears that these online resources are often promoted by organizations who are selling products and are rarely evidence-based. Thus, parents, teachers, and school administrators should be cautious when reviewing information at these sites, and should focus on online resources that are provided by the federal agencies and advocacy groups that use research to guide their recommendations.

Researchers have also turned to educators' awareness and perceptions of cyberbullying to understand how intervention programs can be improved upon (Cassidy et al. 2012; Beale and Hall 2007). Cassidy and colleagues studied the experiences, knowledge of social media, and attention that teachers give to cyberbullying issues. The authors found that most teachers were unfamiliar with the avenues where children can be cyberbullied, and that schools lacked specific programs to address the problem of cyberbullying (Cassidy et al. 2012). These findings highlight the need for new programs supporting research-based interventions catered to educators and focused on identifying warning signs of cyber bullying victimization and perpetration.

Few school-based programs in the United States have been developed and evaluated to reduce cyberbullying specifically; however, it appears that many efficacious bully prevention and intervention programs or approaches could be extended to include outcomes focused on cyberbullying (Paul et al. 2012; Slonje et al. 2013). Scholars who are evaluating bully prevention programs should at the very least add cyberbullying outcome measures and, where possible, bully prevention programs should add lessons on cyber safety and cyberbullying. However, schools need to be supported to implement these programs through a stronger legislation that addresses cyberbullying. Finally, much more guidance is needed for school practitioners to talk to parents about limiting screen time, monitoring their children's use of the technology, talking to their children about Internet safety and privacy, and encouraging open communications when they do experience cyberbullying.

Further, more longitudinal research needs to be conducted to understand the developmental trajectories associated with traditional bullying and cyberbullying, and the risk and factors associated with simultaneous changes of these behaviors. Measurement issues plague the bullying scholarship, which has largely been focused on traditional, face-to-face bullying, and it appears that when bullying involves social media and technology, these measurement issues become even more complex. Thus, it will be critical for scholars to conduct systematic and multi-method and multi-informant studies on cyberbullying.

References

Aboujaoude, E., Savage, M. W., Starcevic, V., & Salame, W. O. (2015). Cyberbullying: Review of an old problem gone viral. *Journal of Adolescent Health, 57*(1), 10–18. https://doi.org/10.1016/j.jadohealth.2015.04.011

Agnew, R. (2001). Building on the foundation of general strain theory: Specifying the types of strain most likely to lead to crime and delinquency. *Journal of Research in Crime and Delinquency, 38*(4), 319–361. https://doi.org/10.1177/0022427801038004001.

Ahlfors, R. (2010). Many sources, one theme: Analysis of cyberbullying prevention and intervention websites. *Journal of Social Sciences, 6*(4), 515–522.

Ang, R. P., & Goh, D. H. (2010). Cyberbullying among adolescents: The role of affective and cognitive empathy, and gender. *Child Psychiatry and Human Development, 41*(4), 387–397. https://doi.org/10.1007/s10578-010-0176-3

Bandura, A. (1978). Social learning theory of aggression. *Journal of Communication, 28*, 12–29. https://doi.org/10.1111/j.1460-2466.1978.tb01621.x.

Bandura, A. (1986). *Social foundations of thought and action: A social cognitive theory*. Englewood Cliffs: Prentice-Hall.

Bandura, A. (2001). Social cognitive theory: An agentic perspective. *Annual Review of Psychology, 52*(1), 1–26. https://doi.org/10.1146/annurev.psych.52.1.1.

Bauer, N. S., Lozano, P., & Rivara, F. P. (2007). The effectiveness of the Olweus bullying prevention program in public middle schools: A controlled trial. *Journal of Adolescent Health, 40*(3), 266–274. https://doi.org/10.1016/j.jadohealth.2006.10.005

Bauman, S. (2010). Cyberbullying in a rural intermediate school: An exploratory study. *The Journal of Early Adolescence, 30*(6), 803–833. https://doi.org/10.1177/0272431609350927.

Bauman, S. (2013). Cyberbullying: What does research tell us? *Theory Into Practice, 52*(4), 249–256. https://doi.org/10.1080/00405841.2013.829727.

Bauman, S., Toomey, R. B., & Walker, J. L. (2013). Associations among bullying, cyberbullying, and suicide in high school students. *Journal of Adolescence, 36*(2), 341–350. https://doi.org/10.1016/j.adolescence.2012.12.001

Beale, A. V., & Hall, K. R. (2007). Cyberbullying: What school administrators (and parents) can do. *The Clearing House: A Journal of Educational Strategies, Issues and Ideas, 81*(1), 8–12. https://doi.org/10.3200/TCHS.81.1.8-12

Bevans, K. B., Bradshaw, C. P., & Waasdorp, T. E. (2013). Gender bias in the measurement of peer victimization: An application of item response theory. *Aggressive Behavior, 39*(5), 370–380. https://doi.org/10.1002/ab.21486

Bowen, G. L., Richman, J. M., Brewster, A., & Bowen, N. (1998). Sense of school coherence, perceptions of danger at school, and teacher support among youth at risk of school failure. *Child and Adolescent Social Work Journal, 15*, 273–286. https://doi.org/10.1023/A:1025159811181

Bowllan, N. M. (2011). Implementation and evaluation of a comprehensive, school-wide bullying prevention program in an urban/suburban middle school. *Journal of School Health, 81*(4), 167–173.

Boxer, P., & Dubow, E. F. (2002). A social-cognitive information-processing model for school-based aggression reduction and prevention programs: Issues for research and practice. *Applied and Preventive Psychology, 10*(3), 177–192. https://doi.org/10.1016/S0962-1849(01)80013-5

Bronfenbrenner, U. (1977). Toward an experimental ecology of human development. *American Psychologist, 32*(7), 513–531. https://doi.org/10.1037/0003-066X.32.7.513

Cappadocia, M. C., Craig, W. M., & Pepler, D. (2013). Cyberbullying prevalence, stability, and risk factors during adolescence. *Canadian Journal of School Psychology, 28*(2), 171–192. https://doi.org/10.1177/0829573513491212

Casas, J. A., Del Rey, R., & Ortega-Ruiz, R. (2013). Bullying and cyberbullying: Convergent and divergent predictor variables. *Computers in Human Behavior, 29*(3), 580–587. https://doi.org/10.1016/j.chb.2012.11.015

Cassidy, W., Brown, K., & Jackson, M. (2012). 'Under the radar': Educators and cyberbullying in schools. *School Psychology International, 33*(5), 520–532. https://doi.org/10.1177/0143034312445245

Cassidy, W., Faucher, C., & Jackson, M. (2013). Cyberbullying among youth: A comprehensive review of current international research and its implications and application to policy and practice. *School Psychology International, 34*(6), 575–612. https://doi.org/10.1177/0143034313479697

Centres for Disease Control and Prevention. (2009a). *Bullying surveillance among youths: Uniform definitions for public health and recommended data elements, Version 1.0.* Atlanta: National Center for Injury Prevention and Control, Centers for Disease Control and Prevention and the United States Department of Education.

Centres for Disease Control and Prevention. (2009b). *Technology and youth: Protecting your child from electronic aggression.* Atlanta: Centres for Disease Control and Prevention.

Chibnall, S., Wallace, M., Leicht, C., & Lunghofer, L. (2006). *I-safe evaluation. Final report.* Caliber Association, Fairfax. Retrieved from http://www.ncjrs.gov/pdffiles1 /nij/grants/213715.pdf

Cohen, L. E., & Felson, M. (1979). Social change and crime rate trends: A routine activity approach. *American Sociological Review, 44*, 588–608.

Committee for Children. (2008). *Second Step: Student success through prevention program.* Seattle: Committee for Children.

Couvillon, M. A., & Ilieva, V. (2011). Recommended practices: A review of schoolwide preventative programs and strategies on cyberbullying. *Preventing*

School Failure: Alternative Education for Children and Youth, 55(2), 96–101. https://doi.org/10.1080/1045988X.2011.539461

Craig, W. M., Pepler, D., & Atlas, R. (2000). Observations of bullying in the playground and in the classroom. *School Psychology International, 21*(1), 22–36. https://doi.org/10.1177/0143034300211002

David-Ferdon, C., & Hertz, M. F. (2009). *Electronic media and youth violence: A CDC issue brief for researchers*. Atlanta: Centers for Disease Control and Prevention.

Dehue, F., Bolman, C., & Völlink, T. (2008). Cyberbullying: Youngsters' experiences and parental perception. *CyberPsychology and Behavior, 11*(2), 217–223. https://doi.org/10.1089/cpb.2007.0008

Dekovic, M. (1999). Risk and protective factors in the development of problem behavior during adolescence. *Journal of Youth and Adolescence, 28*(6), 667–685. https://doi.org/10.1023/A:1021635516758.

Dublin, R. (1978). *Theory building*. New York: Free Press.

Eisenberg, N., & Strayer, J. (1987). Critical issues in the study of empathy. In N. Eisenberg & J. Strayer (Eds.), *Empathy and its development: Cambridge studies in social and emotional development* (pp. 3–13). New York: Cambridge University Press.

Espelage, D. L. (2012). Bullying prevention: A research dialogue with Dorothy Espelage. *Prevention Researcher, 19*, 17–20.

Espelage, D. L., Rao, M. A., & Craven, R. (2012). Theories of cyberbullying. In S. Bauman, D. Cross, & J. L. Walker (Eds.), *Principles of cyberbullying research: Definitions, measures, and methodology* (pp. 78–97). New York: Routledge.

Espelage, D. L., Low, S., Van Ryzin, M. J., & Polanin, J. R. (2015). Clinical trial of second step middle school program: Impact on bullying, cyberbullying, homophobic teasing, and sexual harassment perpetration. *School Psychology Review, 44*(4), 464–479. https://doi.org/10.17105/spr-15-0052.1

Fanti, K. A., Demetriou, A. G., & Hawa, V. V. (2012). A longitudinal study of cyberbullying: Examining risk and protective factors. *European Journal of Developmental Psychology, 9*(2), 168–181. https://doi.org/10.1080/1740562 9.2011.643169

Farrington, D. P., & Ttofi, M. M. (2009). School-based programs to reduce bullying and victimization. *Campbell Systematic Reviews, 2009*, 6.

Feinberg, T., & Robey, N. (2009). Cyberbullying: Intervention and prevention strategies. *National Association of School Psychologists, 38*(4), 22–24.

Felson, M., & Boba, R. (2010). *Crime and everyday life* (4th ed.). Los Angeles: Sage.

Gámez-Guadix, M., Orue, I., Smith, P. K., & Calvete, E. (2013). Longitudinal and reciprocal relations of cyberbullying with depression, substance use, and problematic internet use among adolescents. *Journal of Adolescent Health, 53*(4), 446–452. https://doi.org/10.1016/j.jadohealth.2013.03.030

Gradinger, P., Strohmeier, D., & Spiel, C. (2011). Motives for bullying others in cyberspace. In Q. Li, D. Cross, & P. K. Smith (Eds.), *Cyberbullying in the global playground: Research from international perspectives* (pp. 263–284). Oxford: Wiley-Blackwell.

Groff, E. R. (2007). Simulation for theory testing and experimentation: An example using routine activity theory and street robbery. *Journal of Quantitative Criminology, 23*(2), 75–103. https://doi.org/10.1007/s10940-006-9021-z.

Hay, C., Meldrum, R., & Mann, K. (2010). Traditional bullying, cyber bullying, and deviance. A general strain theory approach. *Journal of Contemporary Criminal Justice, 26*(2), 130–147. https://doi.org/10.1177/1043986209359557

Hinduja, S., & Patchin, J. W. (2008). Cyberbullying: An exploratory analysis of factors related to offending and victimization. *Deviant Behavior, 29*(2), 129–156. https://doi.org/10.1080/01639620701457816

Hinduja, S., & Patchin, J. W. (2009). *Bullying beyond the schoolyard: Preventing and responding to cyberbullying*. Thousand Oaks: Corwin Press.

Hinduja, S., & Patchin, J. W. (2010a). *Cyberbullying research summary: Cyberbullying and strain*. Retrieved from http://www.cyberbullying.org/cyberbullying_and_strain_research_fact_ sheet.pdf

Hinduja, S., & Patchin, J. W. (2010b). Bullying, cyberbullying and suicide. *Archives of Suicide Research, 14*(3), 206–221. https://doi.org/10.1080/13811 118.2010.494133

Hinduja, S., & Patchin, J. W. (2011). Cyberbullying: A review of the legal issues facing educators. *Preventing School Failure: Alternative Education for Children and Youth, 55*(2), 71–78. https://doi.org/10.1080/1045988X.2011.539433

Hinduja, S., & Patchin, J. W. (2013). Social influences on cyberbullying behaviors among middle and high school students. *Journal of Youth and Adolescence, 42*(5), 711–722. https://doi.org/10.1007/s10964-012-9902-4

Hoff, D. L., & Mitchell, S. N. (2009). Cyberbullying: Causes, effects, and remedies. *Journal of Educational Administration, 47*(5), 652–665. https://doi.org/10.1108/09578230910981107

Holladay, J. (2011). Cyberbullying. *Education Digest, 76*(5), 4–9.

Hong, J. S., & Espelage, D. L. (2012). A review of research on bullying and peer victimization in school: An ecological systems analysis. *Aggression and Violent Behavior, 17*, 311–312. https://doi.org/10.1016/j.avb.2012.03.003

Jang, H., Song, J., & Kim, R. (2014). Does the offline bully-victimization influence cyberbullying behavior among youths? Application of general strain theory. *Computers in Human Behavior, 31*, 85–93. https://doi.org/10.1016/j.chb.2013.10.007

Juvonen, J., & Gross, E. F. (2008). Extending the school grounds? – Bullying experiences in cyberspace. *Journal of School Health, 78*(9), 496–505. https://doi.org/10.1111/j.1746-1561.2008.00335.x

Keith, S., & Martin, M. E. (2005). Cyber-bullying: Creating a culture of respect in a cyber world. *Reclaiming Children and Youth, 13*(4), 224–228.

Kowalski, R. M., Limber, S. P., Limber, S., & Agatston, P. W. (2012). *Cyberbullying: Bullying in the digital age* (2nd ed.). Chichester: Wiley.

Kowalski, R. M., Giumetti, G. W., Schroeder, A. N., & Lattanner, M. R. (2014). Bullying in the digital age: A critical review and meta-analysis of cyberbullying research among youth. *Psychological Bulletin, 140*(4), 1073–1137. https://doi.org/10.1037/a0035618

Kulig, J. C., Hall, B. L., & Kalischuk, R. G. (2008). Bullying perspectives among rural youth: A mixed methods approach. *Rural and Remote Health, 8*(2), 1–11.

Lane, D. K. (2011). Taking the lead on cyberbullying: Why schools can and should protect students online. *Iowa Law Review, 96*(5), 1791–1811.

Lenhart, A. (2015). *Teens, social media and technology overview 2015*. Washington, DC: Pew Research Center.

Li, Q. (2006). Cyberbullying in schools a research of gender differences. *School Psychology International, 27*(2), 157–170. https://doi.org/10.1177/0143034306064547.

Low, S., & Espelage, D. (2013). Differentiating cyber bullying perpetration from non-physical bullying: Commonalities across race, individual, and family predictors. *Psychology of Violence, 3*, 39–52. https://doi.org/10.1037/a0030308

Marcum, C. D., Higgins, G. E., & Ricketts, M. L. (2010). Potential factors of online victimization of youth: An examination of adolescent online behavior utilizing routine activity theory. *Deviant Behavior, 31*, 381–410. https://doi.org/10.1080/01639620903004903

Mesch, G. S. (2009). Parental mediation, online activities, and cyberbullying. *CyberPsychology & Behavior, 12*(4), 387–393. https://doi.org/10.1089/cpb.2009.0068

Mishna, F., Cook, C., Saini, M., et al. (2009). *Interventions for children, youth, and parents to prevent and reduce cyber abuse* [Internet]. Oslo: Campbell Systematic Reviews [cited 7 February 2016]. Available from: http://citeseerx. ist.psu.edu/viewdoc/download?doi.10.1.1.688.7950&rep.rep1&type.pdf

Nansel, T. R., Overpeck, M., Pilla, R. S., Ruan, W. J., Simons-Morton, B., & Scheidt, P. (2001). Bullying behaviors among US youth: Prevalence and association with psychosocial adjustment. *JAMA, 285*(16), 2094–2100. https:// doi.org/10.1001/jama.285.16.2094

National Children's Home. (2005). *Putting U in the picture: Mobile bullying survey*. Retrieved from http://www.nch.org.uk/uploads/documents/Mobile% 20bullying%20 report.pdf

Navarro, J. N., & Jasinski, J. L. (2011). Going cyber: Using routine activities theory to predict cyberbullying experiences. *Sociological Spectrum, 32*, 81–94. https://doi.org/10.1080/02732173.2012.628560

Navarro, J. N., & Jasinski, J. L. (2013). Why girls? Using routine activities theory to predict cyberbullying experiences between girls and boys. *Women and Criminal Justice, 23*(4), 286–303. https://doi.org/10.1080/08974454.2013.784225

Noret, N., & Rivers, I. (2006, April). *The prevalence of bullying by text message or email: Results of a four year study*. Poster Presented at the Annual Conference of the British Psychological Society, Cardiff.

Notar, C. E., Padgett, S., & Roden, J. (2013a). Cyberbullying: A review of the literature. *Universal Journal of Educational Research, 1*(1), 1–9. https://doi. org/10.13189/ujer.2013.010101

Notar, C. E., Padgett, S., & Roden, J. (2013b). Cyberbullying: Resources for intervention and prevention. *Universal Journal of Educational Research, 1*(3), 133–145.

Olweus, D. (1993). *Bullying at School: What We Know and What We Can Do.* Cambridge, MA: Blackwell Publishers.

Olweus, D. (2012). Cyberbullying: An overrated phenomenon? *European Journal of Developmental Psychology, 9*, 520–538. https://doi.org/10.1080/17 405629.2012.682358

Olweus, D., & Limber, S. P. (2010). Bullying in school: Evaluation and dissemination of the Olweus Bullying Prevention Program. *American Journal of Orthopsychiatry, 80*(1), 124–134. https://doi.org/10.1111/ j.1939-0025.2010.01015.x

Ortega-Ruiz, R., Del Rey, R., & Casas, J. A. (2012). Knowing, building and living together on internet and social networks: The ConRed cyberbullying prevention program. *International Journal of Conflict and Violence, 6*(2), 302–312. https://doi.org/10.4119/UNIBI/ijcv.250

Paez, G. R. (2016). Cyberbullying among adolescents: A general strain theory perspective. *Journal of School Violence*, 1–12. https://doi.org/10.1080/15388 220.2016.1220317.

Patchin, J. W., & Hinduja, S. (2010a). Cyberbullying and self-esteem. *Journal of School Health, 80*(12), 614–624. https://doi.org/10.1111/ j.1746-1561.2010.00548.x

Patchin, J. W., & Hinduja, S. (2010b). Traditional and non-traditional bullying among youth: A test of general strain theory. *Youth and Society, 41*, 727–751. https://doi.org/10.1177/0044118X10366951

Patchin, J. W., & Hinduja, S. (2012). *Cyberbullying prevention and response: Expert perspectives.* London: Routledge.

Paul, S., Smith, P. K., & Blumberg, H. H. (2012). Revisiting cyberbullying in schools using the quality circle approach. *School Psychology International, 33*(5), 492–504. https://doi.org/10.1177/0143034312445243

Pearce, N., Cross, D., Monks, H., Waters, S., & Falconer, S. (2011). Current evidence of best practice in whole-school bullying intervention and its potential to inform cyberbullying interventions. *Australian Journal of Guidance and Counselling, 21*(01), 1–21. https://doi.org/10.1375/ajgc.21.1.1

Pergolizzi, F., Pergolizzi, J., Gan, Z., Macario, S., Pergolizzi, J. V., Ewin, T. J., & Gan, T. J. (2011). Bullying in middle school: Results from a 2008 survey. *International Journal of Adolescent Medicine and Health, 23*(1), 11–84. https://doi.org/10.1515/ijamh.2011.003

Perren, S., & Gutzwiller-Helfenfinger, E. (2012). Cyberbullying and traditional bullying in adolescence: Differential roles of moral disengagement, moral emotions, and moral values. *European Journal of Developmental Psychology, 9*, 195–209. https://doi.org/10.1080/17405629.2011.643168

Price, M., & Dalgleish, J. (2010). Cyberbullying experiences, impacts and coping strategies as described by Australian young people. *Youth Studies Australia, 29*(2), 51–59.

Raskauskas, J. (2010). Multiple peer victimization among elementary school students: Relations with social-emotional problems. *Social Psychology of Education, 13*(4), 523–539. https://doi.org/10.1007/s11218-010-9124-0

Raskauskas, J., & Stoltz, A. D. (2007). Involvement in traditional and electronic bullying among adolescents. *Developmental Psychology, 43*(3), 564. https://doi.org/10.1037/0012-1649.43.3.564

Renati, R., Berrone, C., & Zanetti, M. A. (2012). Morally disengaged and unempathic: Do cyberbullies fit these definitions? An exploratory study. *Cyberpsychology, Behavior, and Social Networking, 15*(8), 391–398. https://doi.org/10.1089/cyber.2012.0046

Roberto, A. J., Eden, J., Savage, M. W., Ramos-Salazar, L., & Deiss, D. M. (2014). Outcome evaluation results of school-based cybersafety promotion and cyberbullying prevention intervention for middle school students. *Health Communication, 29*(10), 1029–1042. https://doi.org/10.1080/10410236.20 13.831684

Rueckert, L., & Naybar, N. (2008). Gender differences in empathy: The role of the right hemisphere. *Brain and Cognition, 67*(2), 162–167. https://doi.org/10.1016/j.bandc.2008.01.002

Salvatore, A. J. (2006). *An anti-bullying strategy: Action research in a 5/6 intermediate school.* Hartford: University of Hartford.

Schneider, S. K., O'Donnell, L., Stueve, A., & Coulter, R. W. S. (2012). Cyberbullying, school bullying, and psychological distress: A regional census of high school students. *American Journal of Public Health, 102*, 171–177. https://doi.org/10.2105/AJPH.2011.300308

Selkie, E. M., Fales, J. L., & Moreno, M. A. (2016). Cyberbullying prevalence among US middle and high school–aged adolescents: A systematic review and quality assessment. *Journal of Adolescent Health, 58*(2), 125–133. https://doi.org/10.1016/j.jadohealth.2015.09.026

Slonje, R., & Smith, P. K. (2008). Cyberbullying: Another main type of bullying? *Scandinavian Journal of Psychology, 49*, 147–154. https://doi.org/10.1111/j.1467-9450.2007.00611.x

Slonje, R., Smith, P. K., & Frisén, A. (2013). The nature of cyberbullying, and strategies for prevention. *Computers in Human Behavior, 29*(1), 26–32. https://doi.org/10.1016/j.chb.2012.05.024

Smith, P. K., Mahdavi, J., Carvalho, M., & Tippett, N. (2006). *An investigation into cyber-bullying, its forms, awareness, and impact, and the relationship between age and gender in cyber-bullying* (Research Brief No. RBX03-06). London: Department for Education and Skills.

Smith, P. K., Mahdavi, J., Carvalho, M., Fisher, S., Russell, S., & Tippett, N. (2008). Cyberbullying: Its nature and impact in secondary school pupils. *Journal of Child Psychology and Psychiatry, 49*, 376–385. https://doi.org/10.1111/j.1469-7610.2007.01846.x

Smokowski, P. R., Evans, C. B. R., & Cotter, K. L. (2014). The differential impacts of episodic, chronic, and cumulative physical bullying and cyberbullying: The effects of victimization on the school experiences, social support, and mental health of rural adolescents. *Violence and Victims, 29*, 1029–1046. https://doi.org/10.1891/0886-6708.VV-D-13-00076

Snakenborg, J., Van Acker, R., & Gable, R. A. (2011). Cyberbullying: Prevention and intervention to protect our children and youth. *Preventing School Failure:*

Alternative Education for Children and Youth, 55(2), 88–95. https://doi.org/1 0.1080/1045988X.2011.539454

Sourander, A., Klomek, A. B., Ikonen, M., Lindroos, J., Luntamo, T., Koskelainen, M., .Ristkari, T., & Helenius, H. (2010). Psychosocial risk factors associated with cyberbullying among adolescents: A population-based study. *Archives of General Psychiatry, 67*(7), 720–728. doi:https://doi. org/10.1001/archgenpsychiatry.2010.79.

Srabstein, J. C., Berkman, B. E., & Pyntikova, E. (2008). Antibullying legislation: A public health perspective. *Journal of Adolescent Health, 42*(1), 11–20. https://doi.org/10.1016/j.jadohealth.2007.10.007

Steffgen, G., König, A., Pfetsch, J., & Melzer, A. (2011). Are cyberbullies less empathic? Adolescents' cyberbullying behavior and empathic responsiveness. *Cyberpsychology, Behavior, and Social Networking, 14*(11), 643–648. https:// doi.org/10.1089/cyber.2010.0445

Sticca, F., Ruggieri, S., Alsaker, F., & Perren, S. (2013). Longitudinal risk factors for cyberbullying in adolescence. *Journal of Community and Applied Social Psychology, 23*(1), 52–67. https://doi.org/10.1002/casp.2136

Subrahmanyam, K., & Greenfield, P. (2008). Online communication and adolescent relationships. *The Future of Children, 18*(1), 119–146. https://doi. org/10.1353/foc.0.0006

Thorton, T. N., Craft, C. A., Dahlberg, L. L., Lynch, B. S., & Baer, K. (2000). *Best practices of youth violence prevention: A sourcebook for community action.* Atlanta: Centers for Disease Control and Prevention.

Tokunaga, R. S. (2010). Following you home from school: A critical review and synthesis of research on cyberbullying victimization. *Computers in Human Behavior, 26*(3), 277–287. https://doi.org/10.1016/j.chb.2009.11.014

Topcu, Ç., & Erdur-Baker, Ö. (2012). Affective and cognitive empathy as mediators of gender differences in cyber and traditional bullying. *School Psychology International, 33*(5), 550–561. https://doi.org/10.1177/0143034312446882

Torney-Purta, J. (2002). The school's role in developing civic engagement: A study of adolescents in twenty-eight countries. *Applied Developmental Science, 6*, 203–212. https://doi.org/10.1207/S1532480XADS0604_7

Twyman, K., Saylor, C., Taylor, L. A., & Comeaux, C. (2010). Comparing children and adolescents engaged in cyberbullying to matched peers. *Cyberpsychology, Behavior, and Social Networking, 13*(2), 195–199. https:// doi.org/10.1089/cyber.2009.0137

Van Geel, M., Vedder, P., & Tanilon, J. (2014). Relationship between peer victimization, cyberbullying, and suicide in children and adolescents: A meta-analysis. *JAMA Pediatrics, 168*(5), 435–442. https://doi.org/10.1001/ jamapediatrics.2013.4143

Wade, A., & Beran, T. (2011). Cyberbullying: The new era of bullying. *Canadian Journal of School Psychology, 26*, 44–61. https://doi.org/10.1177/0829573510396318

Walrave, M., & Heirman, W. (2011). Cyberbullying: Predicting victimisation and perpetration. *Children & Society, 25*(1), 59–72. https://doi.org/10.1111/j.1099-0860.2009.00260.x

Wang, J., Iannotti, R. J., & Nansel, T. R. (2009). School bullying among adolescents in the United States: Physical, verbal, relational, and cyber. *Journal of Adolescent Health, 45*(4), 368–375. https://doi.org/10.1016/j.jadohealth.2009.03.021

Wikstrom, P. O. H. (2009). Routine activity theories. *Oxford Bibliographies.* https://doi.org/10.1093/OBO/9780195396607-0010

Willard, N. (2011). School response to cyberbullying and sexting: The legal challenge. *Brigham Young University Education & Law Journal, 1*, 75–125.

Williams, K. R., & Guerra, N. G. (2007). Prevalence and predictors of internet bullying. *Journal of Adolescent Health, 41*(6), S14–S21. https://doi.org/10.1016/j.jadohealth.2007.08.018

Wilson, E. (2007). As bullies go high-tech, lawmakers say schools should be fighting back. *The Seattle Times.* Retrieved from http://www.seattletimes.com/seattle-news/as-bullies-go-high-tech-lawmakers-say-schools-should-be-fighting-back/

Wong-Lo, M. (2009). *Cyberbullying: Responses of adolescents and parents toward digital aggression* (Unpublished Doctoral Dissertation). University of North Texas.

Ybarra, M. L., & Mitchell, K. J. (2004). Youth engaging in online harassment: Associations with caregiver-child relationships, Internet use, and personal characteristics. *Journal of Adolescence, 27*, 319–336. https://doi.org/10.1016/j.adolescence.2004.03.007

Ybarra, M. L., Espelage, D. L., & Mitchell, K. J. (2007). The co-occurrence of Internet harassment and unwanted sexual solicitation victimization and perpetration: Associations with psychosocial indicators. *Journal of Adolescent Health, 41*(6), S31–S41. https://doi.org/10.1016/j.jadohealth.2007.09.010

Zhang, A., Musu-Gillette, L., & Oudekerk, B. A. (2016). *Indicators of school crime and safety: 2015* (NCES 2016-079/NCJ 249758). Washington, DC: National Center for Education Statistics, U.S. Department of Education, and Bureau of Justice Statistics, U.S. Department of Justice.

5

Cyberbullying in the United Kingdom and Ireland

Hannah Gaffney and David P. Farrington

Introduction

Research interest in cyberbullying has grown significantly, both in the United Kingdom and internationally, in the past decade. Information communication technologies (ICTs) have become ever more present in our everyday social interactions, with large percentages of young people being very active online. Findings from European research (the EU Kids Online survey) have concluded that a growing number of children and adolescents have access to and are active on the Internet (Livingstone and Haddon 2009a). In the United Kingdom, the survey identified similar trends, with 90% of all children aged 6 to 17 years being active online, and 87% of children aged 6 to 10 years reporting Internet use. The figures for UK adolescents aged 11 to 14 (94%) and 15 to 17 years (95%) were comparable to the figures reported for Irish adolescents.

In addition, a recent systematic review of children's rapidly increasing access to ICTs reported that, in the United Kingdom, the use of the

H. Gaffney • D. P. Farrington (✉)
Institute of Criminology, University of Cambridge, Cambridge, UK

© The Author(s) 2018   101
A. C. Baldry et al. (eds.), *International Perspectives on Cyberbullying*, Palgrave Studies in Cybercrime and Cybersecurity, https://doi.org/10.1007/978-3-319-73263-3_5

Internet at home increased with age, from 37% of 3–4 year old to 58% of 5–7 year olds, 87% of 8–11 year olds, and 95% of 12–15 year olds (Livingstone and Smith 2014, p. 3). The ownership of mobile phones, particularly smartphones, and other Internet-ready devices such as tablets, music players, and games consoles is also on the rise, with 62% of 12–15 year olds in 2012 reporting ownership. Thus, as our interpersonal communications move into the online sphere, it is only to be expected that these platforms will increasingly be used for aggressive forms of behaviours (Asam and Samara 2016).

Cyberbullying has been defined by UK academics as an aggressive, intentional act carried out by a group or individual, *using electronic forms of contact* repeatedly and over time against a victim who cannot easily defend himself or herself (Smith et al. 2008, p. 376). However, the three core elements of the widely accepted definition of traditional school-bullying (i.e. intention to harm, repetitive nature, and clear power imbalance) are not as easily distinguished in cases of cyberbullying. Furthermore, there are several features that are unique to cyberbullying in comparison to traditional school-bullying, such as the ability of the perpetrator to remain relatively anonymous; the lack of physical and social cues in online communication; the breadth of the potential audience and the added complexity of the bystanders' roles in cyberbullying; and the fact that there is 'no place to hide' (Marczak and Coyne 2015, p. 149). A full discussion of these issues is beyond the scope of the current chapter; see Smith et al. (2013) for a full and comprehensive overview.

Previous research has found that cyberbullying is associated with several undesirable psychological, behavioural, and health-related outcomes. For example, studies conducted in Europe have discovered that cyber-victims report higher levels of emotional and social problems, psychological difficulties, headaches, abdominal pain, and sleeping difficulties (Sourander et al. 2010). In addition, the cyberbullies who were identified in this study reported higher frequencies of conduct problems, hyperactivity, smoking, and alcohol use. Additionally, cyberbullying victimization is correlated with several undesirable mental health outcomes, such as depression, anxiety, and suicidal ideation (Betts 2016).

A recent meta-analysis of 80 studies found that, while prevalence rates of cyberbullying were lower than those for traditional school-bullying, there were significant correlations between these types of aggressive behaviours (Modecki et al. 2014). Moreover, the perceived impact of cyberbullying has been frequently reported to be worse than the impact of face-to-face or traditional school-bullying, but this relationship may vary according to the type of cyberbullying experienced (Smith et al. 2006). A qualitative study conducted with youth in the United Kingdom indicated that children were aware that cyberbullying occurred typically as an extension or continuation of offline bullying (Betts and Spenser 2017). Participants in this study reported how, in comparison with school-bullying that has a clear cut-off point (typically when the victim goes home from school), cyberbullying experiences had the potential to occur at any time of the day or night because of constant access to, and engagement with, technology (Betts and Spenser 2017, p. 27). In the Republic of Ireland, participants also thought that all forms of cyberbullying behaviours had more impact than traditional school-bullying, with the exception of bullying via email (Cotter and McGilloway 2011).

The complexity of cyberbullying is partially attributable to the significantly large number of different behaviours that it may encompass (Marczak and Coyne 2015). For example, Willard (2006) identified seven potential forms of cyberbullying behaviours: flaming, online harassment, cyberstalking, denigration, masquerade, outing, and exclusion. However, these categories, although proposed only 11 years ago, may already be outdated or incomplete because of the rapid rise and development of social media platforms and sharing apps that could facilitate cyberbullying. For example, when this typology was suggested, the vastly popular picture-sharing app Snapchat was not in existence.

More recent research suggests the need to identify a wider array of potential cyberbullying behaviours. For example, Rivers and Noret (2010) identified ten categories of behaviours: threat of physical violence, abusive or hate-related, sexual acts, demands or instructions, threats to damaging existing relationships, threats to family or home, and menacing chain messages. Moreover, Nuccitelli (2012) proposes over 36 different behaviours that could be considered cyberbullying. Other studies proposed broader categories, such as sexting, trolling, and griefing (Slonje et al. 2013); or direct and indirect cyberbullying (Langos 2012). Direct cyberbullying includes behaviours that occur exclusively between the perpetrator(s) and the victim(s), for example aggressive content sent via text/instant messages and/or phone calls, or exclusion from online groups. Indirect cyberbullying occurs in the public online environment, for example, publicly posting hurtful or embarrassing posts and/or pictures about an individual or the creation of public forums targeting the victim specifically.

Media reports of several cases of teenage suicide, attributed to experiences of victimization online, have heightened public awareness and concern about cyberbullying. For example, Felix Alexander aged 17 from Worcester (UK) tragically committed suicide in 2016 after years of being bullied. Felix's mother wrote that online bullying had exacerbated the effect that victimization had on her son, and that in an effort to prevent the online attacks he had removed himself from multiple social media sites. However, in doing so, this increased his feelings of social isolation (The Guardian, October 5, 2016).

Thus, cyberbullying is an important area for research. Other chapters in this book review issues surrounding the prevalence of cyberbullying and the associated risk and protective factors in several international settings. The prevalence rates of reported cyberbullying behaviours vary greatly between international studies, from 10% to 72% (Marczak and Coyne 2015). This chapter aims to address these questions in the context of adolescents in the United Kingdom and Ireland. When referring to the United Kingdom, it is worthwhile to note that this term includes England, Scotland, Wales, and Northern Ireland. When discussing cyberbullying in Ireland, we are referring to the Republic of Ireland.

Cyberbullying in the United Kingdom and Ireland

A large-scale international survey conducted by the network company Vodafone Plc, in collaboration with YouGov Plc, in 2015 of 4,720 adolescents aged 13 to 18 years revealed that 26% of Irish adolescents were victimized online, whilst 85% reported having heard of someone else being cyberbullied. In the same study, 15% of UK adolescents reported being cyberbullied themselves and 68% reported that they had heard of someone else being cyberbullied. Of the 11 countries surveyed (Czech Republic, Germany, Greece, Ireland, Italy, Netherlands, New Zealand, South Africa, Spain, United Kingdom, and United States), rates of cyber-victimization in Ireland were the second highest, while the UK figure was the lowest. Furthermore, this international survey revealed that 60% of Irish children and 35% of UK children thought that cyberbullying was worse than face-to-face bullying. The international survey also revealed that 41% of children reported that cyberbullying victimization made them feel depressed, 26% said they felt completely alone, 18% reported suicidal thoughts, 21% had avoided school, and 25% had shut down their social media accounts as a result of cyberbullying.

In the United Kingdom, the charitable organization Childline reported, for the year 2015–16, that it had delivered 4,541 counselling sessions relating to cyberbullying, which was a 13% increase from 2014–15 (National Society for the Prevention of Cruelty to Children 2015, p. 7) and an overall increase of 88% over the past five years. Young people who had contacted Childline about online bullying typically reported knowing the identity of the perpetrator and described how online bullying usually led to offline physical and verbal victimization. Furthermore, victims reported fear because they felt that the bullies '*could reach them anywhere*'. Various forms of victimization were reported by callers to Childline, for example malicious or hurtful messages being posted about them to social media profiles, blogs, pictures, or posts. In some situations, online forums were created as spaces for multiple perpetrators to specifically post bullying content about the victim(s).

Table 5.1 shows the prevalence of cyberbullying perpetration and/or victimization, as measured by 25 independent empirical studies employing samples from the United Kingdom (n = 15; Ackers 2012; Bevilacqua et al. 2017; Brewer and Kerslake 2015; Del Rey et al. 2015; Fletcher et al. 2014; Genta et al. 2012; Lasher and Baker 2015; Monks et al. 2012; Oliver and Candappa 2003; Pornari and Wood 2010; Rivers and Noret 2010; Smith et al. 2008 (Studies 1 and 2); West 2015; Wolke et al. 2017), Northern Ireland (n = 4; Devine and Lloyd 2012; McClure Watters 2011; McGuckin et al. 2010; Purdy and York 2016), and the Republic of Ireland (n = 4; Callaghan et al. 2015; Corcoran et al. 2012; Cotter and McGilloway 2011; O'Moore 2012). One other international study

Table 5.1 Descriptions of cyberbullying studies conducted in the United Kingdom and the Republic of Ireland

Study	Sample	Time frame/Type of assessment	Prevalence of cyberbullying (%)	Prevalence of cybervictimization (%)
Ackers (2012)	325 Year 7 to 9 students from one UK secondary school	13-item structured questionnaire using both open- and closed-ended questions to gain an understanding of students' knowledge and views of cyberbullying, and also any personal experiences they may have (p. 144)	7%	11%
Bevilacqua et al. (2017)	6,667 Year 7 students from a cluster randomized controlled trial in 40 English schools. 47% were male and the mean age was 11.8 years. 39.4% were white British, 25% Asian/Asian British, 14% black/black British, 8.5% white other, and 5.1% other ethnicity	Smith et al. (2008) measured cyberbullying via mobile phones or the Internet in the past 3 months. Responses were measured on a 5-point Likert scale. Authors dichotomized responses to 'not/rarely bullied or bullies' and 'bullied or bullies/ frequently bullied or bullies' (p. 3)	Males 1.13% Females 0.45%	Males 1.94% Females 4.48%
Brewer and Kerslake (2015)	90 students aged 16 to 18 years from further education colleges in the North West of England. 51 were female and 39 were men	The Revised Cyberbullying Inventory (RCBI; Topcu and Erdur-Baker 2010) measures frequency of cyberbullying perpetration and victimization in the past six months. Responses are scaled on a 4-point Likert scale, from never (0) to more than three times (3)	*More than once in past 6 months 13.54%*	*More than once in past 6 months 16.22%*

(continued)

Table 5.1 (continued)

Study	Sample	Time frame/Type of assessment	Prevalence of cyberbullying (%)	Prevalence of cybervictimization (%)
Callaghan et al. (2015)	318 secondary school students aged 15 to 18 years in Ireland	'How often have you been bullied at school in the past couple of months in the ways listed below? Someone sent mean instant messages, wall postings, emails and text messages, or created a web site that made fun of me? Someone took unflattering or inappropriate pictures of me without permission and posted them online? Someone tricked me into sharing personal information in an email or text message and forwarded that?' Responses ranged from 'I have not been bullied in this way in the past couple of months' to 'several times a week' (pp. 200–201)	–	Cyber only: All 9.8% Boys 10.3% Girls 9.2% Traditional and cyber: All 9.5% Boys 6.5% Girls 13.8%
Corcoran et al. (2012)	876 adolescents aged 12 to 16 from rural and urban post-primary schools in Ireland. 61% were male, 39% female, and the mean age was 14.22. The majority of participants were Irish (90.9%)	Participants completed the Cyberbullying Questionnaire (Smith et al. 2006), which asks about the frequency of both cyberbullying and traditional bullying perpetration and victimization experiences in the past three months	2.6%	6.3%

(continued)

Table 5.1 (continued)

Study	Sample	Time frame/Type of assessment	Prevalence of cyberbullying (%)	Prevalence of cybervictimization (%)
Cotter and McGilloway (2011)[a]	122 students from 2 mixed-gender secondary schools in Ireland. 64 students were in 1st and 2nd year (28 male, 36 female, mean age = 13.08 years) and 58 students were in 5th and 6th year (23 male, 35 female, mean age = 16.62 years)	Participants completed the Cyberbullying Questionnaire (Smith et al. 2006), which asks participants to indicate the frequency of cyberbullying in the past six months. Before completing the survey, participants are provided with a definition of both traditional bullying and cyberbullying (p. 46)	Total 9% Inside school 36.8% Outside school 63.2%	Total 17% Inside school 45.4% Outside school 54.5%
Del Rey et al. (2015)	737 students from 5 UK secondary schools that were part of a larger study in six European countries. 44.6% of the UK sample was female	The European Cyberbullying Intervention Project Questionnaire (Brighi et al. 2012). 22-item Likert scale with frequency responses for cyberbullying victimization and aggression from 'never' to 'more than once a week' (p. 143)	*UK:* Aggressors 0.94% Bully/victims 2.03%	*UK:* Victims 6.37%
Devine and Lloyd (2012)	3,657 adolescents in Northern Ireland, 54% were female	Participants were respondents of the annual Kids Life and Times (KLT) survey, and data were collected in 2009. Participants were asked to indicate whether they had been bullied by someone via nasty text messages or posting bad things on the Internet using yes/no response categories (p. 13)	–	Total 13.83% Girls 15% Boys 11%

(continued)

Table 5.1 (continued)

Study	Sample	Time frame/Type of assessment	Prevalence of cyberbullying (%)	Prevalence of cybervictimization (%)
Fletcher et al. (2014)	1,144 Year 8 students aged 12 to 13 years from 8 mixed-sex ethnically diverse secondary schools in the United Kingdom. Mean age was 12.1 years and 54% were male. 44% identified as white British, 18% black/ black-British, 16% Asian/ Asian-British, 9% Dual heritage, and 13% other	Item adapted from the Cyberbullying Questionnaire (Smith et al. 2008) required participants to indicate the prevalence and frequency of cyberbullying others via mobile phones and the Internet. 'Have you ever bullied someone else through your mobile phone or using the Internet?' Participants also completed ten items from the Edinburgh Study of Youth Transitions and Crime (McAra and McVie 2010) concerning school misbehaviour and delinquency and the Strengths and Difficulties Questionnaire (SDQ; Goodman 2006), a measure of psychological functioning and distress (p. 1394)	*Less than once a week* Total 13.5% Males 14% Females 13% *About once a week* Total 0.3% Males 0.3% Females 0.2% *Several times a week or more* Total 0.3%	

(continued)

Table 5.1 (continued)

Study	Sample	Time frame/Type of assessment	Prevalence of cyberbullying (%)	Prevalence of cybervictimization (%)
Genta et al. (2012)	2,227 students from Years 8, 10, and 12 in 14 English secondary schools that took part in a large-scale European study on bullying. Data collected in 2008 and the majority of participants were white British (1,555). The remaining identified as Asian (437), black (116), and mixed race (160). 1,105 were male and 1,114 were female	'Cyberbullying is a new form of bullying which involves the use of mobile phones (texts, calls, video clips) or the Internet (e-mail, instant messaging, chat rooms, websites) or other forms of information and communication technology to deliberately harass, threaten, or intimidate someone' (p. 20). Definition of traditional bullying was also provided, and students were given two examples of behaviours that constitute traditional bullying and cyberbullying perpetration. Participants were asked to indicate the frequency of experiencing or participating in these behaviours in the past two months. Responses were measured on a 5-point Likert scale, from 'never' to 'several times a week'. Due to the lack of respondents indicating 'severe cyberbullying', the analysis also included those indicating 'occasional cyberbullying'	*Mobile bullying:* Occasional 1% Severe 1.5% *Internet bullying:* Occasional 1.5% Severe 1.5% (p. 23)	*Mobile victimization:* Occasional 2.1% Severe 2% *Internet victimization:* Occasional 4% Severe 2.6% (p. 23)

(continued)

Table 5.1 (continued)

Study	Sample	Time frame/Type of assessment	Prevalence of cyberbullying (%)	Prevalence of cybervictimization (%)
Lasher and Baker (2015)	11,166 adolescents from the Longitudinal Study of Young People in England. Data were collected in 2014 when the sample were in Year 10, aged 14 to 15 years	Past 12 months	–	Total 11% Males: 7% Females: 15%
Livingstone et al. (2011)	Adolescent participants to the EU Kids Online survey. Total sample includes 25,142 children aged 9 to 16 years from 25 countries	Children were asked if they had been treated, or had treated other people, in a hurtful or nasty way on the Internet, whether as a single, repeated or persistent occurrence (p. 24)	–	UK 8% Ireland 4%
McClure Watters (2011)	2,201 primary (Year 6; n = 904) and secondary (Year 9; n = 1,297) students from rural and urban schools in Northern Ireland. 1,222 were female and 1,077 were male	All participants completed the Revised Olweus Bully/Victim Questionnaire (OBVQ; Olweus 1996). Definition of bullying was provided and time frame for responses was within the past couple of months. Two global items asked how often participants have been victimized or have bullied others in the past couple of months. OBVQ contains some questions concerning cyberbullying, but supplementary questions were included in this study (p. 24)	Mobile phones 0.77% Computers 0.34%	Mobile phones 1.34% Computers 2.12%

(continued)

Table 5.1 (continued)

Study	Sample	Time frame/Type of assessment	Prevalence of cyberbullying (%)	Prevalence of cybervictimization (%)
McGuckin et al. (2010)[b]	3,440 pupils aged 11 years from 217 Northern Irish primary schools participated	Participants completed the Kids Life and Times (KLT) questionnaire in 2008 and were asked to indicate whether they had ever had been bullied by someone sending them nasty messages or posting bad things about them online (pp. 87–88)	–	10.3%
Monks et al. (2012)	120 students aged 7 to 11 years from 5 primary schools in the southeast of England. 116 were male and 104 were female. Data were collected in 2008	Modified version of Smith et al. (2008) bullying and cyberbullying questionnaire. Participants were asked to indicate the frequency of their involvement in cyberbullying behaviours over the past school term	5%	20.5%

(continued)

Table 5.1 (continued)

Study	Sample	Time frame/Type of assessment	Prevalence of cyberbullying (%)	Prevalence of cybervictimization (%)
O'Moore (2012)	3,004 students from 9 secondary schools in Ireland. Participants were aged 12 to 16 years and 66.4% were male and 33.6% female. Schools were selected to reflect variety of schools in Ireland: fee-paying, single-sex or mixed, urban or rural, and so on (p. 212)	Measured both traditional bullying (OBVQ; Olweus 1996) and cyberbullying (Smith et al. 2006). Definitions of both were provided, cyberbullying was defined as 'bullying through text messages, pictures or video clips via mobile phone cameras, phone calls, e-mail, chat-rooms, Instant Messaging (IM) or websites (blogs, personal websites, personal polling sites, or social networking sites). Cyber-bullying can happen when text messages/ pictures/clips/e- mails/messages etc. are sent to you, but also when text messages/pictures/clips/e- mails/ messages etc. are sent to others, about you'. Responses were on a frequency scale from 'never' to 'several times a week'. Participants were asked: 'How often have you been cyberbullied in the past couple of months?' and 'How often have you cyberbullied others in the past couple of months?' (p. 212)	*Total:* Pure bullies 4.4% Bully victims 4.1% *Boys:* Pure bullies 4.9% Bully victims 3.9% *Girls:* Pure bullies 3.5% Bully victims 4.5% (p. 213)	*Total:* Pure victims 9.8% *Boys:* Pure victims 6.9% *Girls:* Pure victims 15.6% (p. 213)

(continued)

Table 5.1 (continued)

Study	Sample	Time frame/Type of assessment	Prevalence of cyberbullying (%)	Prevalence of cybervictimization (%)
Oliver and Candappa (2003)	953 students from Year 5 students from 6 primary schools (n = 174; mean age 9 years) and from Year 8 students from 6 secondary schools (n = 779; mean age 12 years). 49% of the sample identified as white British, 20% black and Asian, and 23% other ethnicity. 52% were female and 47% male	Mixed-methods study, questionnaire element targeted definitions, perceptions of the prevalence and experiences of bullying. Data collected in 2002 from Year 8 students on frequency of receiving nasty text messages and/or emails (p. 50)	–	Text messages 4% Emails 2%
Pornari and Wood (2010)	339 students in Years 7 to 9 in one UK secondary school. 159 were male and 180 female. Mean age was 13.3 years and 92.3% were white British. 2.9% identified as mixed race and 2.4% identified as other	26-item scale measuring both offline and online peer aggression and victimization. 3 items each measured cyberaggression and cybervictimization frequency measured on a 5-point Likert scale from 'never' to 'very often' in the past 6 months. Cyber items included, for example, sending insulting or threatening messages via email, text, or Internet chat rooms or forums. Participants also completed a 40-item measure of moral disengagement, hostile attribution bias, and outcome expectancies (pp. 84, 85)	Total 31.5% Males 25.8% Females 36.5%	Total 56.2% Males 53.2% Females 58.8%

(continued)

Table 5.1 (continued)

Study	Sample	Time frame/Type of assessment	Prevalence of cyberbullying (%)	Prevalence of cybervictimization (%)
Purdy and York (2016)	425 students in Years 9, 10, and 11 from 2 post-primary schools in Northern Ireland. 47.3% were male and 52.7% of respondents were female	This definition was provided: 'Cyberbullying defined as any behaviour performed through electronic or digital media by individuals or groups that repeatedly communicates hostile, or aggressive messages intended to inflict harm or discomfort on others' (Tokunaga 2010, p. 278) Structured questionnaire; one question referred to cyberbullying; responses measured on a 5-point ('strongly disagree' to 'strongly agree') Likert scale; past 2 months	—	Total 3.7% School A: 2.7% School B: 4.3%
Rivers and Noret (2010)	Year 7 to 10 students from 13 schools in the North of England, aged 11 to 14 years and predominantly white British (98%). Data collection occurred in 2002, 2003, and 2006. Approximately 2,500 students were included per calendar year (p. 651)	'Have you ever received any nasty or threatening text messages or emails?' Coded on a six-point Likert scale, from 0 = 'not bullied' to 6 = 'frequently, several times a week' (p. 653)	—	2002 Boys: 12% Girls: 14.1% 2003 Boys: 10.6% Girls: 14.3% 2004 Boys: 13.8% Girls: 18.8% 2005 Boys: 11.3% Girls: 21.3% 2006 Boys: 10.3% Girls: 20.8%

(continued)

Table 5.1 (continued)

Study	Sample	Time frame/Type of assessment	Prevalence of cyberbullying (%)	Prevalence of cybervictimization (%)
Smith et al. (2008); Study 1	92 pupils from 14 London schools. One teacher from each school randomly selected one boy and one girl from Years 7 to 10 (inclusive) to complete the questionnaire. 43 respondents were male and 49 were female, aged 11 to 16 years. The majority of students were white British (n = 54). Other ethnicities included Afro-Caribbean (n = 10), black African (n = 7), Indian (n = 7), Chinese (n = 1), and mixed race (n = 3) (p. 378)	Global items: (1) Have you experienced bullying of any kind in the past couple of months? (2) Have you experienced bullying via the seven media in the past couple of months? Multiple-choice questions were then asked relating specifically to each of the seven types of media about how often students had been victimized or had cyberbullied others, separately for inside and outside school. All questions measured on a 5-point Likert scale, from 'never' to 'several times a week' (p. 377)	'More than once/twice' *Outside school:* Phone call 1.1% Text 1.1 % Email 1.1% Picture 0% Instant messaging 1.1% Website 0% Chatroom 0% *Inside school:* Phone call 1.1% Text 0% Email 2.2% Picture 0% Instant messaging 0% Website 0% Chatroom 0%	'More than once/ twice' *Outside school:* Phone call 10.9% Text 3.3% Email 4.4% Picture 0% Instant messaging 3.3% Website 1.1% Chatroom 0% *Inside school:* Phone call 3.3% Text 3.3% Email 3.3% Picture 0% Instant messaging 0% Website 0% Chatroom 0%

(*continued*)

Table 5.1 (continued)

Study	Sample	Time frame/Type of assessment	Prevalence of cyberbullying (%)	Prevalence of cybervictimization (%)
Smith et al. (2008); Study 2	533 students from 5 schools in several UK counties from Years 7 to 10. 261 were male and 267 were female (5 missing) and the majority (82.8%) of participants identified as white British (p. 378)	Global items: (1) Have you experienced bullying of any kind in the past couple of months? (2) Have you experienced bullying via the seven media in the past couple of months? Multiple choice questions were then asked relating specifically to each of the seven types of media about how often students had been victimized or had cyberbullied others, separately for inside and outside school. All questions measured on a 5-point Likert scale, from 'never' to 'several times a week' (p. 377)	% Ever cyberbullied someone else by: Phone call 4.3% Text 2.8% Email 2.4% Picture 1.8% Instant messaging 5.3% Website 2.4% Chat room 1.0% (p. 379)	% Ever been cyberbullied by: Phone call 9.5% Text 6.6% Email 4.7% Picture 5.0% Instant messaging 9.9% Website 3.5% Chatroom 2.5% (p. 379)
West (2015)	5,690 adolescents aged 16 to 19 years from 41 colleges. 42.6% of respondents were male and 57.4% were female. 75.8% of participants identified as white British, and the remainder identified as Asian (13.3%), white other (3.9%), mixed race (3.1%), black (2.5%), or other (1.4%). Data collected in 2014	An online questionnaire was distributed comprising 50 items about their experiences of cyberbullying 'while being a college student' (p. 103)	Cyberbullies 1.9% Once 44.4% 2–3 times 25% 4–6 times 5.6% 7–10 times 1.4% More than 10 times 23.6%	Cybervictims 7.9% Once 42.5% 2–3 times 32.6% 4–6 times 10.9% 7–10 times 2.6% More than 10 times 11.4%

(continued)

Table 5.1 (continued)

Study	Sample	Time frame/Type of assessment	Prevalence of cyberbullying (%)	Prevalence of cybervictimization (%)
Wolke et al. (2017)	2,754 students from schools in the Midlands, UK. Participants were aged 11 to 16 years, mean age = 13.5 years. 56.9% were female and 82.5% were white British (p. 900)	Four items on the Bullying and Friendship Interview (Wolke et al. 2000) schedule related to cyberbullying victimization experienced in the past six months: 'Had rumours spread about you online?' 'Had embarrassing pictures been posted online without permission?' 'Had private emails, messages or photos been forwarded to someone else or where others can see it?' 'Got threatening or aggressive emails, instant messages, text messages, or tweets'. Frequency was measured on a 5-point Likert scale. Non-victims were classified as those who indicated these behaviours never or occasionally occurred, and victims were categorized as those responding that these behaviours occurred often or frequently	–	Pure cybervictims 1.13% Offline direct and cybervictims 0.87% Offline relational and cybervictims 0.908%

aPercentages were estimated by the first author

bThis paper also presents results for data collected in 2009 from the KLT survey; however, as Devine and Lloyd (2012) also utilize these data, we do not include these results here

cSchool A = small non-selective mixed-gender school in a rural location; School B = large selective mixed-gender school in an urban area

presented results on cyberbullying in both the United Kingdom and the Republic of Ireland (Livingstone et al. 2011). In addition, O'Neill and Dinh (2015) presented results from the Net Children Go Mobile survey in the United Kingdom and the Republic of Ireland. However, this study has been excluded from subsequent exploration, as it reports percentages for offline and online victimization (United Kingdom 21%; Ireland 22%) combined.

These studies were identified during searches of the online academic literature database Web of Science. Searches were conducted for studies that were published between the years 2000 and 2017 and employed key terms such as '*cyberbullying*'; '*cybervictimization*'; '*online harassment*'; *cyber*, *bully**; *victim**; '*United Kingdom*'; '*UK*'; and '*Ireland*'. The British English spelling of victimization, that is, *victimisation*, was also included as a search term. Additionally, specific searches of key researchers in the United Kingdom and Ireland, for example, Professor Peter Smith and Professor Mona O'Moore respectively, were conducted in order to discover any relevant publications. This chapter will discuss the findings on the prevalence of cyberbullying perpetration and victimization derived from these studies, and the factors that potentially influence prevalence.

Prevalence of Cyberbullying Perpetration and Victimization

An early study of cyberbullying prevalence in the United Kingdom was conducted in 2002, with Year 8 students (n = 779; mean age = 12 years) reporting how often they had received nasty emails or text messages (Oliver and Candappa 2003). This seminal study reported that 4% of children reported receiving nasty text messages and 2% reported receiving nasty emails. Subsequent research studies identified higher prevalence rates from data collected between 2002 and 2006. Rivers and Noret (2010) reported the prevalence of 'receiving nasty text messages or emails' in a sample of British adolescents aged 11 to 14 years. The results are presented for this five-year study independently for each year of data collection and for males and females separately. The results show a steady increase in the rate of cyberbullying victimization experienced by girls from the first point of data collection in 2002 (14.1%) to 2005 (21.3%). The rates declined slightly in 2006 to 20.8% of girls reporting receiving nasty text messages or emails. The figures for boys were less consistent, as is demonstrated by the results shown in Table 5.1.

In 2005, a study conducted with UK adolescents aged 11 to 16 years (Smith et al. 2008; Study 1) found that a maximum of 1.1% of children reported cyberbullying others via phone calls, texts, emails, and/or instant messages outside school, and 2.3% reported cyberbullying others via email inside school more than once or twice. Cyberbullying victimization varied from 1.1% (via websites outside school) to 3.3% (via phone calls, texts, emails inside school), and 10.9% reporting bullying victimization via phone calls outside school more than once or twice in the past couple of months (Smith et al. 2008). This pilot study was subsequently followed up and revealed higher incidence rates of children reporting having 'ever' cyberbullied someone (from 1% via chat rooms to 5.3% via instant messaging) or having ever been a victim of cyberbullying (from 2.5% via chatrooms to 9.5% via phone calls and 9.9% via instant messaging; Smith et al. 2008, p. 379).

The prevalence of cyberbullying perpetration and victimization has varied greatly in more recent studies, from 2.5% (mobile bullying perpetration), 3% (Internet bullying perpetration), 4.1% (mobile bullying victimization), and 6.6% (Internet bullying victimization) for 2,227 Year 8 to 12 students in 2008 (Genta et al. 2012) to 13.5% of 1,144 Year 8 students reporting engaging in cyberbullying perpetration less than once a week (Fletcher et al. 2014). Also in 2008, 5% and 20.5% of primary school children in England, aged 7 to 11 years, self-identified as cyberbullies and cybervictims respectively (Monks et al. 2012). In addition, Ackers (2012) found that 11% of 325 Year 7 to 9 students from one secondary school in the United Kingdom responded that they had been cyberbullied, while 7% of the sample responded that they had cyberbullied someone else. Research conducted with older adolescents (90 students aged 16 to 18 years) found that 13.5% and 16.2% of children reported cyberbullying perpetration and victimization respectively (Brewer and Kerslake 2015).

National data collected via the Longitudinal Study of Young People in England (of Year 10 students in 2014) discovered that 11% of children reported cyberbullying victimization (Lasher and Baker 2015). Moreover, the international EU Kids Online survey concluded that 8% of UK children reported cyberbullying victimization (Livingstone et al. 2011). An exploratory study of cyberaggression and cybervictimization found that 31.5% and 56.2% of 339 Year 7 to 9 students in one UK secondary school reported engaging in and experiencing cyberaggression and cybervictimization respectively (Pornari and Wood 2010). A more recent study (Bevilacqua et al. 2017) discovered that, among a sample of Year 7 students from 40 English schools, 1.6% and 6.4% of children reported cyberbullying perpetration and victimization respectively. Among older children, prevalence rates of cyberbullying perpetration (1.9%) and victimization (7.9%) were slightly higher (West 2015).

Other studies have categorized children according to their self-reported involvement in cyberbullying. Del Rey et al. (2015) found that 0.9% of 737 UK students were categorized as aggressors of cyberbullying, 2.0% were categorized as bully victims, and 6.4% were victims of cyberbullying. In this large-scale European study, the prevalence of cyberbullying perpetration among UK adolescents was relatively low in comparison to the overall sample that included children from countries such as Italy, Greece, Poland, Spain, and Germany. However, the number of children in the United Kingdom who reported cyberbullying victimization was in line with the mean prevalence reported by the total sample (6.4% compared with 6.8%). Wolke et al. (2017) found that 1.1% of 2,754 UK adolescents aged 11 to 16 years were classified as 'pure cybervictims', in other words, being victimized online only.

In Northern Ireland, a government report concluded that 1.1% and 3.5% of primary and secondary school students reported cyberbullying perpetration and victimization respectively (McClure Watters 2011). Additionally, 3.7% of 425 Year 9 to 11 students from two secondary schools reported experiencing cyberbullying victimization. Results from a nationally disseminated survey (Kids Life and Times) showed that 13.8% of Northern Irish adolescents reported cyberbullying victimization (Devine and Lloyd 2012). Moreover, among a sample of nearly 3,500 children, aged 11, attending 217 Northern Irish primary schools, 10.3% reported experiencing cyberbullying victimization (McGuckin et al. 2010).

Seminal research on cyberbullying in the Republic of Ireland in 2011 found that 9% and 17% of secondary school students reported cyberbullying perpetration and victimization, respectively (Cotter and McGilloway 2011). In addition, this study found that most cyberbullying perpetration and victimization reported by participants was experienced outside school (see Table 5.1). Furthermore, O'Moore (2012) reported that 4.4% of over 3,000 secondary school students were classified as pure cyberbullies, 4.1% were categorized as bully victims, and 9.8% were categorized as pure cybervictims. International studies, which included Irish children, have found that 4% of adolescents reported cyberbullying victimization (Livingstone et al. 2011). Similarly, Corcoran et al. (2012) discovered that 2.6% of post-primary Irish adolescents reported cyberbullying perpetration, and 6.3% reported cyberbullying victimization. A recent study conducted in the Republic of Ireland concluded that 9.8% of Irish adolescents aged 15 to 18 years (n = 318) had experienced cyberbullying victimization (Callaghan et al. 2015).

Measuring Cyberbullying and Cybervictimization

Unfortunately, the measurement instruments used in cyberbullying research are far from perfect (Patchin and Hinduja 2015; Gradinger et al. 2010), and thus there are several factors to consider when interpreting the prevalence rates produced. Some researchers in the field suggest that a precise measure of cyberbullying prevalence may be impossible to achieve (Sabella et al. 2013). A recent meta-analysis investigated the prevalence of cyberbullying perpetration and victimization and the potential methodological moderator variables that can impact reporting rates (Foody et al. 2017). This synthesis of 39 empirical studies, conducted in the Republic of Ireland and Northern Ireland, found that 5.2% and 3.9% of primary and post-primary school students, respectively, reported engaging in cyberbullying perpetration. In addition, 13.7% and 9.6% of primary and post-primary school students, respectively, reported cyberbullying victimization. These aggregate figures were lower than those identified for traditional school-bullying perpetration (10.1%) and victimization (26.1%).

The observations noted in this chapter are in line with the conclusions of this recent meta-analysis. In particular, Foody et al. (2017) discovered that a series of moderator variables also influenced the prevalence rates reported by primary studies. For example, the time frame during which participants were asked to disclose their experiences of cyberbullying perpetration and/or victimization was a significant moderator for both outcomes. Namely, the longer the time, the higher was the percentage of cyberbullying perpetration (Q(df = 2) = 19.53, $p < 0.001$) and cyberbullying victimization (Q(df = 2) = 22.88; $p < 0.001$), as measured by seven studies with post-primary students. Issues relating to methodology will be investigated in the following sections of this chapter in relation to cyberbullying research that has been conducted in the United Kingdom and Ireland. For example, prevalence rates of cyberbullying perpetration and victimization may be affected by the time frame specified for experiencing these behaviours, the use of categorical frequency variables, the use of self-report measures, and the year of data collection.

Time Frame of Measurement The period of time during which children were required to report cyberbullying victimization and/or perpetration varied between studies conducted in the United Kingdom and Ireland. Of the studies that used a specified time frame for experiences of cyberbullying, children were asked about their experiences of cyberbullying perpetration and/or victimization in the past 2 (e.g. Genta et al. 2012; Purdy and York 2016), 3 (e.g. Bevilacqua et al. 2017), 6 (e.g. Brewer and Kerslake 2015; Cotter and McGilloway 2011; Pornari and Wood 2010; Wolke et al. 2017), or 12 (e.g. Lasher and Baker 2015) months. Additionally, some studies asked about the frequency of cyberbullying behaviours in other time frames, such as ever (e.g. Fletcher et al. 2014; McGuckin et al. 2010; Rivers and Noret 2010; West 2015), the past couple of months (e.g. Callaghan et al. 2015; O'Moore 2012; Smith et al. 2008), or the past school term (e.g. Monks et al. 2012).

No definitive pattern could be identified in the prevalence rates according to the time frame specified in the measurement instrument. However, in many cases (e.g. Brewer and Kerslake 2015; Cotter and McGilloway 2011; McGuckin et al. 2010; Pornari and Wood 2010; Fletcher et al. 2014), prevalence rates of cyberbullying perpetration and victimization were higher when children were asked to indicate the frequency over longer periods of time (e.g. six months or ever), in comparison with studies employing shorter periods of time (e.g. two months, Genta et al. 2012; or three months, Bevilacqua et al. 2017). Surprisingly, other studies that used longer time frames for experiencing cyberbullying whilst being a college student (e.g. West 2015) or the past couple of months (e.g. Smith et al. 2008) reported quite low prevalence. This suggests that choosing an appropriate time frame for measuring cyberbullying perpetration and victimization may influence the frequency of reporting. Therefore, this issue should be considered when choosing an adequate measurement instrument for empirical research; however, there may be other factors that also influence reporting rates.

Frequency Responses Cyberbullying perpetration and/or victimization prevalence rates could also be influenced by how behaviours are categorized. The majority of measurement tools used in studies reviewed in this chapter employed Likert frequency scales, asking children to indicate whether they had experienced cyberbullying behaviours never to once or more a week (e.g. the European Cyberbullying Intervention Project Questionnaire; Brighi et al. 2012). Typically, most studies found that, when including response categories of lower frequency, more children reported cyberbullying behaviours. For example, Fletcher et al. (2014) discovered that, while only 0.3% of children reported cyberbullying perpetration several times a week or more, 13.5% of children reported cyberbullying perpetration less than once a week. Moreover, when the questions specified ever cyberbullying someone else, or ever being cyberbullied, the prevalence rates were higher in comparison to results for cyberbullying more than once or twice a week (Smith et al. 2008).

Reports of cyberbullying perpetration and victimization in Northern Ireland suggest that when lower levels of these behaviours are included, the overall prevalence increases (McClure Watters 2011). With respect to cyberbullying victimization, 3.5% of children experienced cyberbullying two or three times a month (2.1% by mobile phones; 1.3% on the

Internet). A further 16.6% of children reported cybervictimization via mobile phones or the Internet that only happened once or twice. In addition, 5.5% reported cyberbullying others via mobile phones or the Internet 'only once or twice'. Among the 1.9% and 7.9% of adolescents aged 16 to 19 years who identified as cyberbullies and cybervictims, respectively, the majority of bullies (44.4%) and victims (42.5%) indicated that the behaviours had only occurred once in the time that they had been a college student (West 2015).

Generally, empirical research tends to focus on cyberbullying perpetration and victimization that occurs more frequently over longer periods of time, which is considered to have a more severe effect. However, since the issue of repetition is a contentious factor in defining cyberbullying (Patchin and Hinduja 2015), it may be desirable to also include behaviours that occur less frequently. Cotter and McGilloway (2011) asked participants to indicate the duration of their experiences of cyberbullying. Of 22 cybervictims identified in this study, the majority (n = 16) reported that the cyberbullying victimization lasted for one to two weeks. A minority of participants reported cyberbullying victimization lasting for 'about a month' (n = 2), 'about six months' (n = 2), or for several years (n = 2). The experience of even one incident of cyberbullying victimization may be repeated for the victim and the negative impact exacerbated because of the permanency of online data and the speed and extent of distribution (Willard 2006). Therefore, the restrictions that may be imposed when measuring cyberbullying prevalence should be carefully considered. For example, only counting cyberbullying that occurs 'several times a week or more' (Fletcher et al. 2014) may underestimate the extent of the problem.

Self-Report Measures Each study included in this review employed self-report measures of cyberbullying perpetration and/or victimization. Measurement instruments include the Cyberbullying Questionnaire (Smith et al. 2008), the European Cyberbullying Intervention Project Questionnaire (Brighi et al. 2012), the Revised Olweus Bully/Victim Questionnaire (Olweus 1996), or specific items on cyberbullying from the Bullying and Friendship Interview (Wolke et al. 2000). However, the use of self-report measures may not be the best method for establishing true prevalence rates, because of potential biases, such as social desirability responding. For example, O'Moore (2012) found that between 3.5% and 15.6% of male and female children were categorized as pure cyberbullies or pure cybervictims. However, 39.1% of females and 29.9% of males from the same study reported being aware of someone else who had been victimized online, and 28.4% of children indicated that they were aware of someone who had bullied others online. Moreover, 33% of UK Year 8 students reported knowing someone else who had been cyberbullied, although only 11% reported being cyberbullied themselves (Ackers 2012). Social desirability responding may also potentially explain why cyberbullying victimization is more frequently reported than cyberbullying perpetration (e.g. Smith et al. 2008; Monks et al. 2012). Thus, the reliability and validity of self-report measures should be investigated and taken into consideration when interpreting the reported prevalence of cyberbullying perpetration and/or victimization.

Year of Data Collection An additional factor that needs to be considered when interpreting the rates of cyberbullying perpetration and/or victimization is the year in which data were collected. The last decade has seen a rapid increase in the prevalence and accessibility of Internet-ready devices, such as smartphones, tablets, personal computers, and music players. Therefore, the potential to engage in cyberbullying behaviours or to be cyberbullied is increasingly at our fingertips (Slonje et al. 2013). Analysing the results from the studies shown in Table 5.1, amongst those that report when data collection occurred, it appears that cyberbullying prevalence rates may be influenced by the year in which data were collected.

Genta et al. (2012) reported that 2.1% and 2% of children reported occasional and severe mobile phone victimization and 4% and 2.6% reported occasional and severe Internet victimization, respectively. Additionally, this study also discovered that 95% of children had a computer with Internet access in their homes, but only 38.4% reported having access to the Internet in their own bedrooms. Based on analyses of the overall sample (i.e. including adolescents from Italy and Spain), Genta et al. (2012) found that accessibility to the Internet in one's own bedroom was a significant predictor of higher levels of both cyberbullying victimization and perpetration. However, as the data were collected approximately nine years ago, in 2008, these figures may not be generalizable to the adolescent population in the United Kingdom or Ireland today. For example, national data collected from UK adolescents in 2014 indicated that 11% of children reported cyberbullying victimization (Lasher and Baker 2015). Furthermore, two studies conducted in Northern Ireland analysed results from the Kids Life and Times survey administered in 2008 (McGuckin et al. 2010) and 2009 (Devine and Lloyd 2012). Even within the space of a year the rate of cyberbullying victimization reported rose from 10.3% to 13.8%.

Another element that may affect the prevalence rates of reported cyberbullying, relating to the year in which data are collected, is the medium through which the aggression takes place. For example, Purdy and York (2016) estimated the prevalence of cyberbullying among a sample of 425 Northern Irish adolescents and also explored their social media use: 90.2% reported using Facebook, 69.9% reported using Snapchat, and 55.6% reported using Twitter. Most students reported spending an average of 1 to 2 hours online per day (31.3%) and 1 in 5 students reported spending 2 to 3 hours online per day. Sending hurtful or nasty comments either via text messages or on social networking sites was the most common form of cyberbullying among all students (Purdy and York 2016).

In comparison, earlier studies focused solely on cyberbullying occurring via text messaging or emails (e.g. Oliver and Candappa 2003; Smith et al. 2008). Moreover, the use of specific social media sites changes over time too, which could also influence the prevalence of cyberbullying, as some platforms may be more conducive to this form of aggressive behaviour. For example, Cotter and McGilloway (2011) specifically refer to the social networking site 'Bebo', but this site is no longer used, so that their prevalence rate for cyberbullying may not apply to adolescents in 2017.

Risk Factors

A large-scale review assessed risk factors associated with cyberbullying perpetration and victimization as measured by 53 studies conducted in various international locations (Baldry et al. 2015). This review categorized factors according to a socio-ecological framework (Bronfenbrenner 1979), with risk factors identified at the individual (e.g. technology use, personality traits, values), peer and family (e.g. pro-social peers, peer rejection, parental support), and school (e.g. lack of teacher support, negative school climate) levels. This theoretical framework is commonly used to explain risk factors associated with cyberbullying (e.g. Cross et al. 2015). This chapter will further explore the potential risk factors and predictors that are associated with cyberbullying perpetration and victimization as measured in UK or Irish samples. The included studies measured mainly individual-level factors, such as gender, ethnicity, demographics, traditional bullying perpetration and victimization, and various psychological and cognitive constructs. In addition, some school-level variables have been studied. Because of the general lack of longitudinal studies, it is difficult to draw conclusions about prediction or about causal effects.

Gender Assessing the prevalence rates reported by studies conducted with samples in the United Kingdom and Ireland, it appears that girls report, on average, higher rates of cybervictimization than boys, and boys report, on average, higher rates of cyberbullying perpetration. Bevilacqua et al. (2017) concluded that 1.13% of males and 0.45% of females reported frequent cyberbullying perpetration, and 1.94% of males and 4.48% of females reported frequent cyberbullying victimization. In Northern Ireland, female adolescents (15%) reported statistically significant higher rates of cyberbullying victimization compared to their male peers (11%; χ^2 =18.45, df = 2, $p < 0.001$; Devine and Lloyd 2012, p. 17).

Similar results were found by Pornari and Wood (2010), with females (58.8%) reporting higher rates of cybervictimization compared to males (53.2%). Of the children who were categorized as 'pure cybervictims' (i.e. those reporting experiencing bullying victimization online only) in Wolke and colleagues' study (2017), 58.1% were female. Ackers (2012) concluded that there was a significant main effect for gender in self-reported cyberbullying victimization, with females being more likely to report being victimized. The frequency of receiving nasty or threatening text messages or emails varied between 10.3% and 12% for boys, but it was higher for girls, varying between 14.1% and 21.3% (Rivers and Noret 2010). An exploratory study of 1,144 year 8 students in UK secondary schools concluded that males (14.7%) were more likely than females (13.4%) to report engaging in cyberbullying perpetration (Odds Ratio (OR) = 0.91; CI = 0.64 to 1.28), although this difference was not statistically significant (Fletcher et al. 2014).

In the Republic of Ireland, however, one study found that boys reported more cyberbullying victimization than females, 10.3% and 9.2% respectively (Callaghan et al. 2015). In comparison, employing a sample of Irish adolescents, aged 12 to 16 years, O'Moore (2012, p. 213) classified more girls (15.6%) as pure victims of cyberbullying than boys (6.9%). This study categorized more boys (4.9%) as pure bullies than girls (3.5%); however, more girls (4.5%) were classified as bully victims than boys (3.9%). Similarly, Pornari and Wood (2010) found that girls were more likely to report cyberaggression perpetration than boys (OR = 1.66, $p < 0.05$). However, some studies found no significant association between gender and cyberbullying perpetration or victimization (e.g. Monks et al. 2012, p. 483).

Ethnicity and Demographic Variables A few of the studies conducted in the United Kingdom and Ireland considered the impact of several demographic and sociodemographic variables. Research on ethnicity found that males of mixed ethnicity (4.5%) and females identifying as Black or Black British (0.8%) were more likely to report engaging in frequent cyberbullying perpetration (Bevilacqua et al. 2017). Both males and females identifying as white other (3.4% and 5.2% respectively) were more likely to report frequent cyberbullying victimization. An analysis of the relationship between ethnicity and cyberbullying perpetration concluded that, in comparison with children identifying as white British (11.6%), those of dual heritage (20%; OR = 1.92; CI = 1.09 to 3.40) and other ethnicity (19.1%; OR = 1.76; CI = 1.03 to 3.00) were more likely to report cyberbullying perpetration (Fletcher et al. 2014). The differences between children identifying as white British and those identifying as Asian or Asian British (9.9%; OR = 0.83, CI = 0.47 to 1.48) or as black or black British (17.2%; OR = 1.55, CI = 0.97 to 2.48) were not quite statistically significant.

Fletcher et al. (2014) found no differences in cyberbullying perpetration reported by students according to family structure (i.e. living with two parents, one parent, or other). Adolescents who reported having unemployed parents (21.1%) were more likely to engage in cyberbullying perpetration than students with parents in employment (13.8%; OR = 1.6; CI = 0.98 to 2.6), although this effect was not quite statistically significant.

Traditional School-Bullying and Victimization The most common finding by studies conducted with children in the United Kingdom and Ireland is that there is a significant relationship between school-bullying perpetration and victimization offline and cyberbullying perpetration and victimization. Previous research has found that there is a distinct overlap between offline and online victimization, with individuals participating in both acts as pure offline and pure online bullies and victims, but also various combinations of online and offline bullies, victims, and bully victims (Schultze-Krumbholz et al. 2015). For example, in the study conducted by Wolke et al. (2017), 8.1% and 5.8% of children reported experiencing victimization as a result of direct and relationship bullying respectively, while only 1.1% of children reported experiencing only cybervictimization. In addition, 5.1% of children reported experiencing direct, relational, and online bullying victimization. Typically, reports of offline bullying perpetration and victimization are higher than those reported for online perpetration and victimization (e.g. Bevilacqua et al. 2017; Cotter and McGilloway 2011; Livingstone et al. 2011; Monks et al. 2012; O'Moore 2012).

Pornari and Wood (2010, p. 88) concluded that, among a sample of UK adolescents, high levels of traditional aggression correlated with an increased likelihood of an adolescent being a cyberbully (B = 0.24; SE = 0.03; p < 0.001). Similarly, high levels of traditional victimization correlated with an increased likelihood of being a cybervictim (B = 0.10; SE = 0.02; p < 0.001), but with a decreased likelihood of being a cyberbully (B = −0.09; SE = 0.03; p = 0.001). Fletcher et al. (2014) also investigated the relationships between self-reported aggressive behaviour at school and the frequency of cyberbullying perpetration. Students who reported higher levels of aggressive behaviour in school were significantly more likely to also report cyberbullying perpetration (37.1%; OR = 14.35; CI = 7.96 to 25.86), in comparison with those reporting lesser degrees of in-school aggression. In a sample of primary schoolchildren, being a traditional victim was a significant predictor of being a cybervictim, but not a cyberbully. Furthermore, being a traditional bully was a significant predictor of being a cyberbully, but not a cybervictim (Monks et al. 2012, pp. 483–484). However, when age is taken into consideration, the relationship between traditional bullying and cyberbullying may change. For example, O'Moore (2012, p. 213) found that 32% of post-primary cyberbullies reported traditional bullying victimization, while 28.9% of cybervictims reported engaging in traditional bullying perpetration.

Cognitive and Psychological Factors Five studies reviewed in this chapter (i.e. Brewer and Kerslake 2015; Corcoran et al. 2012; Fletcher et al. 2014; Wolke et al. 2017) investigated the relationship between cyberbullying and different cognitive or psychological factors. Because of the infrequency of longitudinal studies, it is unclear whether these are risk factors for, or outcomes of, cyberbullying perpetration and victimization, but the results are important to guide future research.

In an adjusted multilevel regression model, Wolke et al. (2017) found that pure cybervictimization was significantly related to lower self-esteem ($B = -2.19$, $p = 0.004$) and higher levels of self-reported behavioural difficulties ($B = 4.13$, $p > 0.001$). Furthermore, when effect sizes were adjusted for demographic variables, interesting relationships were observed between self-reported cyberbullying perpetration of UK adolescents and their psychological functioning, overall mental well-being, and several aspects of mental and physical health (Fletcher et al. 2014[1]). Based on a measure of psychological functioning (the Strengths and Difficulties Questionnaire; Goodman 2006), Fletcher et al. (2014) suggested that children with greater overall difficulties (OR = 2.32; CI = 1.97 to 3.24) and greater conduct problems (OR = 1.3; CI = 1.08 to 1.55) were more likely to report bullying others online in comparison with children reporting fewer overall difficulties or fewer conduct problems. Significant negative relationships were observed between cyberbullying perpetration and the quality of life (OR = −3.51; CI = −5.7 to −0.1), psychosocial health (OR = −5.04; CI = −7.26 to −1.6), emotional functioning (OR = −5.6; CI = −9.03 to −0.18), and school functioning (OR = −7.35, CI = −9.27 to −4.95; see Fletcher et al. 2014).

In Northern Ireland, Devine and Lloyd (2012) observed that adolescents who experienced cyberbullying victimization reported significantly poorer overall psychological well-being (t (1, 3382) = 10.77, $p < 0.001$). In the Republic of Ireland, Corcoran et al. (2012) discovered interesting relationships between aspects of participants' self-concepts, measured using the Piers-Harris 2 (Piers et al. 2002) instrument. Cybervictims scored lower on overall general self-concept and the 'freedom of anxiety' subscale, in comparison to non-involved groups. For UK adolescents, Brewer and Kerslake (2015) found that cyberbullying victimization was significantly and positively correlated with loneliness ($r = 0.8$, $p < 0.01$) and negatively correlated with self-esteem ($r = −0.42$, $p < 0.01$). In addition, cyberbullying perpetration was significantly negatively correlated with loneliness ($r = −0.38$, $p < 0.01$) and self-esteem ($r = −0.22$, $p < 0.01$). Based on standard regression models, low self-esteem was significantly related to cyberbullying victimization. Low levels of empathy and self-esteem were also significantly related to cyberbullying perpetration (Brewer and Kerslake 2015, p. 258).

Pornari and Wood (2010) also conducted exploratory analyses of several individual cognitive factors and cyberaggression perpetration and victimization among UK adolescents. The results indicated that the moral justification facets of moral disengagement were related to cyberaggression perpetration ($B = 0.20$, SE = 0.04; $p < 0.001$). Moreover, hostile attribution bias was significantly related to cyberaggression victimization ($B = 0.12$, SE = 0.04, $p < 0.05$). Finally, Corcoran et al. (2012) investigated the relationship between cyberbullying perpetration and victimization and personality, as measured by the Junior Eysenck Personality Questionnaire (Eysenck and Eysenck 1975). Significant differences were observed between groups (i.e. cyberbullies, cybervictims, traditional bullies, traditional victims, non-involved) on both psychoticism and neuroticism scores. Specifically, the cybervictim group reported significantly higher scores on the neuroticism scale compared to the non-involved group.

School-Level Factors Bevilacqua et al. (2017) further investigated the relationship between several school-level variables and the frequency of self-reported cyberbullying perpetration and victimization. Effect sizes, adjusted for all individual-level variables, such as gender and ethnicity, evaluated the relationship between the proportion of children eligible for free school meals, the Income Deprivation Affecting Children Index score, and the most recent overall Ofsted rating, and the prevalence of cyberbullying perpetration and victimization. Moreover, school type (e.g. community, funded by local authorities; voluntary-aided, funded by a charity and partially by local authorities; sponsor-led academies and foundation schools), size, and sex composition were also investigated in relation to cyberbullying and cybervictimization. Significant relationships were found for the impact of the proportion of students eligible for free school meals (adjusted OR = 1.02, CI = 1.002 to 1.05), community schools (adjusted OR = 4.25, CI = 1.54 to 11.71), foundation schools (adjusted OR = 4.73, CI = 1.83 to 12.26), and the 'requires improvement' Ofsted rating (adjusted OR = 4.01, CI 1.05 to 15.24) versus cyberbullying perpetration. These results suggested that cyberbullying perpetration was more likely to occur in schools with lower socioeconomic demographics and poor national ratings. In relation to cyberbullying victimization, no statistically significant effects were found.

The majority (74.2%) of pure cybervictims, categorized by Wolke et al. (2017), were from schools that were not eligible for the pupil premium (an indicator of deprivation and special assistance within schools). This study also investigated the relationship between cyberbullying and parental education. The majority of pure cybervictims reported that their parents had 12 to 13 years of education; 32.3% reported parental education of more than 13 years; and 6.5% reported that their parents had spent less than 11 years in full-time education (Wolke et al. 2017). In Northern Ireland, the prevalence of cybervictimization was higher among students attending a school in an urban location (4.3%) compared to those attending a smaller school in a rural location (2.7%; Purdy and York 2016). These results suggest that adolescents who self-report cyberbullying perpetration are also more likely to report a wide range of psychological and social problems. This is an important observation to better inform cyberbullying intervention and prevention programmes in the United Kingdom and Ireland.

Cyberbullying Intervention and Prevention

Legal Aspects In comparison to the United States, there is currently no law in place in the United Kingdom or Ireland that criminalizes cyberbullying behaviours (Marczak and Coyne 2010). Some researchers have described cyberbullying as being in a state of legal limbo (Asam and Samara 2016, p. 131). However, current legislation in the United Kingdom specifies that all schools must have a clearly defined anti-bullying policy (Marczak and Coyne 2010; the *School Standards and Framework Act, 1998*). Furthermore, the Education and Inspections Act (2006) gives teaching professionals powers to regulate students' behaviour in school, including the ability to confiscate personal ICTs (Asam and Samara 2016). As pointed out in this chapter, there is quite frequently an overlap in experiencing traditional bullying and cyberbullying. Therefore, it is pertinent for UK schools to incorporate elements targeting cyberbullying into these anti-bullying policies. In addition, teachers are key players in cyberbullying intervention and prevention. By removing ICTs from a student's possession they are able to physically stop cyberbullying perpetration from taking place in school.

There are ways in which online aggression, that may amount to cyberbullying, can be prosecuted in the United Kingdom. For example, online hate crimes have recently received media attention, with sources specifying that the Crown Prosecution Service in the United Kingdom will start to seek harsher penalties for abuse perpetrated online via social media sites such as Twitter and/or Facebook. The Director of Public Prosecutions stated recently that the criminal justice system in the United Kingdom must start handling cases of online hate crimes as seriously as it handles offences that occur face-to-face (Dodd 2017). Recent news stories have highlighted the extreme levels of hate and abuse that those in the public eye receive online. For example, Olivia Attwood, who appeared on a reality-style dating show aired on ITV2, received abuse that was so bad that she could not disclose it on live television (BBC 2017). Celebrities are not the only ones who are subject to such abuse. Cyberbullying and general cyberaggression are becoming increasingly common in our society, as communications rapidly increase in the online sphere.

School-Based Intervention and Prevention School-based anti-bullying programmes have been widely researched internationally, with results indicating that they can be effective in reducing traditional bullying perpetration and victimization (e.g. Farrington and Ttofi 2009). Thompson and Smith (2012) conducted a large-scale review of anti-bullying policies in UK schools. Their evaluation found that anti-bullying efforts in UK schools occurred at several different levels, including whole-school, classroom, and playground strategies. As the current chapter has shown, in the United Kingdom and Ireland, traditional and online bullying commonly overlap, so that it is important that schools in the United Kingdom and Ireland integrate cyberbullying into their existing anti-bullying policies. More recently, a content analysis of anti-bullying policies in schools in Northern Ireland revealed that the majority of schools incorporate elements targeting cyberbullying (Purdy and Smith 2016). Additionally, the 'Quality Circles' approach has been employed in schools in order to tackle the problem of cyberbullying (Paul et al. 2010).

Large numbers of parents in the Republic of Ireland report that they are aware of the risk posed by cyberbullying, and they are either worried or unsure about whether their children are exposed (O'Higgins Norman et al. 2016). Moreover, head teachers of secondary schools in Northern Ireland and the Republic of Ireland report that cyberbullying is prevalent in their schools and that they are frustrated with their attempts to handle this complex problem (Purdy and McGuckin 2015). Research has investigated the factors that predict teachers' intention to intervene in bullying, including cyberbullying, scenarios. Boulton et al. (2014) concluded that the three significant predictors of willingness to intervene were ratings of empathy, coping, and severity of the behaviours. Therefore, the inclusion of parents and teachers in school-based cyberbullying intervention and prevention efforts is very important.

The effectiveness of several widely disseminated anti-bullying pro-grammes in reducing cyberbullying perpetration and victimization have been evaluated internationally, including the KiVa programme in Finland (Williford et al. 2013) and the NoTrap! programme in Italy (Menesini et al. 2012; Palladino et al. 2016). However, the effectiveness of cyberbul-lying intervention and prevention programmes in the United Kingdom or Ireland has not yet been evaluated. Moreover, anti-bullying pro-grammes implemented in the United Kingdom have not typically included cyberbullying-related outcome measures (e.g. the INCLUSIVE programme, Bonell et al. 2015; the Emotional Literacy intervention, Knowler and Frederickson 2013). Future research should focus on evalu-ating the effectiveness of anti-bullying programmes in the United Kingdom and Ireland in reducing cyberbullying perpetration and victim-ization. It should also be pointed out that, because research conducted with non-school-aged samples is scarce, this is an important avenue for future research (Myers and Cowie 2016).

Conclusions

We conclude that cyberbullying and cybervictimization are quite preva-lent in the United Kingdom and Ireland, although it is difficult to com-pare conclusions from different studies because of differences in operational definitions and methods of measuring cyberbullying and cybervictimization. Research suggests that girls are more likely to be cybervictims and boys are more likely to be cyberbullies. Cyberbullying is closely related to traditional school-bullying, while cybervictimization is closely related to traditional school victimization. Cyberbullying and cybervictimization are related to cognitive and psychological factors such as low self-esteem, loneliness, and behavioural difficulties, but there is a great need for longitudinal studies to establish causal influences. Cyberbullying and cybervictimization are more prevalent in deprived schools. Since cyberbullying and cybervictimization are known to be related to undesirable psychological and health-related outcomes, it is critical to mount more intervention programmes in the United Kingdom and Ireland and to evaluate them using high-quality methods, in order to reduce cyberbullying and cybervictimization most effectively.

Acknowledgements We are very grateful to Mona O'Moore and Peter Smith for their helpful comments on an earlier version of this chapter.

Notes

1. Only statistically significant relationships are reported here. For a full overview, see Fletcher et al. 2014, table 3, p. 1396.

References

Ackers, M. J. (2012). Cyberbullying: Through the eyes of children and young people. *Educational Psychology in Practice, 28*(2), 141–157. https://doi.org/1 0.1080/02667363.2012.665356.

Asam, A. E., & Samara, M. (2016). Cyberbullying and the law: A review of psychological and legal challenges. *Computers in Human Behavior, 65*, 127–141. https://doi.org/10.1016/j.chb.2016.08.012

Baldry, A. C., Farrington, D. P., & Sorrentino, A. (2015). "Am I at risk of cyberbullying"? A narrative review and conceptual framework for research on risk of cyberbullying and cybervictimization: The risk and needs assessment approach. *Aggression and Violent Behavior, 23*, 36–51. https://doi. org/10.1016/j.avb.2015.05.014

BBC (Producer). (2017). *Love Island's Olivia: I've received death threats.* Retrieved from http://bbcnews.co.uk

Betts, L. R. (2016). Cyberbullying: Approaches, consequences, and interventions. In J. Binder (Ed.), *Palgrave studies in cyberpsychology.* London: Palgrave Macmillan.

Betts, L. R., & Spenser, K. A. (2017). "People think it's a harmless joke": Young people's understanding of the impact of technology, digital vulnerability and cyberbullying in the United Kingdom. *Journal of Children and Media, 11*(1), 20–35. https://doi.org/10.1080/17482798.2016.1233893

Bevilacqua, L., Shackleton, N., Hale, D., Allen, E., Bond, L., Christie, D., Elbourne, D., Fitzgerald-Yau, N., Fletcher, A., Jones, R., Miners, A., Scott, S., Wiggins, M., Bonell, C., & Viner, R. M. (2017). The role of family and school-level factors in bullying and cyberbullying: A cross-sectional study. *BMC Pediatrics, 17*, 160–169. https://doi.org/10.1186/s12887-017-0907-8

Bonell, C., Fletcher, A., Fitzgerald-Yau, N., Hale, D., Allen, E., Elbourne, D., Jones, R., Bond, L., Wiggins, M., Miners, A., Legood, R., Scott, S., Christie,

D., & Viner, R. (2015). Initiating change locally in bullying and aggression through the school environment (INCLUSIVE): A pilot randomised controlled trial. *Health Technology Assessment, 19*(53), 1–110. https://doi.org/10.3310/hta19530

Boulton, M. J., Hardcastle, K., Down, J., Fowles, J., & Simmonds, J. A. (2014). A comparison of preservice teachers' responses to cyber versus traditional bullying scenarios: Similarities and differences and implications for practice. *Journal of Teacher Education, 65*(2), 145–155. https://doi.org/10.1177/0022487113511496

Brewer, G., & Kerslake, J. (2015). Cyberbullying, self-esteem, empathy and loneliness. *Computers in Human Behavior, 48*, 255–260. https://doi.org/10.1016/j.chb.2015.01.073

Brighi, A., Guarini, A., Melotti, G., Galli, S., & Genta, M. L. (2012). Predictors of victimisation across direct bullying, indirect bullying and cyberbullying. *Emotional and Behavioural Difficulties, 17*(3–4), 375–388. https://doi.org/10.1080/13632752.2012.704684

Bronfenbrenner, U. (1979). *Ecology of human development: Experiments by nature and design*. Cambridge, MA: Harvard University Press.

Callaghan, M., Kelly, C., & Molcho, M. (2015). Exploring traditional and cyberbullying among Irish adolescents. *International Journal of Public Health, 60*, 199–206. https://doi.org/10.1007/s00038-014-0638-7

Corcoran, L., Connolly, I., & O'Moore, M. (2012). Cyberbullying in Irish schools: An investigation of personality and self-concept. *Irish Journal of Psychology, 33*(4), 153–165. https://doi.org/10.1080/03033910.2012.677995

Cotter, P., & McGilloway, S. (2011). Living in an 'electronic age': Cyberbullying among Irish adolescents. *The Irish Journal of Education, 39*, 44–56.

Cross, D., Barnes, A., Papageorgiou, A., Hadwen, K., Hearn, L., & Lester, L. (2015). A social–ecological framework for understanding and reducing cyberbullying behaviours. *Aggression and Violent Behavior, 23*, 109–117. https://doi.org/10.1016/j.avb.2015.05.016

Del Rey, R., Casas, J. A., Ortega-Ruiz, R., Schultze-Krumbholz, A., Scheithauer, H., Smith, P., Thompson, F., Barkoukis, V., Tsorbatzoudis, H., Brighi, A., Guarini, A., Pyżalski, J., & Plichta, P. (2015). Structural validation and cross-cultural robustness of the European Cyberbullying Intervention Project Questionnaire. *Computers in Human Behavior, 50*, 141–147. https://doi.org/10.1016/j.chb.2015.03.065

Devine, P., & Lloyd, K. (2012). Internet use and psychological well-being among 10-year-old and 11-year-old children. *Child Care in Practice, 18*(1), 5–22. https://doi.org/10.1080/13575279.2011.621888

Dodd, V. (2017, August 21). CPS to crack down on social media hate crime, says Alison Saunders. *The Guardian*. Retrieved from http://www.theguardian.com

Eysenck, H. J., & Eysenck, S. B. G. (1975). *Manual of the Eysenck Personality Questionnaire*. London: Hodder and Stoughton.

Farrington, D. P., & Ttofi, M. M. (2009). School-based programs to reduce bullying and victimization. *Campbell Systematic Reviews, 2009, 6*.

Fletcher, A., Fitzgerald-Yau, N., Jones, R., Allen, E., Viner, R. M., & Bonell, C. (2014). Brief report: Cyberbullying perpetration and its associations with socio-demographics, aggressive behaviour at school, and mental health outcomes. *Journal of Adolescence, 37*, 1393–1398. https://doi.org/10.1016/j.adolescence.2014.10.005

Foody, M., Samara, M., & O'Higgins Norman, J. (2017). Bullying and cyberbullying studies in the school-aged population on the island of Ireland: A meta-analysis. *British Journal of Educational Psychology*. https://doi.org/10.1111/bjep.12163

Genta, M. L., Smith, P. K., Ortega, R., Brighi, A., Guarini, A., Thompson, F., Tippett, N., Mora-Merchán, J. A., & Calmaestra, J. (2012). Comparative aspects of cyberbullying in Italy, England, and Spain: Findings from a DAPHNE project. In Q. Li, D. Cross, & P. K. Smith (Eds.), *Cyberbullying in the global playground: Research from international perspectives* (pp. 15–31). West Sussex: Wiley-Blackwell.

Goodman, R. (2006). The Strengths and Difficulties Questionnaire: A research note. *Journal of Child Psychology, 38*, 581–586. https://doi.org/10.1111/j.1469-7610.1997.tb01545.x.

Gradinger, P., Strohmeier, D., & Spiel, C. (2010). Definition and measurement of cyberbullying. *Cyberpsychology: Journal of Psychosocial Research on Cyberspace, 4*(2), article -1.

Knowler, C., & Frederickson, N. (2013). Effects on an emotional literacy intervention for students identified with bullying behaviour. *Educational Psychology, 33*(7), 862–883. https://doi.org/10.1080/01443410.2013.785052

Langos, C. (2012). Cyberbullying: The challenge to define. *Cyberpsychology, Behavior, and Social Networking, 15*(6), 285–289. https://doi.org/10.1089/cyber.2011.0588.

Lasher, S., & Baker, C. (2015). *Bullying: Evidence from the longitudinal study of young people in England 2, wave 2* (Research brief). London: Department of Education. Retrieved from www.gov.uk/government/publications

Livingstone, S., & Haddon, L. (2009a). EU Kids Online. *Zeitschrift Für Psychologie/Journal of Psychology, 217*(4), 236–239.

Livingstone, S., & Haddon, L. (2009b). *EU Kids Online: Final report 2009*. London: EU Kids Online, London School of Economics and Political Science. Retrieved from http://eprints.lse.ac.uk

Livingstone, S., & Smith, P. K. (2014). Annual research review: Harms experienced by child users of online and mobile technologies: The nature, prevalence and management of sexual and aggressive risks in the digital age. *Journal of Child Psychology and Psycyhiatry, 55*(6), 635–654. https://doi.org/10.1111/jcpp.12197

Livingstone, S., Haddon, L., Görzig, A., & Ólafsson, K. (2011). *EU Kids Online: Final report*. London: EU Kids online, London School of Economics and Political Science.

Marczak, M., & Coyne, I. (2010). Cyberbullying at school: Good practice and legal aspects in the United Kingdom. *Australian Journal of Guidance & Counselling, 20*(2), 182–193. https://doi.org/10.1375/ajgc.20.2.182

Marczak, M., & Coyne, I. (2015). A focus on online bullying. In A. Attrill (Ed.), *Cyberpsychology* (pp. 145–163). Oxford: Oxford University Press.

McAra, L., & McVie, S. (2010). Youth crime and justice: Key messages from the Edinburgh study of youth transitions and crime. *Criminology and Criminal Justice, 10*, 179–209.

McClure Watters. (2011). *The nature and extent of pupil bullying in schools in the North of Ireland* (Research report No. 56). Bangor: Department of Education for Northern Ireland.

McGuckin, C., Cummins, P. K., & Lewis, C. A. (2010). f2f and cyberbullying among children in Northern Ireland: Data from the Kids Life and Times survey. *Psychology, Society, & Education, 2*(2), 83–96.

Menesini, E., Nocentini, A., & Palladino, B. E. (2012). Empowering students against bullying and cyberbullying: Evaluation of an Italian peer-led model. *International Journal of Conflict and Violence, 6*(2), 313–320. https://doi.org/10.4119/UNIBI/ijcv.253

Modecki, K. L., Minchin, J., Harbaugh, A. G., Guerra, N. G., & Runions, K. C. (2014). Bullying prevalence across contexts: A meta-analysis measuring cyber and traditional bullying. *Journal of Adolescent Health, 55*(5), 602–611. https://doi.org/10.1016/j.jadohealth.2014.06.007

Monks, C. P., Robinson, S., & Worlidge, P. (2012). The emergence of cyberbullying: A survey of primary school pupils' perceptions and experiences. *School Psychology International, 33*(5), 477–491. https://doi.org/10.1177/0143034312445242

Myers, C., & Cowie, H. (2016). How can we prevent and reduce bullying amongst university students? *International Journal of Emotional Education, 8*(1), 109–119.

National Society for the Prevention of Cruelty to Children. (2015). *What children are telling us about bullying: Childline bullying report 2015/16*. London: Author.

Nuccitelli, M. (2012). Cyber bullying tactics. *Forensic Examiner, 21*(3), 24–27.

O'Higgins Norman, J., O'Moore, M., & McGuire, L. (2016). *Cyberbullying in Ireland: A survey of parents internet usage and knowledge*. Dublin: ABC, National Anti-bullying research and resource centre.

O'Moore, M. (2012). Cyber-bullying: The situation in Ireland. *Pastoral Care in Education, 30*(3), 209–223. https://doi.org/10.1080/02643944.2012.688065

O'Neill, B., & Dinh, T. (2015). Mobile technologies and the incidence of cyberbullying in seven European countries: Findings from Net Children Go Mobile. *Societies, 5*, 384–398. https://doi.org/10.3390/soc5020384

Oliver, C., & Candappa, M. (2003). *Tackling bullying: Listening to the views of children and young people* (Research Report RR400). London: Department for Education and Skills.

Olweus, D. (1996). *The revised bully/victim questionnaire for students*. Bergen: University of Bergen.

Palladino, B. E., Nocentini, A., & Menesini, E. (2016). Evidence-based intervention against bullying and cyberbullying: Evaluation of the NoTrap! program in two independent trials. *Aggressive Behavior, 42*(2), 194–206. https://doi.org/10.1002/ab.21636

Patchin, J. W., & Hinduja, S. (2015). Measuring cyberbullying: Implications for research. *Aggression and Violent Behavior, 23*, 69–74. https://doi.org/10.1016/j.avb.2015.05.013

Paul, S., Smith, P. K., & Blumberg, H. H. (2010). Addressing cyberbullying in school using the quality circle approach. *Australian Journal of Guidance and Counselling, 20*(2), 157–168. https://doi.org/10.1375/ajgc.20.2.157

Piers, E. V., Harris, D. B., & Herzberg, D. S. (2002). *Piers-Harris children's self concept scale* (Rev. ed.). Los Angeles: Western Psychological Services.

Pornari, C. D., & Wood, J. (2010). Peer and cyber aggression in secondary school students: The role of moral disengagement, hostile attribution bias, and outcome expectancies. *Aggressive Behavior, 36*, 81–94. https://doi.org/10.1002/ab.20336

Purdy, N., & McGuckin, C. (2015). Cyberbullying, schools and the law: A comparative study in Northern Ireland and the Republic of Ireland. *Educational Research, 57*(4), 420–436. https://doi.org/10.1080/00131881.2015.1091203

Purdy, N., & Smith, P. K. (2016). A content analysis of school anti-bullying policies in Northern Ireland. *Educational Psychology in Practice, 32*(3), 281–295. https://doi.org/10.1080/02667363.2016.1161599

Purdy, N., & York, L. (2016). A critical investigation of the nature and extent of cyberbullying in two post-primary schools in Northern Ireland. *Pastoral Care in Education, 34*(1), 13–23. https://doi.org/10.1080/02643944.2015.1127989

Rivers, I., & Noret, N. (2010). 'I h8 u': Findings from a five-year study of text and email bullying. *British Educational Research Journal, 36*(4), 643–671. https://doi.org/10.1080/01411920903071918

Sabella, R. A., Patchin, J. W., & Hinduja, S. (2013). Cyberbullying myths and realities. *Computers in Human Behavior, 29*(6), 2703–2711. https://doi.org/10.1016/j.chb.2013.06.040

Schultze-Krumbholz, A., Göbel, K., Scheithauer, H., Brighi, A., Guarini, A., Tsorbatzoudis, H., Barkoukis, V., Pyżalski, J., Plichta, P., Del Rey, R., Casas, J. A., Thompson, F., & Smith, P. K. (2015). A comparison of classification approaches for cyberbullying and traditional bullying using data from six European countries. *Journal of School Violence, 14*(1), 47–65. https://doi.org/10.1080/15388220.2014.961067

Slonje, R., Smith, P. K., & Frisén, A. (2013). The nature of cyberbullying, and strategies for prevention. *Computers in Human Behavior, 29*(1), 26–32. https://doi.org/10.1016/j.chb.2012.05.024

Smith, P. K., Mahdavi, J., Carvalho, M., & Tippett, N. (2006). *An investigation into cyber-bullying, its forms, awareness, and impact, and the relationship between age and gender in cyber-bullying* (Research Brief No. RBX03-06). London: Department for Education and Skills.

Smith, P. K., Mahdavi, J., Carvalho, M., Fisher, S., Russell, S., & Tippett, N. (2008). Cyberbullying: Its nature and impact in secondary school pupils. *Journal of Child Psychology and Psychiatry, 49*, 376–385. https://doi.org/10.1111/j.1469-7610.2007.01846.x

Smith, P. K., del Barrio, C., & Tokunaga, R. S. (2013). Definitions of bullying and cyberbullying: How useful are the terms? In S. Bauman, D. Cross, & J. Walker (Eds.), *Principles of cyberbullying research: Definitions, measures and methodology* (pp. 26–40). New York: Routledge.

Sourander, A., Klomek, A. B., Ikonen, M., Lindroos, J., Luntamo, T., Koskelainen, M., .Ristkari, T., & Helenius, H. (2010). Psychosocial risk factors associated with cyberbullying among adolescents: A population-based study. *Archives of General Psychiatry, 67*(7), 720–728. https://doi.org/10.1001/archgenpsychiatry.2010.79.

The Guardian. (2016, October 5). Mother of teenager who killed himself appeals for kindness online. Retrieved from https://www.theguardian.com/society/2016/oct/05/felix-alexander-mother-lucy-open-letter-worcester

Thompson, F., & Smith, P. K. (2012). Anti-bullying strategies in schools: What is done and what works. *British Journal of Educational Psychology, Monograph Series, 11*(9), 154–173.

Tokunaga, R. S. (2010). Following you home from school: A critical review and synthesis of research on cyberbullying victimization. *Computers in Human Behavior, 26*(3), 277–287. https://doi.org/10.1016/j.chb.2009.11.014

Topcu, C., & Erdur-Baker, O. (2010). The Revised Cyberbullying Inventory (RCBI): Validity and reliability studies. *Procedia: Social and Behavioral Sciences, 5*, 660–664. https://doi.org/10.1016/j.sbspro.2010.07.161

West, D. (2015). An investigation into the prevalence of cyberbullying among students aged 16–19 in post-compulsory education. *Research in Post-Compulsory Education, 20*(1), 96–112. https://doi.org/10.1080/13596748.2015.993879

Willard, N. E. (2006). *Cyberbullying and Cyberthreats: Responding to the challenge of online social cruelty, threats, and distress.* Centre for Safe and Responsible Internet Use. Available at: https://www.internetsafetyproject.org/wiki/center-safe-and-responsible-internet-use

Williford, A., Elledge, L. C., Boulton, A. J., DePaolis, K. J., Little, T. D., & Salmivalli, C. (2013). Effects of the KiVa antibullying program on cyberbullying and cybervictimization frequency among Finnish youth. *Journal of Clinical Child and Adolescent Psychology, 42*(6), 820–833. https://doi.org/10.1080/15374416.2013.787623

Wolke, D., Woods, S., Bloomfield, L., & Karstadt, L. (2000). The association between direct and relational bullying and behaviour problems among primary school children. *Journal of Child Psychology and Psychiatry, 41*(8), 989–1002. https://doi.org/10.1111/1469-7610.00687

Wolke, D., Lee, K., & Guy, A. (2017). Cyberbullying: A storm in a teacup? *European Child and Adolescent Psychiatry, 26*, 899–908. https://doi.org/10.1007/s00787-017-0954-6

Part III

The Implementation of the EU Project for Risk Assessment of Cyberbullying: The TABBY Project

6

Cyberbullying in Cyprus

Andreas Kapardis and George Poyiadjis

The Prevalence of Cyberbullying and Cybervictimization in Cyprus

Human behaviour, including deviant and criminal behaviour, reflects such factors as the type of society and economy as well as the age composition of the population; the technologies available and in use; risk and protective factors at the level of the individual, the family, school, and the broader community; and, finally, the priorities and emphases of agents of social control. The advent of the Internet and the explosion in the social media has vastly increased the scope for bullying, which has traditionally been talked about in the context of the school. As Baldry et al. (2016) remind us, '[c]yberbullying affects boys and girls of different ages all around the world since communication among peers has changed, and so have the

A. Kapardis (✉)
University of Cyprus, Nicosia, Cyprus

G. Poyiadjis
Nicosia, Cyprus

© The Author(s) 2018
A. C. Baldry et al. (eds.), *International Perspectives on Cyberbullying*, Palgrave Studies in Cybercrime and Cybersecurity, https://doi.org/10.1007/978-3-319-73263-3_6

risks of online communication' (p. 7). Cyberbullying has been defined by Smith et al. (2008, p. 376)[1] as *'an aggressive act or behavior that is carried out using electronic means by a group or an individual repeatedly and over time against a victim who cannot easily defend him or herself.'*

At the same time, as Baldry et al. (2017) found, cyberbullying overlaps with cybervictimization for both boys and girls. Their study involved 2,785 Italian students aged 11–17 recruited from seven secondary schools, who anonymously self-reported about school and cyberbullying as victims and/or perpetrators. Classifying their respondents as 'only bullies,' 'only victims,' 'bully/victims,' or 'not involved' in school and/or online, they reported that, for girls, 'school only bullies' were not overlapping with 'cyber only bullies,' and 'school only victims' were not overlapping with 'cyber only victims,' but these categories were related for boys. 'School bully/victims' were significantly overlapping with 'cyber bully/victims' for both boys and girls. Baldry et al. (2017) concluded that the role continuity approach is most appropriate to explain these two disturbing problems in adolescents, especially for boys.

Research into bullying in Cyprus is relatively new (see Kapardis and Poyiadjis 2013) and was preceded by research into juvenile delinquency and school antisocial behaviour (see Kapardis 1985, 1986, 2008, 2013). In fact, it would not be an exaggeration to say that the present authors are the only ones to have concerned themselves with cyberbullying and cybervictimization. Risk and protective factors have been studied in relation to juvenile delinquency in schools (see Baldry and Kapardis 2013; Kapardis 2008, 2013; Kapardis and Poyiadjis 2013). Kapardis (2013) reported that delinquency risk factors are significantly related to the school and protective factors to the family.

The Observatory for School Violence in Schools within the Ministry of Education in Cyprus, in collaboration with and using the questionnaire of the International Observatory for School Violence of Eric Debarbieux, reported in 2012 a survey of 2,068 secondary school students during the school year 2010–2011. The prevalence of cyberbullying in the form of ironic messages or threats among secondary school students was found to be 14.7%, with 2.4% reporting such victimization over ten times a year. Concerning *gender differences*, as researchers have reported in other countries, boys were significantly more likely

($p < 0.05$) to be cybervictims than girls (15.9% vs. 13.2%). Interestingly, the cyberbully was another pupil in 2.6%, a group of pupils (2.1%), and for 0.7% a teacher. Concerning measurements of cyberbullying prevalence, it should not be forgotten that, as Baldry et al. (2016) emphasize, '*cyberbullying remains complex because there is no consensus regarding how it should be defined and measured*' (p. 57). In this context, it should be noted that while researchers have investigated the conceptions of children regarding bullying, very few have formally examined how well children's conceptions of bullying coincide with researchers' operationalization.

Research just completed by Monica Shiakou and her associates (in press) at the European University of Cyprus with 71 children (50 boys, 21 girls) between the ages of 6 and 12 from two after-school clubs in Nicosia, Cyprus, randomly divided into 8 focus groups, revealed that the three main criteria communicated by researchers as being integral to the construct and definition of bullying were mentioned very little by the participant children. More specifically, only 3% of the children mentioned repetition, 12.6% intent, and 32% power imbalance while 91% mentioned negative acts in their definitions. Shiakou and colleagues' findings emphasize the need to clarify clearly the criteria and assumptions of what exactly will be measured before students are asked for information about bullying and cyberbullying.

In another study, the first of its kind, Shiakou and Pikkis (in press) sought to evaluate the involvement of theatrical drama as a means of education and prevention of bullying with a sample 150 primary school-children in Cyprus. Based on the literature on bullying, a theatrical scenario was created demonstrating the key constructs of its definition, the groups of children involved, and possible interventions. Using semi-structured questions, the children were then asked to answer on the meanings and characteristics of school bullying depicted in the scenario. The results showed that the dramatized text created for the purpose proved to be a useful prevention and information tool for school bullying. The findings obtained with a theatrical scenario by Shiakou and Pikkis (in press) point to important and promising results for the future use of such tools (related to the education, understanding/interpretation, and measurement of school bullying) in primary education.

In the light of limited literature on cyberbullying in Cyprus, the society most comparable to the population of Cyprus in the free areas of the island[2] is Greece. Drawing on Sorrentino and Athansiades (Chap. 8 in this volume), we learn that the first cyberbullying study was carried out in 2005, it involved 450 students aged 16–19 years, and reported high (54%) prevalence rates. More recently, Antoniadou et al. (2016) surveyed 146 Greek high school students and found that cyberbullying was predicted by being a male, online disinhibition, online activity, and psychopathic traits, while traditional bullying was predicted by being male, online disinhibition, and sensation-seeking. Cybervictimization was predicted by online disinhibition, assertion, and few peer relations, while traditional victimization by Internet skills and impulsive/irresponsible traits. An interesting study of bullying on Facebook in Greece among 226 university undergraduates by Kokkinos et al. (2016) found that one-third of the sample reported they had bullied through Facebook at least once during the past month, with male students reporting more frequent involvement than females. Interestingly, bullying through Facebook was predicted by low agreeableness and more time spent on Facebook for males only while none of the variables studied predicted engagement in bullying on Facebook by female undergraduates.

Implementation of the Threat Assessment of Bullying Behaviour in Youngsters (TABBY) Project

The TABBY project had clear aims and objectives from design to implementation. These were the same in all European countries participating, targeting both teachers and students in sensitizing them for a safer use of the Internet and to increase awareness for online risky behaviours, thus reducing the risk of being cyberbullied and experiencing other negative experiences on the Internet. Due to excessively long delays in being granted access to state schools, four participating schools in Cyprus (Grammar School and Heritage in Limassol, Grammar School in Nicosia, and Xenion in Famagusta) were chosen to participate from the private sector, representing at least a major school from each of four districts. The design of the project included Control and Experimental Groups (one in each school) and the questionnaire was completed online by the students.

Implementation of the project included training most teachers from each school, with the non-participating classes taking part at the end of the project. This was given as an incentive for the schools, as well as training for parents during evening hours. Teachers were presented and informed about the use of the TABBY toolkit as well as the consequences of cyberbullying and cybervictimization and all the relevant information of the EU-funded project. This was welcomed quite enthusiastically by the teachers as well as the administrative staff. Each school participated with controlled and experimental groups, with the control group students being presented with the video as well as the training upon completion of the project, thus ensuring that the entire school population was informed and trained under the TABBY guidelines.

In considering the findings reported, caution is warranted because the Cyprus TABBY researchers faced some unpredictable difficulties. Although agreement had been reached with all four schools to participate in the study, some teachers instructed their classes to decline taking part in the second phase of the project on the ground that it was May 2015 and school examinations were scheduled. Also, due to excessive concern by the schools about securing the anonymity of all participating students in order to comply with private data legislation, the personal code generator for the participants made it impossible to match a number of participants as it allowed each participant to use different identification numbers for the two phases of the study. Consequently, although 190 students participated in the first phase (November), 162 did so in the second phase, and it was only possible to match 124 for before-and-after comparisons, reducing the final amount of usable data. Of the matched participants, only 25% were in the Experimental Group. However, despite its limitations, the study remains the only one of its kind and the need for more such research in Cyprus that will underpin evidence-based intervention policies cannot be overstated.

The Present Study

Participants and Their Digital Uses

For the TABBY Trip project, 124 Cypriot students (56.5% males, 43.5% females), aged 11 to 17 years (M = 14.83, SD = 2.17) participated in the study in full. Regarding the use of cyber communication, 56.7% of all respondents reported having at least one profile on a social network. Of these, only 18.2% said that among all their profile's contacts they personally knew all of them. The average number of hours students reported spending online ranged from 0 to 12, with a total of 43.7% admitting to being online between 0 to 4 hours a day. Full details of the whole sample are presented in Table 6.1.

Table 6.1 Descriptive statistics for the sample in Cyprus

	N = 124
Gender (males)	50.0%
Age	M = 14.83 (sd = 2.17)
Presence of social network profile(s)	56.7% at least one
Personally know all friends on social network	18.2% everyone
Perceived popularity among peers	8.6% not at all
Parents/significant adult among kid's online contacts	19.9% no
Parents talk with kid about Internet safety	10.0% never
Teachers talk with kid about Internet safety	21.2% never
Hours a day online	43.7% 2/4 h
School achievement	8.2% below average
School bullying	85.8% never
	8.7% once or twice
	5.5% > than twice
School victimization	84.9% never
	7.6% once or twice
	7.6% > than twice
Cyberbullying	52.3% never
	34.9% once or twice
	12.8% > than twice
Cybervictimization	3.4% never
	82.8 % once or twice
	13.8% > than twice
Internet addiction	M = 16.07 (sd = 4.42)
Risk perception	M = 2.25 (sd = 2.64)

Procedure

Participants were recruited from five private schools from four of the five districts of Cyprus. Parental consent was obtained before data collection, and only students authorized by their parents and who wanted to participate in the research completed the TABBY online checklist.

The collection of data was conducted during the months of November/December 2014 and six months later in May 2015. Students filled in the online questionnaire during their Information Technology class, under the supervision and assistance of the Project researcher. Prior to the completion of the TABBY questionnaire, students were informed about anonymity and the importance of the honesty of their answers. The project researcher actively provided clarification for some questions when needed.

Measures

To measure cyberbullying, the same methodology and instruments adopted for the whole project were used, and it is therefore explained in the TABBY self-assessment of threats questionnaire. The Likert-type scale to measure cyberbullying consisted of five items for cyberbullying and five items for cybervictimization (total $\alpha = 0.90$). Students filled in the questionnaire in the presence of one of the researchers and a teacher who oversaw the data collection. Students were assured about the confidentiality of the study and the anonymity of the answers provided and were told that only the researchers could access the answers once provided which went automatically into a database to be analysed in an aggregated way. Students were given the opportunity to pose questions if they had any. After completing the questionnaire, all students returned to their classes and debriefing was provided, if required. Finally, based on students' responses in each phase of the research, the degree of online exposure risk for the matched respondents was calculated using a colour scheme (classified as 'Green', 'Yellow', 'Orange', and 'Red'[3]), making possible a comparison between the control and the experimental groups.

Appendix

- **Green Tabby** (score 0–10)

Bullying and cyberbullying are phenomena unrelated to you. It is very likely that your relationships in the real world as well as your online behaviour combined with proper knowledge of useful strategies for Internet security will 'protect you' from acting out and experiencing these behaviours. Keep it up and never give up if you ever find yourself in some kind of trouble!

- **Yellow Tabby** (score 11–20) ·

Although you are not very involved in bullying and cyberbullying, it is likely that you have experienced them as a victim or a perpetrator, in a mild form or as a 'joke' among friends. Remember that both phenomena cause pain and suffering to the victim and lead to risk of deviant behaviour in the so-called bullies. So be careful; for you it is a low risk, but you are still running some kind of risk!

- **Orange Tabby** (score 21–40)

Bullying and cyberbullying are phenomena well known to you, and you are most likely to do or suffer from one or both of them frequently. You are, therefore, in such a state of high risk that it would be helpful to talk about this with a trusted adult in order to establish together the most appropriate way to deal with the situation, and thus to avoid enduring a condition that exposes you to further negative consequences. The threats you have experienced might lead to further and more-severe actions. Or you yourself might be breaching too much the limits of licit behaviour.

- **Red Tabby** (score 41–62)

Bullying and cyberbullying are your daily bread! It does not matter whether you are Nelson or Milhouse, what counts is that you need urgent help because you are in a condition that puts you at a very high level of risk both of cyberbullying others or being bullied. Do not think you can solve your problems alone; ask for help!

Findings

Prevalence of School Bullying and Cyberbullying

Students' involvement in cyberbullying and cybervictimization was analysed, also considering gender differences (see Table 6.2). To this aim, the categorical classification was used, cut-off at least sometimes, for the four possible levels of involvement in cyberbullying and then for cybervictimization to look for gender differences. Odds ratios (OR) was used to measure the strengths of relationships because (unlike chi-squares) they are not influenced by sample sizes.

Table 6.2 shows that boys were more involved than girls in overall cyberbullying as the odds for cyberbullies were 1.87 times greater for

Table 6.2 Gender differences in cyberbullying and cybervictimization involvement in Cyprus

		Male	Female
Total cyberbullying			
	N	25	12
	%	12.9	7.5
	OR (C.I.)	0.58 (0.30–1.11)	
Flaming			
	N	17	5
	%	8.8	3.1
	OR (C.I.)	0.33* (0.12–0.92)	
Denigration			
	N	8	3
	%	4.1	1.9
	OR (C.I.)	0.44 (0.12–1.69)	
Impersonation			
	N	4	0
	%	2.1	0
	OR (C.I.)	0.13 (0–2.45)	
Outing			
	N	8	4
	%	4.1	2.5
	OR (C.I.)	0.59 (0.17–2.00)	
Exclusion			
	N	5	1
	%	2.6	0.6
	OR (C.I.)	0.24 (0.03–2.04)	

(continued)

Table 6.2 (continued)

		Male	Female
Total cybervictimization			
	N	34	27
	%	17.5	16.8
	OR (C.I.)	0.95 (0.60–1.51)	
Flaming			
	N	11	7
	%	5.7	4.3
	OR (C.I.)	0.76 (0.28–1.99)	
Denigration			
	N	16	15
	%	8.2	9.3
	OR (C.I.)	1.14 (0.55–2.39)	
Impersonation			
	N	13	2
	%	6.7	1.2
	OR (C.I.)	0.17* (0.04–0.78)	
Outing			
	N	15	12
	%	7.7	7.5
	OR (C.I.)	0.96 (0.43–2.11)	
Exclusion			
	N	13	5
	%	6.7	3.1
	OR (C.I.)	0.45 (0.15–1.28)	

Notes: *OR* odds ratio, *C.I.* confidence interval

boys than for girls. The results also document that boys were involved in all cyberbullying types. Looking also at gender differences, the most frequent forms of cyberbullying among the Cypriot students were flaming (12.1% vs. 7.1%) and denigration (11.3% vs. 6.0%); the respective odds were 1.81 and 3.60 greater for boys than for girls. However, girls were more involved than boys in overall cybervictimization; the odds for cybervictims were 0.73 greater for girls than for boys. Flaming (7.9% vs 9.7%) and impersonation (7.1% vs 6.4%) were the most common cybervictimization types, both among boys and girls. However, no significant gender differences were found with regard to cyber-victimization types.

Risk and Protective Factors

On the basis of the international literature, it would have been expected that a number of factors would be found to be statistically correlated with (but not causes of) cyberbullying. Table 6.3 shows that the following *risk factors* were significantly correlated with cyberbullying: the presence of social network profiles which, in turn, applied significantly more to the older students; hours spent on line (especially by boys and older students); school bullying (especially the older a student is); having been victimized at school (especially for boys); those scoring low on risk perception, which characterized more the older students as well as those with low academic achievement and those who were school bullies or, finally, had themselves been victimized at school; and, also, students whose parents/significant adult was not among their online friends.

The cyberbullying *protective factors* identified by the analysis (see Table 6.3) are good academic achievement, which is negatively associated with hours a day online; having parents who talk with their kids about Internet safety; perceiving one's self to be popular among one's peers; and, finally, having teachers who talk with the students about Internet safety, and such students know personally all their friends on their social network, have high academic achievement, their parents talk to them about Internet safety, and perceive themselves to be popular among their peers.

Cybervictimization was found (see Table 6.4) to be statistically associated to a significant degree with the following *risk factors*: having social network profiles, which, in turn, is more likely to be the case with older students; not knowing personally all of one's friends on one's social network; being a boy or of older age and spending more hours a day online; bullying at school, which is likely to be the case with older students; being a school victim, which correlates with being a boy and, also, not knowing all one's friend's on one's social network; Internet addiction, which goes with being a boy, having social network profile/s, and spending more hours a day online; and not perceiving a risk which is associated with being older, of low academic achievement, bullying at school, and a school-bullying victim.

Table 6.3 Correlations between cyberbullying and risk factors in Cyprus

	1.	2.	3.	4.	5.	6.	7.	8.	9.	10.	11.	12.	13.	14.	15.
1. Cyberbullying	–														
2. Gender (male = 1)	0.09	–													
3. Age	−0.06	0.02	–												
4. Presence of social network profile(s)	−0.06	−0.09	0.14**	–											
5. Personally know all friends on social network	−0.06	−0.07	−0.02	0.09	–										
6. Hours a day online	0.15**	−0.13*	0.26**	0.16**	−0.06	–									
7. Good academic achievement	−0.04	0.06	−0.03	0.01	0.02	−0.13*	–								
8. School bullying	0.13*	0.09	−0.28**	0.03	−0.08	−0.02	−0.10	–							
9. School victim	0.12*	0.15**	−0.07	−0.01	−0.11*	0.02	−0.13*	0.47**	–						
10. Internet addiction	0.09	−0.13*	0.24**	0.22**	−0.03	0.50**	−0.03	−0.04	0.02	–					
11. Risk perception	0.16**	0.05	−0.19**	−0.008	−0.06	0.05	−0.18**	0.43**	0.38**	0.05	–				
12. Parents talk with kid about Internet safety	−0.08	−0.14**	−0.02	0.006	0.09	−0.11*	0.15**	−0.05	−0.05	−0.03	−0.06	–			

(continued)

Table 6.3 (continued)

	1.	2.	3.	4.	5.	6.	7.	8.	9.	10.	11.	12.	13.	14.	15.
13. Parents/ significant adult not among kid's online contacts	-0.08	-0.06	0.07	-0.04	0.08	0.12*	0.05	-0.008	0.003	0.07	-0.08	0.16**	–		
14. Perceived popularity among peers	0.09	0.03	-0.16**	0.15**	0.18**	0.15**	0.08	0.07	0.07	0.04	0.16**	0.07	0.07	–	
15. Teachers talk with kid about Internet safety	0.11*	-0.06	-0.02	0.08	0.14**	-0.06	0.16**	-0.04	-0.02	0.09	0.03	0.31**	0.07	0.21**	–

Notes: $p < 0.10$; *$p < 0.05$; **$p < 0.01$; ***$p < 0.000$. All variables are standardized

Table 6.4 Correlations between cybervictimization and risk factors in Cyprus

	1.	2.	3.	4.	5.	6.	7.	8.	9.	10.	11.	12.	13.	14.	15.
1. Cybervictimization	–														
2. Gender (male = 1)	0.01	–													
3. Age	−0.04	0.02	–												
4. Presence of social network profile(s)	0.12*	−0.09	0.14**	–											
5. Personally know all friends on social network	−0.13*	−0.07	−0.02	0.09	–										
6. Number of hours/day online	0.05	−0.13*	0.26**	0.16**	−0.06	–									
7. Good academic achievement	−0.09	0.06	−0.03	0.009	0.02	−0.13*	–								
8. School bullying	0.20**	0.09	−0.28**	0.03	−0.08	−0.02	−0.10	–							
9. School victim	0.19**	0.15**	−0.07	−0.01	−0.11*	0.02	−0.13*	0.47**	–						
10. Internet addiction	0.16**	−0.13*	0.24**	0.22**	−0.03	0.50**	−0.03	−0.04	0.02	–					
11. Risk perception	0.24**	0.05	−0.19**	−0.008	−0.06	0.05	−0.18**	0.43**	0.38**	0.05	–				
12. Parents talk with kid about Internet safety	−0.03	−0.14**	−0.02	0.006	0.09	−0.11*	0.15**	−0.05	−0.05	−0.03	−0.06	–			
13. Parents/significant adult not among kid's online contacts	−0.11	−0.06	0.07	−0.04	0.08	0.12*	0.05	−0.008	0.003	0.07	−0.08	0.16**	–		
14. Perceived popularity among peers at school	0.03	0.03	0.07	0.15**	0.18**	0.15**	0.08	0.07	0.07	0.04	0.16**	0.07	0.07	–	
15. Teachers talk with kid about Internet safety	0.05	−0.06	−0.02	0.08	0.14**	−0.06	0.16**	−0.04	−0.02	0.09	0.03	0.31**	0.07	0.21**	–

Notes: *p* < 0.10; *p* < 0.05; **p* < 0.01; ***p* < 0.000. All variables are standardized

As far as *protective factors* for cybervictimization are concerned, the ones shown in Table 6.4 are personally knowing all of one's friends on social network/s; having good academic achievement, which is correlated with spending less hours a day online; having parents and having teachers who talk with the student about Internet safety but they are unlikely to do so in the case of boys; perceiving popularity among peers at school, which is significantly associated with personally knowing all friends on a social network, spending less hours a day online, and perceiving a risk if online, and this trend correlates negatively with age.

Logistic regression was used in an attempt to identify what factors best predict cyberbullying (see Table 6.5) and cybervictimization (see Table 6.6) with the same predictors for both, thus providing more specific guidance in considering the policy implications of the findings.

Table 6.5 Logistic regression for cyberbullying in Cyprus

| | | | 95 C.I. for OR | |
| | | | Lower | Upper |
Variable	B(SE)	OR	bound	bound
Gender (male = 1)	0.29 (0.49)	1.34	0.51	3.51
Age	−0.33 (0.29)	0.72	0.40	1.29
Presence of social network profile(s)	0.43 (0.54)	1.54	0.53	4.48
Personally know all friends on social network	−0.16 (0.26)	0.85	0.51	1.41
Hours a day online	0.61 (0.28)	1.83*	1.06	3.16
Good academic achievement	−0.23 (0.24)	0.80	0.50	1.27
School bullying	0.19 (0.22)	1.20	0.78	1.86
School victim	0.18 (0.22)	1.20	0.77	1.86
Internet addiction	0.21 (0.33)	1.23	0.65	2.35
Risk perception	0.05 (0.26)	1.05	0.63	1.73
Parents talk with kid about Internet safety	−0.25 (0.27)	0.78	0.46	1.33
Parents/significant adult not among kid's online contacts	−0.74 (0.53)	0.48	0.17	1.35
Perceived popularity among peers at school	0.09 (0.25)	1.09	0.67	1.76
Teachers talk with kid about Internet safety	0.50 (0.24)	1.65	1.03	2.63

Notes: $p < 0.10$; *$p < 0.05$; **$p < 0.01$; ***$p < 0.000$. $R^2 = 0.10$ (Cox and Snell), 0.219 (Nagelkerke), $\chi^2(14) = 30.26$***. All variables are standardized
OR odds ratio, *C.I.* confidence interval, *S.E.* standard error

Table 6.6 Logistic regression for cybervictimization in Cyprus

Variable	B(SE)	OR	95 C.I. for OR Lower bound	Upper bound
Gender (male = 1)	−0.15 (0.34)	0.86	0.44	1.69
Age	−0.08 (0.19)	0.92	0.63	1.35
Presence of social network profile(s)	0.43 (0.36)	1.53	0.76	3.08
Personally know all friends on social network	−0.31 (0.18)	0.73	0.51	1.05
Hours a day online	−0.28 (0.22)	0.75	0.49	1.15
Good academic achievement	−0.20 (0.17)	0.82	0.59	1.14
School bullying	0.27 (0.18)	1.31	0.92	1.86
School victim	0.25 (0.17)	1.28	0.93	1.77
Internet addiction	0.59 (0.23)	1.81	1.16	2.82
Risk perception	0.28 (0.18)	1.33	0.93	1.90
Parents talk with kid about Internet safety	0.08 (0.18)	1.03	0.72	1.46
Parents/significant adult not among kid's online contacts	−0.57 (0.39)	0.57	0.26	1.21
Perceived popularity among peers at school	0.06 (0.18)	1.07	0.75	1.52
Teachers talk with kid about Internet safety	0.07 (0.17)	1.07	0.76	1.50

Notes: $p < 0.10$; *$p < 0.05$; **$p < 0.01$; ***$p < 0.000$. $R^2 = 0.127$ (Cox and Snell), 0.207 (Nagelkerke), $\chi^2(14) = 40.96$**. All variables are standardized
OR odds ratio, *C.I.* confidence interval, *S.E.* standard error

In support of Antoniadou et al. (2016) finding in their study of cyberbullying among junior high school students who reported that online activity was one of the factors that predicted cyberbullying, Table 6.5 shows that only hours a day online can significantly predict cyberbullying ($p < 0.01$).

Table 6.6 shows that the logistic regression yielded no significant results for any of the potential cybervictimization predictors.

Conclusions

The research project reported, despite its limitations, has provided some data both on the prevalence of school bullying among Cypriot secondary school students, online risk-taking behaviours, and the participants' prevalence as far cyberbullying and cybervictimization are concerned. Our findings confirm those reported in 2012 by the Observatory for Violence in Schools within the Ministry of Education in Cyprus concerning the prevalence of cyberbullying (14.7%) and that boys are significantly more likely to be cybervictims than girls. However, the TABBY project revealed that 15% had bullied and as many had been victims of school bullying in the past six months. These figures are significantly higher than those reported in this volume for Greece, a culturally comparable society, by Sorrentino and Athnasiades (Chap. 8 in this volume) (8% and 9% for school bullying and school victimization respectively). Also, junior high school students in Cyprus exhibit cyberbullying to a significantly higher prevalence (48% at last once in the last six months) than their counterparts in Greece and much higher cybervictimization prevalence (97%) than 35% reported in Greece. The TABBY research in Cyprus also found that flaming (9%) and impersonation (7%) were the most common cybervictimization types, both among boys and girls. However, while girls were significantly more involved in cybervictimization, no significant gender differences were found with regard to cybervictimization types.

As far as cyberbullying *risk factors* are concerned, in agreement with the findings reported by other TABBY partner countries, they were not having one's parents among online friends, being a school bully and a school bully victim, and being of low academic achievement. Cybervictimization was found to be alarmingly high, so it is interesting to ask what correlates have been identified. Concerning *risk factors*, again, in agreement with the findings reported by other TABBY partner countries, they were not knowing all of one's friends on one's social network, spending more hours a day online, not perceiving a risk when online, and being a school bully and a school victim. Interestingly, the *protective factors* for cybervictimization were found to be almost identical to the protective factors for cyberbullying, namely, not spending many hours online, knowing all of one's friends on one's social network, having good academic achievement, not spending many hours online, having parents and teachers who talk about Internet safety, and perceiving a risk if online.

A close examination of the findings obtained shows that parents and teachers are less likely to talk to their sons about Internet safety than to their daughters. This gender-based differential approach may well reflect parents' and teachers' belief in a sexist society that 'girls need protection from various dangers' more than boys do.

The very high prevalence of cybervictimization to a degree casts doubt on the conclusion of the 2012 Cyprus Ministry of Education report on School violence, based on teachers' perception that violence in schools, including bullying and cyberbullying, is non-existent or at extremely low levels. Of course, with the passage of time and significant increases in adolescents' greater use of the Internet and social media, one would expect both the prevalence and seriousness of both cyberbullying and cybervictimization to increase. The apparently extremely high prevalence of cybervictimization found may be a reflection of a very broad interpretation of the meaning of the term and/or a strong tendency by female secondary school students attending private schools in Cyprus to perceive themselves as victims online. Nevertheless, it is also likely that the very high cybervictimization prevalence is attributable to the presence of a number of risk factors, namely that 60% had at least one social network profile, only 18% personally knew all friends on their social network, only 20% had parents/significant adult among their online contacts, despite the fact that 90% of the parents and 79% of the teachers, according to the students, talk with the children about Internet safety. It would appear that simply talking to adolescents about Internet safety does not impact on their perception of risks when online. This is an interesting finding in view of the finding by Baldry et al. (2016) in Italy that *even if parental supervision is a potential protective factor [for cyberbullying and cybervictimization], it may not be one in practice*' (p. 71). Perhaps due to the small size of the matched respondents, none of the 15 factors in the logistic regression was found to be statistically significant. The study points to the need for more research with a larger student population.

Policy Implications and Recommendations

The Observatory for School Violence that is located within the Ministry of Education has the prime responsibility for violence study, prevention, and reduction among the school population in Cyprus. The Observatory's 2012 report recommended the formulation of a national anti-school violence strategy and the implementation of a comprehensive intervention programme with the co-ordinated participation of the Ministry's Educational Psychological Services and the Pedagogical Institute. Unfortunately, at the time of writing, no such national strategy has been formulated, only a circular on school-bullying incidents sent to all schools by the Ministry in early 2015. Noting that cyberbullying is not an offence in Cyprus, this presents an opportunity for such a strategy to go beyond the Ministry's circular and address cyberbullying and cybervictimization.

Based on the findings reported for TABBY Cyprus, the following suggestions are made concerning policy recommendations at the level of the community, the school, the class, the parents, and the students:

a) Community level:

- Utilize a systematic media campaign to raise the general public's awareness about (i) Internet safety and (ii) the digital literacy and (ii) the phenomena of both cyberbullying and cybervictimization.
- With the cooperation of the parents' associations in each school, provide seminars aimed at raising parents' and older teachers' digital literacy.

b) School level:

- Guidelines compiled jointly by the Ministry of Education specialist personnel and the Pedagogical Institute to be provided to all schools.
- Make obligatory a cyberbullying and cybervictimization baseline check at the beginning of each school year.
- The high prevalence of cybervictimization attests to the importance of investing in improving the school anti-violence climate and open discussion about bullying, cyberbullying, and cybervictimization, emphasizing anti-violence values, attitudes, and behaviours but also promoting students' and teachers' empathy through specialist activities.

- Enable teachers to actively contribute to cyberbullying prevention by training them to communicate effectively about Internet safety with their students and how best to prevent and manage cyberbullying successfully.
- Address school violence and bullying, cyberbullying, and cyber-victimization in the school curriculum, encouraging individual and group projects on relevant topics and speaking out against violence.
- Establish a helpline at the school for cyberbullies and cyberbullying victims, utilizing the expertise and availability of the school psychologist.

c) Class level:

- Utilizing the peer group factor, develop structured in-class activities to provide opportunities for students to share knowledge and experience about Internet safety, cyberbullying prevention, and cybervictimization support in open discussion.
- Use technological advances to benefit from debates on cyberbullying with students of the same age group at overseas schools with which there are exchange agreements.

d) Parents level:

- Improve parents' digital literacy.
- Raise their Internet safety knowledge and improve their awareness of the adverse impact of both cyberbullying and cybervictimization on those involved and how both can be prevented.

In conclusion, the Internet has become an essential part of modern life and the authorities' response to the cyberbullying and cybervictimization phenomena need to be a continuous part of a well-thought-out and implemented national strategy that includes independent evaluation of the effectiveness of measures implemented at the different levels listed. Panacea solutions do not exist and researchers have a significant role to play in the fight to reduce and prevent both cyberbullying and cybervictimization.

Acknowledgements This publication and the study presented have been produced with the financial support of the DAPHNE programme of the European Union. European Daphne III Programme (Project JUST/2011/DAP/AG/3259) Tabby Trip. Threat Assessment of Bullying Behaviour among Youngsters. Transferring Internet Preventive procedures in Europe. The contents of this article are the sole responsibility of the authors of the article and can in no way be taken to reflect the views of the European Commission. No conflict of interest is present.

Notes

1. Cited by Baldry et al. (2016).
2. Its northern part has been occupied by the Turkish army since 1974.
3. See Appendix for explanation of what each designation means.

References

Antoniadou, N., Kokkinos, C. M., & Markos, A. (2016). Possible common correlates between bullying and cyber-bullying among adolescents. *Psicología Educativa, 22*(1), 27–38. https://doi.org/10.1016/j.pse.2016.01.003

Baldry, A. C., & Kapardis, A. (2013). The juvenile young violent offender: From bullying to delinquency. In A. C. Baldry & A. Kapardis (Eds.), *Risk-assessment for juvenile violent offenders* (pp. 1–5). London: Routledge.

Baldry, A. C., Sorrentino, A., & Farrington, D. P. (2016). Cyberbullying does parental online supervision and youngsters' willingness to report to an adult reduce the risk? In A. Kapardis & D. P. Farrington (Eds.), *The psychology of crime, policing and courts* (pp. 57–74). Oxon: Routledge.

Baldry, A. C., Sorrentino, A., & Farrington, D. P. (2017). School bullying and cyberbullying among boys and girls: Roles and overlap. *Journal of Aggression, Maltreatment and Trauma*, 1–15. https://doi.org/10.1080/10926771.2017.1 330793

Kapardis, A. (1985). Lambousa Reform School, Cyprus: A study of its population (1979–1983) and its effectiveness. *Cyprus Law Review, 4*, 1821–1832.

Kapardis, A. (1986). Juvenile delinquency and delinquents in Cyprus. *Cyprus Law Review, 4*, 2371–2379.

Kapardis, A. (2008). Youth delinquency in Cyprus. In M. Steketee, M. Moll, & A. Kapardis (Eds.), *Juvenile delinquency in six new EU member states: Crime, risky behavior and victimization in the capital cities of Cyprus, Czech Republic, Estonia, Lithuania, Poland and Slovenia* (pp. 51–55). Utrecht: Verwey-Jonker Institute.

Kapardis, A. (2013). Delinquency and victimization in Cyprus. *European Journal on Criminal Policy and Research, 19*(2), 171–182. https://doi.org/10.1007/s10610-013-9201-y.

Kapardis, A., & Poyiadjis, G. (2013). The EARN project in Cyprus. In A. C. Baldry & A. Kapardis (Eds.), *Risk-assessment for juvenile violent offenders* (pp. 117–136). London: Routledge.

Kokkinos, C. M., Baltzidis, E., & Xynogala, D. (2016). Prevalence and personality correlates of Facebook bullying among university undergraduates. *Computers in Human Behavior, 55*(B), 840–850. https://doi.org/10.1016/j.chb.2015.10.017

Smith, P. K., Mahdavi, J., Carvalho, M., Fisher, S., Russell, S., & Tippett, N. (2008). Cyberbullying: Its nature and impact in secondary school pupils. *Journal of Child Psychology and Psychiatry, 49*, 376–385. https://doi.org/10.1111/j.1469-7610.2007.01846.x

7

Cyberbullying in France

Catherine Blaya

The Prevalence of Cyberbullying and Cybervictimization in France

Although the cyberspace opens up new perspectives and opportunities, it can sometimes turn into a hostile environment and a playground for bullying (Tokunaga 2010). Young people are prone to take risks online and can fall prey to bullies and predators and their online safety has become a key preoccupation these last decades. Since the late 1990s, many studies were completed in North America (Kowalski et al. 2008; Li 2007; Shariff 2008; Mishna et al. 2012; Hinduja and Patchin 2008), Europe (Smith et al. 2008) as well as in Latin America (Torres and Vivas 2016) and Asia (Hong et al. 2006; Wright 2015; Lee 2016) on the use of the Internet and its possible risks and opportunities (Livingstone et al. 2011a, b).

In France, research shows the same percentage of cyberbullied young people as the European average, that is 6% (Livingstone et al. 2011a, b; Blaya and Alava 2012). A study by Kubiszewski et al. (2012), on the prevalence of cyberbullying and its consequences among secondary

C. Blaya (✉)
HEPL, Lausanne, Switzerland

© The Author(s) 2018
A. C. Baldry et al. (eds.), *International Perspectives on Cyberbullying*, Palgrave Studies in Cybercrime and Cybersecurity, https://doi.org/10.1007/978-3-319-73263-3_7

school students, concludes that 16.4% of the surveyed young people were victims of cyberviolence, 4.9% were cyberbullies and 5.6% had both statuses. Contrary to most studies on the overlap between traditional bullying and cyberbullying (Hinduja and Patchin 2008, 2012a, b; Mishna et al. 2009; Tokunaga 2010; Melioli et al. 2015), their findings were that most adolescents involved in cyberbullying were not involved in traditional bullying although both groups showed similar patterns of internalizing and externalizing problems, that is general aggressiveness and antisocial behaviour for (cyber)bullies and (cyberbully/victims).

More recent research (Blaya 2013) including 3,200 participants aged 11–16 reveals much higher percentages of victims, with 42% of the participants who reported having experienced cyberviolence, that is to say occasional online violence, and 6% who declared they were cyberbullied. As for perpetration, 7% of the respondents declared they had cyberbullied someone. Findings show an overlap between victimization and perpetration, with 25% of the involved children who were both victims and authors. Another research study investigated the consequences of cyberbullying in the school environment (Blaya 2015) and concluded that the victims of cyberbullying have a significantly worse opinion about their school than the others. The school factors most affected by cyberbullying appeared to be

1. The quality of the relationships among students and students and staff;
2. The perception of the quality of learning;
3. Students' wellbeing at school;
4. The students who reported being cyberbullied also declared they were frightened of going to school.

This last point confirms the findings from Rémond et al. (2015) showing that victims of cyberbullying were adopting avoidance behaviours, and experiencing fear and anxiety. They also found a significant correlation. As for previous studies, they found a strong overlap between online bullying and offline bullying. A report from the Ministry of Education (MENESR-DEPP 2014), highlighted that cyberviolence (SMS, insults, and humiliations) had increased from 9% to 14% in 2013 compared to

2011. When adding happy slapping and the posting of humiliating videos, 18% of the students were cybervictimized. The report concluded on a higher risk for females to be cybervictimized and on a negative impact of this type of violence on the overall school climate.

The TABBY Project (Threat Assessment of Bullying Behaviour in Youngsters)

The TABBY project's objectives were to increase the awareness of the risks to be cyberbullied, to assess these risks, and to improve information levels and skills towards a positive use of the Internet. The assessment of such risks, of the prevalence of cyberbullying, and cybervictimization were part of the project. It also included teacher and student training sessions in order to increase the understanding of the possible negative experiences on the Internet and the way to protect oneself.

Quite a few school staff benefited from the training (97 in secondary schools and 17 in primary schools, 10 management staff). Three sets of training sessions were organized on Internet safety issues and on the use of the videos and the videogame that are part of the project. The involved staff found the training relevant, which is easily understandable since most of them did not know how to use the safety parameters on Facebook, for instance, and had little idea of how cyberbullying could affect not only the individuals but also the school climate as a whole. School staff then approached Internet safety issues with their students and included it into the curriculum during technology classes. The students were informed using the TABBY booklet and videos about online risky behaviours and how to use safety parameters properly as well as on the behaviours that could contribute to stop cyberbullying. Moreover, they were trained on the emotional, social, and legal consequences for cyberbullying victims and perpetrators.

At the level of the children, they showed high interest in the project and the levels of awareness and knowledge increased. The concern for cyberbullying was strong among the school community and even in primary schools, reflecting that the onset for digital communication is early among very young children (Mascheroni et al. 2014).

As part of the project, we assessed over 4,000 students on their digital practices, cyberbullying and cybervictimization experiences and this chapter is dedicated to the presentation of the findings.

The Present Study

Participants and Their Digital Uses

The survey was completed by 4.232 students (50.5% females, 49.5% males) aged 11–19 took part to the survey (M = 14.83, SD = 2.17).

In terms of digital uses, over one respondent out of three (33.4%) reported having at least one profile on a social network and nearly one out of two (47.9%) declared they knew all their friends personally. This last point highlights that over half of the respondents did not know all their friends. The time spent for an average of 2–4 hours per day online involves 36.8% of the young people online, which is higher than for other surveys (Ipsos 2006).

Full details of the whole sample are presented in Table 7.1.

Procedure

The survey was completed in 12 schools located in the south of France. Five schools were primary schools, and seven other schools were secondary schools. In the primary school, only children aged eight to ten took part to the survey. The sample is a convenience sample in the sense that the participating schools had the choice to accept or reject the opportunity to take part in the TABBY project. A consent letter was distributed to the parents through the school authorities and only the students whose parents had given an active formal consent and who wished to participate completed the questionnaire. They were informed they could opt out of the survey at any time. All the questionnaires were anonymous. The data collection was conducted in spring 2014. The questionnaires were completed online under the supervision of a

Table 7.1 Descriptive statistics for the sample in France

	N = 4.232
Gender (males)	49.5%
Age	M = 14.83 (sd = 2.17)
Presence of social network profile(s)	33.4% at least one
Personally know all friends on social network	47.9% everyone
Perceived popularity among peers (both at school and online)	6.4% not at all
Parents/significant adult among kid's online contacts	16.0% no
Parents talk with kid about Internet Safety	15.8% never
Teachers talk with kid about Internet Safety	14.2% never
Hours a day online	36.8% 2/4 h
School achievement	8.3% below average
School bullying	89.0% never
	6.6% once or twice
	4.4% > than twice
School victimization	81.0% never
	11.6% once or twice
	7.4% > than twice
Cyberbullying perpetration	66.1% never
	17.3% once or twice
	16.6% > than twice
Cybervictimization	52.5% never
	19.3% once or twice
	28.2% > than twice
Internet addiction	M = 15.23 (sd = 4.68)
Risk perception	M = 2.19 (sd = 2.65)

research assistant but without the presence of any school staff in order to reassure the participants that no one from the school could check on their individual responses. A research assistant was there to assist participants with the definition of cyberbullying (based on the definition by Smith et al. 2008) and to help with any possible misunderstanding of the questions. The software we used was *Sphinx survey online* and the questionnaire completion took approximately 40 minutes per session. In a perspective of counter-gift to thank the schools for the time and organization they dedicated to the project, each of them was provided with a full report of its individual situation in terms of online risk taking and involvement in cyberbullying as well as a global report including all the schools (Mauss 1950/1997).

Measures

The measurement tool used for this survey was the TABBY questionnaire. The prevalence of cyberbullying was assessed by a 5 items scale for cyberbullying (α = 0.82) and a 5 items scale for cybervictimization (total α = 0.73). The Likert type scales for victimization were ranging from 0 (it never happened during this period), 1 (it happened only once or twice), 2 (it happened sometimes), 3 (it happened about once a week), to 4 (it happened several times a week).

The period of time for measurement was the 6 months prior to the survey. The various variables that were included for online behaviours including digital uses and risky behaviours were

1. Time spent online, having a SNs profile;
2. Risks (risk perception, dialogue with parents about online activities, Internet addiction);
3. Online victimization and perpetration (six types of cyberbullying: flaming, sending hurtful messages, threats, social exclusion, impersonation, and sexting);
4. Offline involvement in bullying (victimization and perpetration);
5. Perceived popularity at school and online. The whole questionnaire's reliability is good with α = 0.79. For a more in-depth description of the questionnaire see Chap. 2 of this book.

Findings

Prevalence of School Bullying and Cyberbullying

Findings reveal that one out of ten students (11%) were involved in school bullying at least once during the previous 6 months, with 4.4% of them who reported it happened more than twice. As for school victimization, 19% of all respondents reported being involved at least once or twice and 7.4% more than twice in the previous 6 months.

For cyberbullying, percentages of involvement are much higher, with only 66.1% of the participants to the survey who stated they had never been involved, 17.3% that they were involved once or twice and 16.6% more than twice. Cybervictimization has affected nearly half of the surveyed young people with 19.3% who reported a negative experience once or twice in the last 6 months and 28.2% more than twice.

In terms of risk taking, children from the age of 8 reported having a profile on a social network and over 30% before the age of 13. The majority stated not knowing all their "friends" on their social network. The data showed that 14% of the respondents reported being victims of repeated cyberviolence that is cyberbullying while they were less numerous in secondary schools (5%). Findings also showed higher percentages of secondary school students who reported cyberviolence (isolated event) with 42% of the respondents who reckoned they had been victimized during the last 6 months.

Our research also assessed what were the most common forms of cyberbullying among the young people. The reported types of victimization (at least a few times) were by ranking order of prevalence: denigration (8.4%), flaming (6%), exclusion (5.3%), impersonation (4.7%) and outing (4.6%). As for perpetration, the most prevalent types of cyberbullying that happened more than twice during the last 6 months of the survey were flaming (7.2%), followed by online exclusion (4.7%), denigration and outing (2.3%), and impersonation (2.2%).

We examined potential gender differences in the involvement in cyberbullying as perpetrators and victims (see Table 7.2). Our analysis used the categorical classification, cut-off at least sometimes, for the four possible levels of involvement in cyberbullying (perpetration) and for cybervictimization. We used odds ratios (OR) to measure strengths of relationships because (unlike Chi-squares) they are not influenced by sample sizes. The analyses show that the odds of being involved in cyberbullying are 1.56 greater for males than for females and that males scored greater than females for all items. In the order of importance, the most frequent types of cyberbullying were flaming, denigration, impersonation, outing, exclusion. We shall note that that the biggest difference in online cyberbullying between males and females are in exclusion (7.3% vs. 2.2%, odds: 3.59), denigration (3.1% vs. 1.6%, odds: 1.95), and outing (3.1% vs. 1.5%, odds: 2.01). As for cybervictimization, results show a

Table 7.2 Gender differences in cyberbullying and cybervictimization involvement in France

		Male	Female
Total cyberbullying			
	N	411	289
	%	19.7	13.5
	OR (C.I.)		1.56*** (1.33–1.84)
Flaming			
	N	179	126
	%	8.6	5.9
	OR (C.I.)		1.49*** (1.18–1.89)
Denigration			
	N	64	34
	%	3.1	1.6
	OR (C.I.)		1.95**(1.28–2.97)
Impersonation			
	N	60	34
	%	2.9	1.6
	OR (C.I.)		1.82**(1.19–2.79)
Outing			
	N	64	33
	%	3.1	1.5
	OR (C.I.)		2.01***(1.31–3.07)
Exclusion			
	N	153	46
	%	7.3	2.2
	OR (C.I.)		3.59***(2.56–5.02)
		Male	**Female**
Total cybervictimization			
	N	538	656
	%	25.7	30.8
	OR (C.I.)		0.78***(0.68–0.89)
Flaming			
	N	107	146
	%	5.1	6.8
	OR (C.I.)		0.73*(0.57–0.95)
Denigration			
	N	133	220
	%	6.4	10.3
	OR (C.I.)		0.59***(0.47–0.74)

(continued)

Table 7.2 (continued)

		Male	Female
Impersonation			
	N	100	99
	%	4.8	4.6
	OR (C.I.)		1.03(0.78–1.37)
Outing			
	N	84	110
	%	4.0	5.2
	OR (C.I.)		0.77(0.58–1.03)
Exclusion			
	N	140	84
	%	6.7	3.9
	OR (C.I.)		1.75***(1.33–2.31)

Notes: *OR* odds ratio, *C.I.* confidence interval

greater involvement of females with odds 0.78 greater than for males. There are significant gender differences as far as flaming and denigration are concerned with respectively 0.73 and 0.59 greater odds for females to be flamed and denigrated online, the most significant difference being for denigration. On the contrary, males are more at odds to be excluded than females (6.7% vs. 3.9%, odds: 1.73), this last finding being in line with the gender differences for cyberbullying: boys are more involved in excluding and in being excluded.

Risk and Protective Factors

The TABBY questionnaire assesses several dimensions that can be considered as risk factors for the involvement of the young people in cyberbullying and cybervictimization. We proceeded to correlation analyses to examine the relationship between the potential risk factors (low school achievement, age, communicating with strangers online, involvement in school bullying, Internet addiction, lack of parental communication, and involvement in online activities and safety, feeling of being popular among peers and teachers' involvement in Internet safety, and the perception of the risk of being victimized online. Results presented in Tables 7.3 and 7.4, below show the strength of the relationship between proximal and distal risk factors. The correlational nature of our data did not permit

Table 7.3 Correlations between cyberbullying and risk factors in France

	1.	2.	3.	4.	5.	6.	7.	8.	9.	10.	11.	12.	13.	14.	15.
1. Cyberbullying	–														
2. Gender (male = 1)	0.08**	–													
3. Age	0.13**	0.04**	–												
4. Presence of social network profile(s)	0.20**	-0.02	0.39**	–											
5. Personally know all friends on social network	-0.03*	0.001	0.16**	0.22**	–										
6. Hours a day online	0.24**	0.05**	0.21**	0.32**	0.02	–									
7. Good academic achievement	-0.13**	-0.04**	-0.18**	-0.12**	0.004	-0.16**	–								
8. School bullying	0.30**	0.07**	0.002	0.08**	-0.05**	0.19**	-0.10**	–							
9. School victim	0.14**	0.11**	-0.09**	0.02	-0.07**	0.11**	-0.06**	0.33**	–						
10. Internet Addiction	0.30**	-0.01	0.27**	0.42**	0.06**	0.47**	-0.15**	0.15**	0.09**	–					
11. Risk perception	0.23**	-0.06**	0.02	0.08**	-0.09**	0.12**	-0.12**	0.31**	0.25**	0.21**	–				
12. Parents talk with kid about Internet safety	-0.11**	-0.13**	-0.11**	-0.10**	0.06**	-0.13**	0.13**	-0.10**	-0.05**	-0.13**	-0.03*	–			
13. Parents/significant adult not among kid's online contacts	-0.09**	-0.06**	0.01	0.02	0.17**	-0.02	-0.02	-0.10**	-0.03	-0.02	-0.02	0.06**	–		
14. Perceived popularity among peers (at school and online)	0.16**	0.07**	-0.02	0.11**	0.002	0.17**	0.03	0.14**	0.05**	0.16**	0.02	-0.002	0.01	–	
15. Teachers talk with kid about Internet Safety	-0.10**	-0.04*	-0.01	-0.05**	0.04*	-0.06**	0.06**	-0.07**	-0.02	-0.08**	-0.005	0.24**	0.02	-0.01	–

Note: $^{+}p < 0.10$; $^{*}p < 0.05$; $^{**}p < 0.01$; $^{***}p < 0.001$. All variables are standardized

Table 7.4 Correlations between cybervictimization and risk factors in France

	1.	2.	3.	4.	5.	6.	7.	8.	9.	10.	11.	12.	13.	14.	15.
1. Cybervictimization	–														
2. Gender (male = 1)	-0.06**	–													
3. Age	0.02	0.04**	–												
4. Presence of social network profile(s)	0.14**	-0.02	0.39**	–											
5. Personally know all friends on social network	-0.06**	0.001	0.16**	0.22**	–										
6. Hours a day online	0.17**	0.05**	0.21**	0.32**	0.02	–									
7. Good academic achievement	-0.08**	-0.04**	-0.18**	-0.12**	0.004	-0.16**	–								
8. School bullying	0.21**	0.07**	0.002	0.08**	-0.05*	0.19**	-0.10**	–							
9. School victim	0.27**	0.11**	-0.09**	0.02	-0.07*	0.11**	-0.06**	0.33**	–						
10. Internet Addiction	0.26**	-0.01	0.27**	0.42**	0.06**	0.47**	-0.15**	0.15**	0.09**	–					
11. Risk perception	0.29**	-0.06**	0.02	0.08**	-0.09*	0.12**	-0.12**	0.31**	0.25**	0.21**	–				
12. Parents talk with kid about Internet Safety	0.03	-0.13**	-0.11**	-0.10**	0.06**	-0.13**	0.13**	-0.10**	-0.05**	-0.13**	-0.03*	–			
13. Parents/significant adult not among kid's online contacts	0.008	-0.06**	0.01	0.02	0.17**	-0.02	-0.02	-0.10**	-0.03	-0.02	-0.02	0.06**	–		
14. Perceived popularity among peers (at school and online)	0.07**	0.07**	-0.02	0.11**	0.002	0.17**	0.03	0.14**	0.05**	0.16**	0.02	-0.002	0.006	–	
15. Teachers talk with kid about Internet Safety	-0.03*	-0.04**	-0.01	-0.05**	0.04*	-0.06**	0.06**	-0.07**	-0.02	-0.08**	-0.005	0.24**	0.02	-0.01	–

Note: $^\dagger p < 0.10$; $^* p < 0.05$; $^{**} p < 0.01$; $^{***} p < 0.001$. All variables are standardized

to establish a causal relationship. As showed in Table 7.3, cyberbullying is negatively associated to academic achievement ($r = -0.13$), parental and teacher involvement in Internet safety information ($r = -11$; $r = -10$), parents as contacts online ($r = -0.09$), and although the association is weaker, being in contact with strangers online ($r = -0.03$). We found an equivalent correlation between being a cyberbully and Internet addiction and school bullying ($r = 0.30$). It is also correlated to the time spent online ($r = 0.24$), the level of risk perception ($r = 0.23$), the perceived popularity among peers (both at school and online) by the respondents ($r = -0.16$) and in a lesser extent to all the other aspects (school victimization, age, being a male).

As for cybervictimization, it is associated with low academic achievement ($r = -0.08$), being female ($r = -0.06$) not knowing all friends on social networks ($r = -0.06$), and less significantly to little teachers' involvement in Internet safety issues ($r = -0.03$). Correlations are strong with the perception of risk ($r = 0.29$), school victimization and bullying ($r = 0.27$; $r = 0.21$), and Internet Addiction ($r = 0.26$). It is also associated with the time spent online, which is in line with the association to Internet addiction, and to have a social network profile.

In order to evaluate the role of the measured risk factors in the involvement of the participants to the survey in cyberbullying and cybervictimization, we performed a logistic regression analysis. The same predictors were used for both cyberbullying perpetration and cybervictimization. As the readers can see in Table 7.5, the addiction to the Internet is strongly associated to being a cyberbully (OR = 1.74), to being a male (OR = 1.57), to school bullying (OR = 1.40), to the perception of risk (OR = 1.39) and the feeling of being popular in the group of school peers (OR = 1.34), while teachers being involved in Internet safety or the social control of parents as being among contacts seem to act as protective factors since they are negatively associated with cyberbullying. However, the parental mediation role seems insignificant.

As for cybervictimization (see Table 7.6), being a victim is strongly associated with high levels of risk perception (OR = 1.67), Internet addiction (OR = 1.53), being a victim offline (OR = 1.48), and the use of social networks (OR = 1.34).

Table 7.5 Logistic regression for cyberbullying in France

Variable	B(SE)	OR	Lower bound	Upper bound
			95 C.I. for OR	
Gender (male = 1)	0.45(0.11)	1.57***	1.26	1.96
Age	0.18(.006)	1.19**	1.05	1.35
Presence of social network profile(s)	0.15(0.09)	1.16	0.97	1.39
Personally know all friends on social network	−0.28(0.07)	0.75***	0.66	0.86
Hours a day online	0.09(0.05)	1.09	0.98	1.20
Good academic achievement	−0.11(0.05)	0.90*	0.81	0.99
School bullying	0.33(0.05)	1.40***	1.26	1.55
School victim	0.03(0.05)	1.03	0.93	1.14
Internet Addiction	0.55(0.07)	1.74***	1.51	2.00
Risk perception	0.33(0.05)	1.39***	1.25	1.54
Parents talk with kid about Internet Safety	−0.07(0.06)	0.93	0.83	1.04
Parents/significant adult not among kid's online contacts	−0.13(0.05)	0.87**	0.79	0.97
Perceived popularity among peers (at school and online)	0.29(0.05)	1.34***	1.20	1.49
Teachers talk with kid about Internet Safety	−0.23(0.06)	0.79***	0.71	0.89

Notes: [i]$p < 0.10$; *$p < 0.05$; **$p < 0.01$; ***$p < 0.000$. R^2: = 0.17 (Cox and Snell), 0.26 (Nagelkerke), $\chi^2(14) = 494.68$***. All variables are standardized
OR odds ratio, *C.I.* confidence interval, *S.E.* standard error

Conclusions and Policy Implications for France

This research project one of whose objectives was to assess online risk taking and the prevalence of the involvement of young people in cyberbullying as victims or perpetrators highlights the fact that the issue is to be taken seriously since the percentages of involved students are high. Cyberbullying supersedes offline perpetration and victimization, which might be due to a stronger social control within the school than online and also to the fact that the children might better control their social behaviour when face to face than when online. Moreover, the sample is composed of young children under the age of ten and research shows that their online social skills are much lower than for their older counterparts and thus their risk of being cyberbullied is greater (Blaya and Fartoukh 2015). This sets

Table 7.6 Logistic regression for cybervictimization in France

Variable	B(SE)	OR	95 C.I. for OR Lower bound	Upper bound
Gender (male = 1)	−0.27(0.09)	0.76**	0.63	0.92
Age	−0.07(0.06)	0.93	0.83	1.04
Presence of social network profile(s)	0.29(0.08)	1.34***	1.15	1.56
Personally know all friends on social network	−0.23(0.06)	0.79**	0.70	0.89
Hours a day online	0.07(0.05)	1.07	0.97	1.18
Good academic achievement	−0.05(0.05)	0.95	0.87	1.05
School bullying	0.13(0.05)	1.14*	1.03	1.25
School victim	0.40(0.05)	1.48***	1.35	1.64
Internet Addiction	0.43(0.06)	1.53***	1.36	1.73
Risk perception	0.51(0.05)	1.67***	1.52	1.84
Parents talk with kid about Internet Safety	0.20(0.05)	1.23***	1.11	1.36
Parents/significant adult not among kid's online contacts	0.08(0.05)	1.08	0.95	1.19
Perceived popularity among peers (at school and online)	0.07(0.05)	1.07	0.97	1.18
Teachers talk with kid about Internet Safety	−0.06(0.05)	0.94	0.86	1.04

Notes: $^{1}p < 0.10$; $*p < 0.05$; $**p < 0.01$; $***p < 0.001$. R^2: = 0.17 (Cox and Snell), 0.25 (Nagelkerke), $\chi 2(14) = 511.54***$. All variables are standardized
OR odds ratio, *C.I.* confidence interval, *S.E.* standard error

the focus on the necessity to start prevention and online positive skills teaching from the earliest onset of digital uses and not to wait for the children to attend secondary school to start awareness raising activities. Being a male is strongly associated with cyberbullying perpetration while females are more associated with cybervictimization. Our findings also show some differences in the types of cyberbullying perpetration and victimization with females being more affected by flaming and denigration while there is a greater involvement of males in social exclusion. This confirms the need for adapted intervention and prevention programmes since experiences seem to differ according to gender and online activities. Males are more involved in online video games (Buckingam 2008), where competition and relationships are tough, and the weakest are excluded. Cyberbullying as bullying is about status, and being competitive in online games is part of it.

The young people involved in cyberbullying as perpetrators or/and as victims show greater levels of addiction to the Internet. Perpetrators feel more popular and also bully offline while victims online are also more often victims offline too. These findings meet previous research conclusions (Smith et al. 2008; Vandebosch and Van Cleemput 2008; Mishna et al. 2012) as well as the lifestyle theory according to which perpetrators tend to cumulate risky behaviours that increase their own risk of victimization due to their lifestyle choices (Cusson 1983). This is also valid for victims, as we have seen victimization is linked to having a social network profile and Internet addiction. Findings show that being a victim is also strongly associated with the perception of the risk to be cyberbullied but as we could not perform causal analyses we cannot conclude if the perception of risk existed before victimization or if it is a consequence of prior victimization since, logically, the more you are a victim, the more your feeling of insecurity grows.

The role of parental mediation does not appear predominant. As shown by Smahel and Wright (2014), if younger children are more open to parental mediation, teenagers perceive it as intrusive. However, the fact that teachers are involved in teaching about Internet safety is negatively associated with cyberbullying. This confirms the key role that schools can play in providing guidance for a positive and safe use of the Internet, promoting citizenship both offline and online (Hinduja and Patchin 2012a, b). Our experience when teaching staff within this project showed evidence that there is still a long way to go towards digital literacy and online safety skills for adults since quite a few of the participants had no clue on how to manage online safety parameters.

In France, quite a few actions have been undertaken these last few years. A law penalizing school bullying was voted in 2014 and cyberbullying is looked upon as an aggravating circumstance (art. 41222-33-2-2 of the Penal Code, law n°2014-873, 4/08/ 2014). Although this does set limits and above all enables the formal recognition of the status of victim to the children who are (cyber)bullied, and is thus of paramount importance, we remain convinced that education will prove more effective.

The Ministry of Education provides two helplines for the young people and their parents: *Stop bullying*: 3020 and *net écoute*: 0820 200 000. Various awareness raising campaigns against (cyber)bullying have been organized and all secondary schools are supposed to teach about Internet safety.

Some primary schools have also started prevention activities in partnership with non-lucrative associations and the school authorities but also with private companies such as the AXA insurance company that has set up as part as its prevention schemes and free of charge the "Internet licence" to raise awareness about the potential online risks and to teach positive and ethical online behaviours. Teachers' initial training includes digital uses and safety issues. However, the focus should be more relevant for staff who entered their teaching career ten years ago than on today's newly appointed teachers who are digital natives and likely to be better informed (Spears et al. 2015). Intervention outcomes are scarcely immediate and changing behaviours requires time. Let us hope that these measures will prove effective in reducing and preventing negative online experiences so that children can make the most of the huge opportunities electronic media offer.

Acknowledgements This publication and the study presented has been produced with the financial support of the DAPHNE programme of the European Union. European Daphne III Program (Project JUST/2011/DAP/AG/3259) TABBY in the Internet. Threat Assessment of Bullying Behaviour among youngsters. Transferring Internet Preventive procedures in Europe. The contents of this article are the sole responsibility of the authors of the article and can in no way be taken to reflect the views of the European Commission. No conflict of interests present.

References

Blaya, C. (2013). *Les ados dans le cyberespace – prises de risqué et cyberviolence.* Bruxelles: De Boeck.
Blaya, C. (2015). (coord.). Cyberviolence et école. *Les Dossiers des Sciences de l'Education,* 33. Presses Université du Mirail.
Blaya, C., & Alava, S. (2012). *Risks and safety for children on the Internet: The FR report. Full findings from the EU Kids Online survey of 9–16 year olds and their parents in France.* Retrieved from www.eukidsonline.net

Blaya, C., & Fartoukh, M. (2015). Digital uses, victimization and online aggression: A comparative study between primary school and lower secondary school students in France. *European Journal on Criminal Policy and Research, 22*(2), 285–300. https://doi.org/10.1007/s10610-015-9293-7

Buckingham, D. (2008). *Youth identity and digital media.* Cambridge, MA: MIT Press.

Cusson, M. (1983). *Le contrôle social du crime.* Paris: Presses universitaires de France.

Hinduja, S., & Patchin, J. W. (2008). Cyberbullying: An exploratory analysis of factors related to offending and victimization. *Deviant Behavior, 29*(2), 129–156. https://doi.org/10.1080/01639620701457816

Hinduja, S., & Patchin, J. (2012a). *School climate 2.0: Preventing cyberbullying and sexting one classroom at a time.* Thousand Oaks: Corwin Press.

Hinduja, S., & Patchin, J. W. (2012b). Cyberbullying: Neither an epidemic nor a rarity. *European Journal of Developmental Psychology, 9*(5), 539–543. https://doi.org/10.1080/17405629.2012.706448

Hong, Y., Li, X., Mao, R., & Stanton, B. (2006). Internet use among Chinese college students: Implications for sex education and HIV prevention. *CyberPsychology and Behavior, 10*(2), 161–169. https://doi.org/10.1089/cpb.2006.9973

Ipsos Insight. (2006). *Mobile phones could soon rival the PC as world's dominant internet platform.* Retrieved from https://www.ipsos.com/en-us/mobile-phones-could-soon-rival-pc-worlds-dominant-internet-platform

Kowalski, R. M., Limber, S. P., & Agatston, P. W. (2008). *Cyber bullying: Bullying in the digital age.* Malden: Blackwell Publishing.

Kubiszewski, V., Fontaine, R., Huré, K., & Rusch, E. (2012). Le cyber-bullying à l'adolescence : problèmes psycho-sociaux associés et spécificités par rapport au bullying scolaire. *L'Encéphale, 39*(2), 77–84. https://doi.org/10.1016/j.encep.2012.01.008

Lee, S. H. (2016). Cyberbullying in Eastern countries: Focusing on South Korea and other Eastern cultures. In R. Navarro et al. (Eds.), *Cyberbullying across the globe* (pp. 149–167). Cham: Springer.

Li, Q. (2007). New bottle but old wine: A research of cyberbullying in schools. *Computer in Human Behavior, 23*(4), 1777–1791. https://doi.org/10.1016/j.chb.2005.10.005

Livingstone, S., Haddon, L., Gorzig, A., & Ölafsson, K. (2011a). *Risks and safety on the internet: The perspective of European children. Full findings.* London: EU Kids Online.

Livingstone, S., Haddon, L., Görzig, A., & Ólafsson, K. (2011b). *EU Kids Online: Final report*. London: EU Kids online, London School of Economics and Political Science.

Mascheroni, G., Micheli, M., & Milesi, D. (2014). *Young children (0–8) and digital technology: A qualitative exploratory study – National report – ITALY*. Retrieved from http://centridiricerca.unicatt.it/osscom_2232.html

Mauss, M. (1950/1997). *Sociologie et anthropologie*. Paris, France: Presses Universitaires de France.

Melioli, T., Sirou, J., Rodgers, R. F., & Chabrol, H. (2015). Étude du profil des personnes victimes d'intimidation réelle et d'intimidation sur Internet. *Neuropsychiatrie de l'Enfance et de l'Adolescence, 63*(1), 30–35. https://doi.org/10.1016/j.neurenf.2014.07.007

MENESR-DEPP. (2014). *Note d'information n 39. Direction de l'Evaluation, de la Prospective et de la Performance*. Paris: Ministère de l'Education Nationale.

Mishna, F., Saini, M., & Solomon, S. (2009). Ongoing and online: Children and youth's perceptions of cyberbullying. *Children and Youth Services Review, 31*, 1222–1228. https://doi.org/10.1016/j.childyouth.2009.05.004

Mishna, F., Khoury-Kassabri, M., Gadalla, T., & Daciuk, J. (2012). Risk factors for involvement in cyberbullying: Victims, bullies and bully-victims. *Children &Youth Services Review, 34*(1), 63–70. https://doi.org/10.1016/j.childyouth.2011.08.032

Rémond, J. J., Kern, L., & Romo, L. (2015). Etude sur la «cyber-intimidation»: Cyberbullying, comorbidités et mécanismes d'adaptations. *L'Encéphale, 41*(4), 287–294. https://doi.org/10.1016/j.encep.2014.08.003

Shariff, S. (2008). *Cyber-bullying: Issues and solutions for the school, the classroom and the home*. New York: Routledge.

Smahel, D., & Wright, M. F. (Eds.). (2014). *Meaning of online problematic situations for children. Results of qualitative cross-cultural investigation in nine European countries*. London: EU Kids Online, London School of Economics and Political Science.

Smith, P. K., Mahdavi, J., Carvalho, M., Fisher, S., Russell, S., & Tippett, N. (2008). Cyberbullying: Its nature and impact in secondary school pupils. *Journal of Child Psychology and Psychiatry, 49*, 376–385. https://doi.org/10.1111/j.1469-7610.2007.01846.x

Spears, B., Campbell, M., Tangen, D., Slee, P., & Cross, D. (2015). La connaissance et la compréhension des conséquences du cyberharcèlement sur le climatscolaire chez les futurs enseignants en Australie. *Les Dossiers des Sciences de l'Education, 33*, 109–130.

Tokunaga, R. S. (2010). Following you home from school: A critical review and synthesis of research on cyberbullying victimization. *Computers in Human Behavior, 26*(3), 277–287. https://doi.org/10.1016/j.chb.2009.11.014

Torres, F. C., & Vivas, G. M. (2016). Cyberbullying and education: A review of emergent issues in Latin America research. In R. Navarro, S. Yubero, & E. Larranaga (Eds.), *Cyberbullying across the globe* (pp. 131–147). Switzerland: Springer International Publishing.

Vandebosch, H., & Van Cleemput, K. (2008). Defining cyberbullying: A qualitative research into the perceptions of youngsters. *Cyberpsychology and Behavior, 11*(4), 1349–1371. https://doi.org/10.1177/1461444809341263

Wright, M. F. (2015). Cyber victimization and adjustment difficulties: The mediation of Chinese and American adolescents' digital technology usage. *Cyberpsychology: Journal of Psychosocial Research on Cyberspace, 9*(1), article 7. https://doi.org/10.5817/CP2015-1-7.

8

Cyberbullying in Greece

Anna Sorrentino and Christina Athanasiades

The Prevalence of Cyberbullying and Cybervictimization in Greece

To our knowledge, the first study on cyberbullying prevalence in Greece, as reported by Sygkollitou et al. (2010) and Antoniadou and Kokkinos (2015), was conducted in 2005. This study, which involved 450 students between 16 and 19 years old, was carried out within the European Action SAFE NET HOME. Findings showed high prevalence rates of cyber-victimization (54.0%) among Greek students. Different results emerged from the European research Eu Kids Online, according to which Greece was classified among the '*non-high degree of online risk*' countries (Lobe et al. 2011; Livingstone and Haddon, 2009).

A. Sorrentino
Department of Psychology, Università degli Studi della Campania Luigi Vanvitelli, Caserta, Italy

C. Athanasiades (✉)
Department of Psychology, Aristotle University of Thessaloniki, Thessaloniki, Greece

189
A. C. Baldry et al. (eds.), *International Perspectives on Cyberbullying*, Palgrave Studies in Cybercrime and Cybersecurity, https://doi.org/10.1007/978-3-319-73263-3_8

Kapatzia and Sygkollitou (2008), in their study involving 544 high school students, found that 15.2% and 20.5% of participants were cyberbullies and cybervictims. Floros and Siomos (2013), comparing results from their cross-sectional study involving the entire adolescent high school student population of the island of Kos (N = 2.017), found a significant rise in reported experiences of Internet cyberbullying over two-year period. More particularly, cyberbullying rates increased from 10.5% in 2008 to 34.1% in 2010.

In a more recent study on 314 Greek secondary school students, Athanasiades et al. (2015) found that the most common cyberbullying typologies were sending nasty or cruel messages to someone (25.5%), and denigration and outing (14.0%), while the most common typologies of cybervictimization were denigration (19.7%) and impersonation (19.4%). In another study, involving 220 Greek elementary school students, Kokkinos et al. (2016) found that the most frequent cyberbullying and cybervictimization types were sending and/or receiving malicious comments about the victim via SMS or Internet. Finally, a study conducted in primary education, with a sample of 452 students, found that the percentage of cybervictimization among students ranges from 11% to 25%, while the percentage of cyberbullying ranges from 5% to 16% (Touloupis and Athanasiades, 2014). In addition, it was found that cyberbullying is positively related to pathological use of the Internet while it is not related to the students' academic achievement.

The TABBY Project (Threat Assessment of Bullying Behaviour in Youngsters)

The TABBY Trip in EU Project aimed (a) to sensitize students and teachers on a safe and conscientious use of the Internet and (b) to increase adults and youth' awareness about the "online traps" they face, when they underestimate their online risky behaviours. The project was implemented in 6 middle schools located in Thessaloniki. Implementation included initially a teachers' training session aimed at increasing teachers' awareness about risky online behaviours, cyberbullying and cybervictimization and educating them with useful strategies in order to protect pupils from possible online negative experiences. In particular, three sets of training sessions were organized for Greek teachers on cyberbullying types and features, Internet safety issues, on the use of the TABBY toolkit (i.e., TABBY checklist, videos and the videogame described in Chap. 2) and on the legal consequences related to cyberbullying and cybervictimization. Once the training was completed, teachers organized in (experimental) classes a set of activities for students such as the completion of the TABBY checklist, viewing of the videos and group discussions about the students' online risky behaviours and Internet safety issues.

The TABBY Project had been well received in Greek schools and educational institutions, since the project and its activities had been granted the official permission of the Greek Ministry of Education. Furthermore, the programme, its goals and main results were disseminated at a national level thanks to the researchers' participation to several scientific conferences and seminars for school personnel.

The Present Study

Participants and Their Digital Use

For the TABBY Trip Project, 981 Greek students (47.2% males, 52.8% females), aged 11–17 years (M = 12.78, SD = 0.71) participated in the study in the first wave of data collection. With regard to the use of cyber communication, 78.4% of all respondents reported having at least one profile on a social network. Of these, only 24.0% said that among all of their profile's contacts they personally knew all of them. The average number of hour's students reported spending online ranged from 0 to 12, with a total of 90.6% referring that they are online between 0 and 4 hours a day. Full details of the whole sample are presented in Table 8.1.

Procedure

Participants were recruited from six public middle schools located in the Greater Metropolitan Area of Thessaloniki, the second largest city in

Table 8.1 Descriptive statistics for the sample in Greece

	N = 981
Gender (males)	47.2%
Age	M = 12.78(SD = 0.71)
Presence of social network profile(s)	39.4% only one
Personally know all friends on social network	24.0% everyone
Perceived popularity among peers	6.2% not at all
Parents/significant adult among kid's online contacts	17.6% no
Parents talk with kid about Internet Safety	17.6% never
Teachers talk with kid about Internet Safety	8.7% never
Hours a day online	46.6% 2/4 h a day
School achievement	25.9% below average
School bullying	92.2% never
	6.1% once or twice
	1.7% > than twice
School victimization	91.1% never
	6.6% once or twice
	2.2% > than twice
Cyberbullying	76.6% never
	14.5% once or twice
	8.9% > than twice
Cybervictimization	64.8% never
	19.9% once or twice
	15.3% > than twice
Internet addiction	M = 9.65 (SD = 4.66)
Risk perception	M = 3.06 (SD = 2.91)

Greece. The Greek Ministry of Education, through its corresponding agency of the Pedagogical Institution, granted official permission for the TABBY research project and the implementation of the intervention in schools. Parental consent was obtained before data collection, and only students authorized by their parents and who wanted to participate in the research completed the online checklist TABBY.

Data collection was conducted during the months of November/December 2014. Students filled in the online questionnaire during school time, under the assistance and supervision of research assistants. Before filling in the questionnaire, the terms school bullying (based on the definition of Olweus, 1995) and cyberbullying (based on the definition of Smith et al., 2008) were explained to students in order to have a common understanding of what was investigated. Students were reassured about the anonymity of their answers and were encouraged to answer all the questions truthfully. Researcher assistants also assisted students in order to avoid possible misunderstanding of the questions.

Measures

To measure cyberbullying we refer to the same methodology and instruments adopted for the whole project, and it is therefore explained in the TABBY self-assessment of threats questionnaire. The scale to measure cyberbullying consisted of 5 items for cyberbullying and 5 items for cybervictimization (total α = 0.65). Students filled in the questionnaire in the presence of one researcher and a teacher who monitored the data collection. Students were assured about the confidentiality of the study and the anonymity of their answers. After completing the questionnaire all students returned to their classes, and debriefing was provided if required.

Findings

Prevalence of School Bullying and Cyberbullying

The findings revealed that 6.1% of students were involved in school bullying at least once or twice during the previous 4 months, with 1.7% of them reporting that it happened more than twice. As for school victimization, 6.6% of all respondents reported being involved at least once or twice while 2.2% more than twice in the previous 4 months.

For cyberbullying, percentages of involvement are much higher; while 76.6% of the participants to the survey stated they had never been involved in cyberbullying, 14.5% declared that they were involved once or twice and 8.9% more than twice. Cybervictimization has affected nearly half of the surveyed young people, since 19.9% of them reported a negative experience once or twice in the last 4 months and 15.3% reported being involved more than twice.

Our research also assessed what were the most common forms of cyberbullying among the young people. The reported types of cyberbullying were by ranking order of prevalence: denigration (8.4%), flaming (6%), exclusion (5.3%), impersonation (4.7%), and outing (4.6%). As for perpetration, the most prevalent types of cybervictimization that happened more than twice during the last 4 months of the survey were flaming (7.2%), followed by online exclusion (4.7%), denigration and outing (2.3%), and impersonation (2.2%).

Students' involvement in cyberbullying and cybervictimization was also analysed with respect to gender differences (see Table 8.2). According to the results, boys were more involved than girls in overall cyberbullying; the odds were for cyberbullies 2.87 times greater for boys than for girls. More particularly, boys were more involved than girls in flaming, denigration, and exclusion, while no significant gender differences were found with regard to students' involvement as cyberbullies in impersonation and outing. With regard to cybervictimization, no significant gender differences were found both in overall cybervictimization and its types.

Risk and Protective Factors

Two separate correlation analyses were performed in order to analyse the relationship between students' involvement in cyberbullying and/or cybervictimization and the dimensions included in the TABBY checklist as risk factors for cyberbullying and cybervictimization (see Tables 8.3 and 8.4).

Cyberbullying was correlated with being male ($r = 0.18$), spending time online ($r = 0.23$), high levels of Internet addiction ($r = 0.26$), and high levels of risk perception ($r = 0.20$). Both school bullying ($r = 0.36$) and victimization ($r = 0.09$) were correlated with students' cyberbullying involvement, while students' perception of being popular among peers was negatively related to students' involvement as cyberbullies ($r = -0.11$).

Cybervictimization was positive associated to the time spent online ($r = 0.25$), Internet addiction ($r = 0.26$) and high levels of risk perception ($r = 0.26$). Furthermore, cybervictimization was also related to school victimization ($r = 0.19$) and bullying ($r = 0.22$) and to low levels of perceived popularity among peers ($r = -0.12$).

Two separate logistic regression analyses were then performed, to evaluate the role that the risk factors measured by our survey could have in students' involvement in cyberbullying and cybervictimization. To this

Table 8.2 Gender differences in cyberbullying and cybervictimization involvement in Greece

		Male	Female
Total cyberbullying			
	N	61	26
	%	13.2%	5.0%
	OR (C.I.)		2.87*** (1.78–4.63)
Flaming			
	N	9	1
	%	1.9%	0.2%
	OR (C.I.)		10.25* (1.29–81.21)
Denigration			
	N	9	1
	%	1.9%	0.2%
	OR (C.I.)		10.25* (1.29–81.21)
Impersonation			
	N	3	2
	%	0.6%	0.4%
	OR (C.I.)		0.75 (0.12–4.48)
Outing		2	1
	N	0.4%	0.2%
	%		
	OR (C.I.)		2.24 (0.20–24.82)
Exclusion			
	N	12	4
	%	2.6%	0.8%
	OR (C.I.)		3.42* (1.09–10.68)

		Male	Female
Total cybervictimization			
	N	61	26
	%	13.1	5.0
	OR (C.I.)		1.14 (0.81–1.62)
Flaming			
	N	10	9
	%	2.2	1.7
	OR (C.I.)		1.25 (0.50–3.10)
Denigration			
	N	11	20
	%	2.4	3.9
	OR (C.I.)		0.61 (0.29–1.28)
Impersonation		4	4
	N	0.08	0.08

(continued)

Table 8.2 (continued)

		Male	Female
	%		
	OR (C.I.)		1.12 (0.28–4.50)
Outing			
	N	5	2
	%	1.1	0.04
	OR (C.I.)		2.82 (0.54–14.59)
Exclusion		10	7
	N	2.2	1.4
	%		
	OR (C.I.)		1.61 (0.61–4.27)

Notes: *OR* odds ratio, *C.I.* confidence interval

purpose, the same predictors were used for both cyberbullying and cybervictimization.

As shown in Table 8.5, boys were more at risk of being involved in cyberbullying (OR = 2.62). Furthermore, not knowing all online contacts personally (OR = 1.41) and spending more time per day on the Internet (OR = 1.29) were also associated with involvement in cyberbullying. Students reporting previous involvement in school bullying and Internet addiction were respectively 1.56 and 1.61 times more at risk of being involved in cyberbullying.

As for cybervictimization (see Table 8.6), being a victim was strongly associated with high levels of risk perception (OR = 1.47), Internet addiction (OR = 1.42), being a school bully (OR = 1.26) and victim (OR = 1.25), and low levels of perceived popularity among peers (OR = 0.74).

Conclusions and Policy Implications for Greece

Minors' Legal Responsibility for Cyberbullying and Other Offences

People under the age of 8 (infants) cannot commit any (punishable) action. They are simply dependent on parental care, as this age is indifferent to criminal law.

Table 8.3 Correlations between cyberbullying and risk factors in Greece

	1.	2.	3.	4.	5.	6.	7.	8.	9.	10.	11.	12.	13.	14.	15.
1. Cyberbullying	–														
2. Gender (male = 1)	0.18**	–													
3. Age	0.11**	0.05	–												
4. Presence of social network profile(s)	0.12**	0.13**	0.09**	–											
5. Personally know all friends on social network	0.003	−0.13**	−0.009	−0.66**	–										
6. Hours a day online	0.23**	−0.009	0.22**	0.24**	−0.05	–									
7. Good academic achievement	0.09**	0.09**	0.11**	0.001	0.06	0.20**	–								
8. School victim	0.09**	0.05	0.05	0.06	−0.03	0.04	0.001	–							
9. School bullying	0.36**	0.16**	0.11**	0.09**	−0.01	0.11**	0.12**	0.19**	–						
10. Internet Addiction	0.26**	0.02	0.17**	0.21**	−0.004	0.45**	0.19**	0.04	0.14**	–					
11. Risk perception	0.20**	−0.02	0.08*	−0.001	0.06	0.11**	0.19**	0.16**	0.14**	0.23**	–				
12. Parents talk with kid about Internet Safety	0.16**	0.18**	0.06	0.05	0.06*	0.15**	0.12**	0.04	0.12**	0.22**	0.07*	–			
13. Parents/significant adult not among kid's online contacts	0.12**	0.07*	0.01	0.19**	−0.12**	0.10**	0.05	−0.05	0.12**	0.09**	0.05	0.13**	–		
14. Perceived popularity among peers	−0.11**	−0.14**	−0.06	−0.45**	0.46**	−0.15**	−0.03	−0.04	−0.08*	−0.10**	−0.01	0.01	−0.12**	–	
15. Teachers talk with kid about Internet Safety	0.01	0.03	0.09**	0.03	0.06	0.12**	0.09**	0.02	−0.002	0.16**	0.06	0.28**	0.001	0.04	–

Note: *$p < 0.05$; **$p < 0.01$; ***$p < 0.000$. All variables are standardized

Table 8.4 Correlations between cybervictimization and risk factors in Greece

	1.	2.	3.	4.	5.	6.	7.	8.	9.	10.	11.	12.	13.	14.	15.
1. Cybervictimization	–														
2. Gender (male = 1)	0.02	–													
3. Age	0.07*	0.05	–												
4. Presence of social network profile(s)	0.13**	0.13**	0.09**	–											
5. Personally know all friends on social network	0.01	−0.13**	−0.009	−0.66**	–										
6. Hours a day online	0.25**	−0.009	0.22**	0.24**	−0.05	–									
7. Good academic achievement	0.05	0.09**	0.11**	0.001	0.06	0.20**	–								
8. School bullying	0.22**	0.16**	0.11**	0.09**	−0.01	0.11**	0.12**	–							
9. School victim	0.19**	0.05	0.05	0.06	−0.03	0.04	0.001	0.19**	–						
10. Internet Addiction	0.26**	0.02	0.17**	0.21**	−0.004	0.45**	0.19**	0.14**	0.04	–					
11. Risk perception	0.26**	−0.02	0.08*	−0.001	0.06	0.11**	0.19**	0.14**	0.16**	0.23**	–				
12. Parents talk with kid about Internet Safety	0.06*	0.18**	0.06	0.05	0.06*	0.15**	0.12**	0.12**	0.04	0.22**	0.07*	–			
13. Parents/significant adult not among kid's online contacts	0.06*	0.07*	0.01	0.19**	−0.12**	0.10**	0.05	0.12**	−0.05	0.09**	0.05	0.13**	–		
14. Perceived popularity among peers at school	−0.12**	−0.14**	−0.06	−0.45**	0.46**	−0.15**	−0.03	−0.08*	−0.04	−0.10**	−0.01	0.01	−0.12**	–	
15. Teachers talk with kid about Internet Safety	0.04	0.03	0.09**	0.03	0.06	0.12**	0.09**	−0.002	0.02	0.16**	0.06	0.28**	0.001	0.04	–

Note: $^†p < 0.10$; $^*p < 0.05$; $^{**}p < 0.01$; $^{***}p < 0.000$. All variables are standardized

Table 8.5 Logistic regression for cyberbullying in Greece

| | | | 95 C.I. for OR | |
| | | | Lower | Upper |
Variable	B(SE)	OR	bound	bound
Gender (male = 1)	0.96 (0.28)	2.62***	1.50	4.57
Age	0.09 (0.12)	1.10	0.86	1.40
Presence of social network profile(s)	0.18 (0.17)	1.20	0.86	1.68
Personally know all friends on social network	0.34 (0.18)	1.41†	0.99	1.99
Hours a day online	0.25 (0.13)	1.29*	1.00	1.65
Good academic achievement	−0.01 (0.12)	0.99	0.77	1.26
School bullying	0.44 (0.09)	1.56***	1.29	1.87
School victim	0.07 (0.10)	1.07	0.88	1.32
Internet Addiction	0.47 (0.15)	1.61**	1.19	2.18
Risk perception	0.29 (0.12)	1.34*	1.07	1.69
Parents talk with kid about Internet Safety	0.17 (0.14)	1.18	0.90	1.55
Parents/significant adult not among kid's online contacts	0.24 (0.31)	1.27	0.70	2.32
Perceived popularity among peers at school	−0.13 (0.14)	0.88	0.66	1.16
Teachers talk with kid about Internet Safety	−0.07 (0.13)	0.93	0.71	1.21

Notes: †$p < 0.10$; *$p < 0.05$; **$p < 0.01$; ***$p < 0.000$. R^2: = 0.12 (Cox and Snell). 0.27 (Nagelkerke). $\chi2(14) = 128.51$***. All variables are standardized
OR odds ratio, *C.I.* confidence interval, *S.E.* standard error

Minors aged 8–13 (children) are absolutely criminally irresponsible. The child cannot be considered as subject of a certain crime and thus he/she is subject only to reformative or therapeutic measures (122§1, 126§2, Penal Code).

Minors aged between 13 and 18 (adolescents) are either criminally irresponsible or criminally responsible. The article 126§3 of the Penal Code (P.C.) stipulates that a teen who has committed an offence is subject to reformative or therapeutic measures, however, the article 127§1 provides for criminal sanction. Criminal sanction consists of imprisonment to a special detention facility for young people and is imposed according to personality and circumstances on minors who have reached the age of 15.

An adult who sexually harasses a minor —who has been entrusted with the task of supervising or keeping him/her, even temporarily—is

Table 8.6 Logistic regression for cybervictimization in Greece

| | | | 95 C.I. for OR | |
| | | | Lower | Upper |
Variable	B(SE)	OR	bound	bound
Gender (male = 1)	0.03 (0.20)	1.03	0.69	1.54
Age	0.00 (0.09)	1.00	0.83	1.20
Presence of social network profile(s)	0.14 (0.13)	1.16	0.89	1.50
Personally know all friends on social network	0.28 (0.14)	1.32*	1.01	1.72
Hours a day online	0.27 (0.10)	1.31**	1.07	1.59
Good academic achievement	−0.08 (0.10)	0.93	0.76	1.13
School bullying	0.23 (0.08)	1.26**	1.08	1.48
School victim	0.22 (0.08)	1.25**	1.06	1.46
Internet Addiction	0.35 (0.11)	1.42*	1.14	1.78
Risk perception	0.38 (0.09)	1.47***	1.23	1.75
Parents talk with kid about Internet Safety	−0.05 (0.10)	0.95	0.78	1.17
Parents/significant adult not among kid's online contacts	0.007 (0.25)	1.01	0.62	1.65
Perceived popularity among peers at school	−0.30 (0.11)	0.74*	0.60	0.91
Teachers talk with kid about Internet Safety	−0.09 (0.10)	0.91	0.75	1.11

Note: *$p < 0.05$; **$p < 0.01$; ***$p < 0.000$. R^2: = 0.11 (Cox and Snell). 0.19 (Nagelkerke). $\chi2(14) = 112.99$***. All variables are standardized
OR odds ratio, $C.I.$ confidence interval, $S.E.$ standard error

punishable as follows: (a) if the victim is less than 14 years old, the offender is punished with at least 10 years' imprisonment; (b) if the victim is over 14 but less than 18 years old, the offender is punished with imprisonment (342§1 P.C.).

The phenomenon of bullying is manifested through verbal, physical, psychological, sexual harassment, and vandalism. It includes (a) physical assault, such as pushing, kicking, punching, (b) verbal assault, such as mocking, insulting, ridiculing, and very often (c) sexual assault, through unwanted touching. All these acts of bullying constitute different crimes of the Penal Code. For example, beatings can constitute the crime of bodily harm (308 P.C.); derogating and mocking, the crime of insult (361 P.C.); vandalism, the crime of damaging another's property (381 P.C.), while threatening messages can constitute the crime of threatening (333

P.C.). In general, we could say that in all acts of bullying there is violence, therefore, the crime of illegal violence (330 P.C.) is documented.

In recent years, the Greek legislation has been significantly modernized in terms of the protection of underage Internet users. Thus, crimes such as child pornography, sexual harassment, and seduction of minors through the Internet, violent and racist content, violation of personal data and privacy, breach of confidentiality of communications, vulgarity, slander, etc are prosecuted by the Greek police authorities. In this context, relevant hotlines and websites for online illegal content complaints have been created and operated.

Teachers' Responsibilities

According to teachers' duties and tasks, as these are described in official documents (FEK 1340/2002), teachers perform a task of high social responsibility, which includes both teaching as well as educating students. Progress, economic growth, civilization, and social cohesion depend to a large extent on the quality of the education provided and, by extension, on the contribution and effort of the teachers. Therefore, the tasks and responsibilities of teachers must be in line with these objectives.

Furthermore, the role and responsibility of teachers towards students is derived from the General Law on Education 1566/1985. Of course, there are other laws and decrees on this issue, such as the Presidential Decree 201/1998 regarding teachers on duty as well as the Law 3500/2006 on the liability of teachers for violation of their obligation to denounce any abuse against pupils.

Generally, teachers replace the family (*in loco parentis*) at least for the time that children are at school and have a particular legal obligation to look after the physical and psychological health of the pupil. Therefore, in case they fail to fulfil, partly or completely, the above obligations, their criminal liability will be sought. However, beyond criminal responsibility, there is also disciplinary responsibility, since teachers have the status of a civil servant. In this case, if they commit a disciplinary offence they are subject to disciplinary sanctions, such as reprimand, fine, downgrading, and even permanent cessation, as provided in the Civil Code (L.3528/2007).

Policy Implications and Recommendations

From a policy recommendation point of view, we suggest the following steps for Greece:

(a) *Involve teachers and school staff in preventing cyberbullying:*

- Involve the entire school staff in anti-violence activities by improving their level of digital literacy;
- Train teachers in the implementation of such activities.

(b) *Improve school climate:*

- Develop and implement specialized activities that promote students' empathy;
- Develop and implement in-class group activities or interventions aimed at developing a positive, supportive school climate in which there are open discussions about cyberbullying;
- Incorporate various programmes or actions into the school curriculum that address the phenomenon of violence in general;
- Develop and implement activities aimed at both bullying and cyberbullying prevention;
- Develop and implement specific school policies and regulations that address specifically the cyberbullying phenomenon;
- Involve the entire school community in the battle against school violence to develop a school culture that opposes all forms of violence and boosts students' confidence in adults' help.

(c) *Promote youngsters' active participation in preventing cyberbullying:*

- Train students on how to become part of the solution themselves, by improving their level of digital literacy and by placing emphasis not only on online risks but on the educational value of the Internet and on its benefits for students' academic and future professional lives.

(d) *Involve parents in fighting cyberbullying:*

- Develop and implement school activities and provisions that contribute to the improvement of the quality of communication between students and parents/teachers;
- Involve parents in anti-violence activities by raising their digital literacy level and awareness of safe and risky Internet use, so that they can monitor their children's ICT use and its impact on their lives.

Acknowledgements This publication and the study presented has been produced with the financial support of the DAPHNE programme of the European Union. European Daphne III Program (Project JUST/2011/DAP/AG/3259) TABBY TRIP. Threat Assessment of Bullying Behaviour among youngsters. Transferring Internet Preventive procedures in Europe. The contents of this article are the sole responsibility of the authors of the article and can in no way be taken to reflect the views of the European Commission. No conflict of interest is present.

References

Antoniadou, N., & Kokkinos, C. M. (2015). A review of research on cyberbullying in Greece. *International Journal of Adolescence and Youth, 20*(2), 185–201. https://doi.org/10.1080/02673843.2013.778207

Athanasiades, C., Kamariotis, H., Psalti, A., Baldry, A. C., & Sorrentino, A. (2015). Internet use and cyberbullying among adolescent students in Greece: The "Tabby" project. *Hellenic Journal of Psychology, 12*(1), 14–39.

Floros, G., & Siomos, K. (2013). The relationship between optimal parenting, Internet addiction and motives for social networking in adolescence. *Psychiatry Research, 209*(3), 529–534. https://doi.org/10.1016/j.psychres.2013.01.010

Kapatzia, K., & Sygkollitou, E. (2008). *Cyberbullying in middle and high schools: Prevalence, gender and age differences* (Unpublished master's thesis). Department of Psychology, Aristotle University, Greece.

Kokkinos, C. M., Antoniadou, N., Asdre, A., & Voulgaridou, K. (2016). Parenting and Internet behavior predictors of cyber-bullying and cybervictimization among preadolescents. *Deviant Behavior, 37*(4), 439–455. https://doi.org/10.1080/01639625.2015.1060087

Livingstone, S., & Haddon, L. (2009). *EU Kids Online: Final report 2009.* London: EU Kids Online, London School of Economics and Political Science. Retrieved from http://eprints.lse.ac.uk

Lobe, B., Livingstone, S., Ólafsson, K., & Vodeb, H. (2011). *Cross-national comparison of risks and safety on the internet: Initial analysis from the EU Kids Online survey of European children.* London: EU Kids Online.

Olweus, D. (1995). Bullying or peer abuse at school: Facts and intervention. *Current Directions in Psychological Science, 4*(6), 196–200. https://doi.org/10.1111/1467-8721.ep10772640

Smith, P. K., Mahdavi, J., Carvalho, M., Fisher, S., Russell, S., & Tippett, N. (2008). Cyberbullying: Its nature and impact in secondary school pupils. *Journal of Child Psychology and Psychiatry, 49*, 376–385. https://doi.org/10.1111/j.1469-7610.2007.01846.x

Sygkollitou, E., Psalti, A., & Kapatzia, A. (2010). Cyberbullying among Greek adolescents. In J. A. Mora-Merchán & T. Jager (Eds.), *Cyberbullying – A cross-national comparison* (pp. 101–113). Landau: Verlag Empirische Padagogik.

Touloupis, T., & Athanasiades, C. (2014). The risky use of new technology among elementary school students: Internet addiction and cyberbullying [in Greek]. *Hellenic Journal of Psychology, 11*, 83–110.

9

Cyberbullying in Hungary

Katalin Parti, Andrea Schmidt, and Bálint Néray

The Prevalence of Cyberbullying and Cybervictimization in Hungary

Research on cyberbullying among students does not have a great tradition in Hungary. Current research on bullying among students is usually limited to offline behaviours witnessed in school environments (Figula 2004; Buda 2009; Gyurkó and Virág 2009; Paksi 2010; Simon et al. 2012). The perception and significance of bullying in schools is usually lower than that of other disruptive student behaviours according to the studies.

K. Parti (✉)
National Institute of Criminology, Budapest, Hungary

A. Schmidt
Moholy-Nagy Művészeti Egyetem Elméleti Intézet, Budapest, Hungary

B. Néray
Department of Medical Social Sciences, Feinberg School of Medicine, Institute for Sexual and Gender Minority Health and Wellbeing, Northwestern University, Evanston, IL, USA

© The Author(s) 2018
A. C. Baldry et al. (eds.), *International Perspectives on Cyberbullying*, Palgrave Studies in Cybercrime and Cybersecurity, https://doi.org/10.1007/978-3-319-73263-3_9

Mérei Ferenc Pedagogic Consulting Institute sent questionnaires to primary schools in 2009, where educators had the opportunity to rank problematic student behaviours. According to this assessment, certain forms of bullying among students ranked in the middle of the list of problematic student behaviours. This means that school bullying is behind vandalism, smoking, theft, regularly changing schools, and excessive gaming. Alcohol consumption, drug abuse, disrespect towards school staff and pregnancy on the other hand represent less severe problems (Mayer et al. 2009, pp. 60–61)

We can establish that research on cyberbullying among peers only started to increase when, in the 2010s, more than half of Hungarian households had Internet access.[1] Hungary is one of the few countries where Internet use among young people exceeded the Internet use of the adult population for a long time.[2] When the adult population started using the Internet on a daily basis, the different types and volume of online abuse, online risks and threats received more attention (Virág and Parti 2011)

According to the 2015 findings of the European School Survey on Alcohol and other Drugs (ESPAD), the great majority (97.9%) of grade 9–10 students (aged 15–16) in Hungary is a regular Internet user (Király et al. 2016, p. 79). Adolescents in grades 9 and 10 spend an average 23.26 hours a week, i.e. 3.3 hours a day online. The average number of hours a week is the highest in the case of social media websites (23.16 hours), followed by online games (15.58 hours), and downloading music and films (11.64 hours). Out of online activities, the use of social media websites is the most widespread (98.6%), followed by the uploading and downloading of music and films (92%), and searching for information, browsing (85.3%) (Király et al. 2016, p. 80) Girls tend to spend more time on social media websites, while boys tend to spend significantly more time in a week shopping or selling online (Király et al. 2016, p. 91).

According to the 2014 findings of the survey Health Behaviour in School-Aged Children (HBSC), 12.2% of students in grades 5–11 (aged 11–16) become perpetrators of school (offline) bullying, while 14.2% of them become victims (N = 6.012). Only every tenth student became both a victim and a perpetrator, while the majority of students, nearly two-thirds of them, are not directly involved in bullying (Várnai and Zsíros 2014, p. 97).

Considering only the rate of victimisation – independent of whether we are talking about victims or perpetrator-victims – we can establish that three quarters of students were *not* bullied by a classmate in the past 12 months, and one quarter of them were bullied once or twice. In about 5% of the cases, victims are bullied regularly or several times a week (Várnai and Zsíros 2014, p. 98). The ratio of bullied students, similarly to that of the perpetrators of bullying, significantly drops with progressing age (Várnai and Zsíros 2014, p. 99).

The sample shows a difference between sexes: compared to boys, the ratio of girls who have never participated in bullying is significantly higher (boys: 70.7%, girls: 82.8%) while with boys, the ratio of those participating in bullying (perpetrators) is significantly higher (boys: 7.33%, girls: 4.43%) (Várnai and Zsíros 2014, p. 100). Compared to offline bullying indices, the ratio of cyberbullying is lower ($N = 6.046$): a smaller ratio of students reported being a victim of cyberbullying: 11.7% of them received abusive messages, and 5% of students saw unpleasant or embarrassing pictures of them being shared, while another 5% were victims of both forms of cyberbullying. This confirms the trends identified by the comprehensive international survey EU Kids Online, according to which 6% of Hungarian children between the ages of 9 and 16 have been bullied by their peers online in the past 12 months (Ságvári and Galácz 2011). The rate of falling victim to certain forms of cyberbullying differs between the sexes, and is higher with girls: girls received more abusive messages in the 11th grade (girls: 20.7%, boys: 13.1%), while embarrassing pictures among younger students (7th grade) were shared more of girls (girls: 12.3%, boys: 7.6%), and in 11th grade more of boys (girls: 9%, boys: 12.7%) (Várnai and Zsíros 2014, p. 101).

According to the findings of the HBSC in Hungary, 61.6% of students were not exposed to any form of bullying ($N = 5.972$). Traditional bullying – committed in schools – has a higher occurrence than cyberbullying – 7.5% of respondents received abusive messages, and embarrassing pictures were shared of 3.2% of them (Várnai and Zsíros 2014, p. 101). According to the study, only 2% of students were bullied in all three ways: harassed by abusive messages, by embarrassing pictures of them being shared, and by being bullied at school.

The TABBY Project (Threat Assessment of Bullying Behaviour in Youngsters)

For the Tabby programme (Tabby in Internet[3] and Tabby Trip in the EU[4]) we recruited schools from the whole country by sending direct emails to the principals of all high schools (6-grade high schools accommodating 7–12th grade students, 4-year high schools accommodating 9–12th grade students, and vocational schools accommodating 9–11th grade students). Furthermore, we announced the project details at educational conferences and workshops. The call for participation was also displayed on the Hungarian project partner's, ESZTER Foundation's,[5] website and on the relevant Facebook pages with educational background and crime-prevention interests. In terms of governmental support, we have found common ground in cooperation with the Hungarian Ministry of Human Resources responsible for educational matters. The Ministry supported our efforts in connecting and contacting high schools in Hungary. We also established cooperation with the second largest telecommunications firm in the country, Telenor Hungary Co.[6] Telenor helped find links to schools interested in joining the programme as well. Telenor provided 30 laptops motivating the schools to join the project. In the beginning of the programme, a 12-hour training was held for the teachers and a 6-hour training for 14–15-year-old peer mentors from the experimental schools.

The accredited, interactive trainings, based on the Tabby booklet including a CD with short thought-provoking videos, were necessary to clarify the prevalence and patterns of bullying and cyberbullying incidents, and to consult the participants on the methods of early recognition, managing and preventing bullying. The trainings consisted of a technical and a methodological block as well on how to administer the Tabby toolkit at schools, and an additional section on tasks promoting anti-bullying behaviour to be carried out jointly by Tabby teachers and

Tabby peer mentors between the first and the follow up data collections, also known as the experimental period. Peer mentors had to be prepared to act assertively and help the victims in a proper way when encountering a bullying or cyberbullying situation. All students who participated in the trainings had to hold a parent consenting certificate. Along the 4 consecutive years of the projects "Tabby in Internet" (2011–2012) and "Tabby Trip in EU" (2013–2014) 71 teachers were trained from 37 schools, and 52 students were trained as peer mentors in Budapest and in the countryside.[7]

Besides the experimental schools, control schools were included to the sample as well, whose teachers and students were not trained, although control schools were offered awareness raising workshops based on the Tabby booklet, after finishing the project.

The first data collection (T1) was conducted after the teacher and peer mentor trainings, followed by the second data collection (T2) after 4 months. Within this 4-month experimental period, students at experimental schools were given anti-bullying lectures and workshops lead by the Tabby teachers. Tabby teachers usually included peer mentors into their activities in order to make connections with students easily. In the experimental period, the activities of the experimental schools were monitored monthly, so that we could measure their deployed efforts. The most frequented activities were holding interactive classes at schools aimed at solving difficult bullying situations, organizing open school days devoted to safer Internet use, learning the etiquette of social networking, and managing awareness raising activities for students and their parents together. It was well proven that the Tabby booklet and the short Tabby videos were beloved by the participants, and were the most frequently utilized as a trigger for discussion classes.

As a by-product, a network was created among the participating teachers where they could share their experiences, discuss difficult situations and also get to know possible scenarios of incidents at early stages with the assistance of the project leaders at ESZTER foundation if that was necessary. As a most welcome development of the project, participating schools started to introduce etiquettes on dos and don'ts on cyberspace, how to identify risky behaviour and how to prevent bullying. Some schools developed protocols for bullying and cyberbullying situations and included that in the house rules.

The Present Study

Participants and Their Digital Uses

For the Tabby Trip in EU project, 902 Hungarian students (41.2% males, 58.4% females), aged 11–19 (M = 15.31, SD = 2.043) participated in the study in the first wave of data collected. With regard to the use of cyber communication, the vast majority of the respondents (94.7%) reported having at least one profile on a social network. 46.2% reported having more than one profile. Of those who had at least one online profile, only 18.5% said they personally knew all their contacts. The average number of hours students reported spending online ranged from 0 to 12 hours, with a total of 78.7% referring that they are online 1–4 hours a day. Within that, more than half of the answerers (51.1%) spent 2–4 hours a day online. Full details of the whole sample are presented in Table 9.1.

Procedure

Participants were recruited from the whole country by call for participation letters supported by the Ministry of Human Resources (supervising educational institutions). Due to the voluntary participation of the project, our sample turned out to be one of convenience, containing schools from Budapest and 5 municipalities in the country and consists of 11–18-year-old students attending 6-year or 4-year high schools and vocational schools. In order to conduct research with minors, both approval from the Ministry of Human Resources, and the directorate of the participating school were obtained before data collection. Parental consent was also a condition for being able to participate in the study. For the current study, data were gathered via the online procedure and was scheduled before the winter/Christmas break, during the months of November/December 2014.

Table 9.1 Descriptive statistics for the sample in Hungary

	N = 902
Gender (males)	41.4% male
Age	M = 15.31 (sd = 2.043)
Presence of social network profile(s)	94.7% at least one
Personally know all friends on social network	18.5% everyone
Perceived popularity among peers	2.0% not at all
Parents/significant adult among kid's online contacts	5.3% no
Parents talk with kid about Internet Safety	28.5% never
Teachers talk with kid about Internet Safety	31.7% never
Hours a day online	51.1% 2/4 h
School achievement	3.4% below average
School bullying	86.6% never
	8.0% once or twice
	5.4% > than twice
School victimization	82.0% never
	9.9% once or twice
	8.1% > than twice
Cyberbullying	63.8% never
	33.4% once or twice
	2.8% > than twice
Cybervictimization	66.3% never
	31.1% once or twice
	2.6% > than twice
Internet addiction	M = 14.36 (sd = 4.78)
Risk perception1 (1–5 Likert scale)	M = 6.0 (sd = 2.65)
Risk perception2 (0–4 Likert scale)	M = 2.00 (sd = 2.65)

Tabby teachers were trained how to administer the survey at their schools with the students from the experimental classes. During school time, they ordered the experimental classes to move into the school computer-technology room to fill out the online questionnaire in groups sized 10–20 students, depending on the number of the computer stations available. Here, each student was seated in front of a PC connected to the *www.tabby.eu* website and was told to fill in the online Tabby Trip anonymous self-report questionnaire dealing with their experiences in bullying, including the use of the new communication technologies and online experiences. The online questionnaire itself does not contain the terms of bullying, but the supervisor teacher had to provide the following, standardized description to the students before filling out the questionnaire, in order to have a common understanding of what was investigated. The following definitions were provided:

> *A student is being bullied or victimized when he or she is exposed, repeatedly and over time, to negative actions on the part of one or more other students. Negative actions can include physical contact, words, making faces or dirty gestures, and intentional exclusion from a group. An additional cri terion of bullying is an imbalance in strength: The student who is ex posed to the negative actions has dif ficulty defending himself or herself.* (Olweus 1995, p. 197)

> *Cyberbullying as an aggressive and intentional act, carried out by a group or an individual, using electronic forms of contact, repeatedly over time against a victim who cannot easily defend himself/herself.* (Smith et al. 2008, p. 376)

Various types of cyberbullying activity were mentioned as per examples of online bullying behaviours, without interpreting and explaining the ethical issues. The latter came after the students finished with the online questionnaire (T1), in order not to pollute their original set of answer, which were to measure their involvement in risky and harmful online situations. Tabby videos and the booklet were utilized in discussion at class only after the first data collection.

Measures

To measure risk assessment, we have developed the Tabby toolkit, which was available online for everybody who visited the project's website. In this way, everybody could measure the level of risk their online behaviour comprised of, including the involvement in bullying at school and cyberbullying, on the side of both the victim and the offender.

The scale to measure cyberbullying consisted of 5 items for cyberbullying and 5 items for cybervictimization (total $\alpha = 0.26$; $p < 0.000$). Students filled out the online questionnaire in the presence of a teacher who monitored the data collection. We have separated the sample of the experimental and the control group by assigning a special identification number to each and every student who was to participate in the study.

The identification number had to be included in the questionnaire.[8] Nevertheless, students were assured about the confidentiality of the study and the anonymity of the answers provided and were told that no-one but the researchers could have access to the answers that, once provided, went automatically into a database were analysed them in an aggregated way. The presence of a supervisor teacher was necessary in order to answer the students' questions if they had any. Teachers then were recommended to hold a debriefing session in case students needed more explanation or group discussions on the various behaviours and acts listed in the questionnaire and how they were related to the risks of bullying and cyberbullying involvement.

Findings

Prevalence of School Bullying and Cyberbullying

With regard to school bullying, 13.4% of all participating students reported being involved in school bullying at least once or twice, in the previous 4 months, while 18.0% of all participating students reported being involved in school victimization at least once or twice, in the previous 4 months.

With regard to cyberbullying, 33.4% of all participating students reported being involved in cyberbullying at least once or twice, and 2.8% more than twice in the previous 4 months (63.8% never bullied anybody online). With regard to cybervictimization, 31.1% of all participating students reported being involved in cybervictimization at least once or twice, and 2.6% more than twice in the previous 4 months (66.3% never was a cybervictim). Overall frequency analysis showed that the most common cyberbullying types in our sample were sending mean, cruel, or threatening messages online to someone they know (flaming: 32.3%), followed by denigration (putting down someone online by sending or posting cruel gossip, rumours, or other harmful material: 6.0%), exclusion (helping to exclude someone from an online group: 5.9%), outing (sharing someone's personal secrets or images online without permission: 4.7%) and impersonation (creation of a fake profile to send or post materials to damage someone's reputation or friendships: 2.8%).

Unlike for cyberbullying typologies, regarding cybervictimization the most frequent form in the sample was denigration (spreading cruel gossips, rumours, or other harmful material online: 18.1%), and outing (sharing someone's personal secrets or images without permission online: 12.2%), followed by flaming (9.9%), social exclusion (5.8%) and impersonation (5.7%).

We then analysed students' involvement in cyberbullying and cybervictimization, also considering gender significant differences (see Table 9.2). To this aim, we used the categorical classification, cutoff at least sometimes, for the four possible levels of involvement in cyberbullying and then for cybervictimization to look for gender differences. We used odd ratios (OR) to the measure strengths of relationships because (unlike chi-squares) they are not influenced by sample sizes.

Boys were more involved than girls in overall cyberbullying activities; the odds were 1.78 times greater for boys than for girls to be involved in cyberbullying. Boys were significantly more engaged in all cyberbullying activities than girls. The greatest gender differences were observed in impersonation (OR = 5.37) and outing (OR = 3.53), where boys were significantly more active than girls. However, the most frequent types of cyberbullying were flaming reported to be committed by 45.2% of boys and only 23.0% of girls; the respective odds were 1.96 greater for boys than for girls. Boys were also more involved in denigration (boys 7.8%, girls 4.8, OR = 1.64), in exclusion (boys 8.1, girls 4.4, OR = 1.84), in outing (boys 8.1, girls 2.3, OR = 3.54), and impersonation (boys 5.1%, girls 1.0%, OR = 5.37). Girls were slightly more involved than boys in overall cybervictimization; the odds for cybervictims were .95 greater for girls than for boys. In denigration, impersonation, and exclusion boys reported more victimization than girls (18.5% vs. 17.8%, 8.3% vs. 3.8%, 6.7% vs. 5.1%). Outing was equally suffered by both genders (12.4% vs. 12.4%), and only flaming was more suffered by girls than boys (girls 11.0%, boys 8.3%). However, no significant gender differences were found with regard to cybervictimization types.

Table 9.2 Gender differences in cyberbullying and cybervictimization involvement in Hungary

		Male	Female
Total cyberbullying			
	N	181	144
	%	48.7	27.4
	OR (C.I.)		1.78*** (1.49–2.12)
Flaming	*N*	168	121
	%	45.2	23.0
	OR (C.I.)		1.96*** (1.62–2.38)
Denigration	*N*	29	25
	%	7.8	4.8
	OR (C.I.)		1.64* (0.98–2.75)
Impersonation	*N*	19	5
	%	5.1	1.0
	OR (C.I.)		5.37*** (2.02–14.26)
Outing	*N*	30	12
	%	8.1	2.3
	OR (C.I.)		3.54*** (1.83–6.81)
Exclusion	*N*	30	23
	%	8.1	4.4
	OR (C.I.)		1.84* (1.09–3.12)
		Male	**Female**
Total cybervictimization			
	N	122	182
	%	32.8	33.8
	OR (C.I.)		0.95 (0.79–1.14)
Flaming	*N*	31	58
	%	8.3	11.0
	OR (C.I.)		0.76 (0.50–1.15)
Denigration	*N*	69	94
	%	18.5	17.8
	OR (C.I.)		1.04 (0.79–1.38)
Impersonation	*N*	31	20
	%	8.3	3.8
	OR (C.I.)		2.20*** (1.27–3.79)
Outing	*N*	46	64
	%	12.4	12.4
	OR (C.I.)		1.02 (0.71–1.45)
Exclusion	*N*	25	27
	%	6.7	5.1
	OR (C.I.)		1.31 (0.77–2.22)

Notes: *OR* odds ratio, *C.I.* confidence interval

Risk and Protective Factors

Tables 9.3 and 9.4 show the relationship between the risk factors and the involvement in cyberbullying and cybervictimization. Due to the correlational nature of these data, it is not possible to establish a causal relationship, but the strength of the relationship between proximal and distal risk factors. With regard to cyberbullying, being a girl ($r = -0.23$), parents' talk about Internet safety ($r = -0.14$), and personally knowing all friends on social network ($r = -0.09$) were negatively correlated to students' cyberbullying activities. Cyberbullying was related with all factors listed, except for the presence on social networking sites – whereas 94.7% of the respondents are present on at least one social network. However, correlation was high with the following possible risk factors: being engaged in school bullying ($r = 0.57$), the student's own risk perception ($r = 0.47$), the length they were online a day ($r = 0.30$), showing the signs of Internet addiction ($r = 0.28$), and having been suffered school bullying in the last 4 months ($r = 0.25$). (see Table 9.3).

Cybervictimization was strongly related to school victimization ($r = 0.47$), the student's own risk perception ($r = 0.45$),[9] being involved in school bullying activities ($r = 0.39$), and the number of hours spent online ($r = 0.26$). As per protective factors, personally knowing all friends on the social network ($r = -0.18$) and gender (being a girl: $r = -0.05$) meant a lower risk for cybervictimization as well, however parents' talking about online safety ($r = -0.03$), although being protective, was not statistically significantly correlated as protective factor. Instead, teachers talking about online safety ($r = -0.09$), and good academic achievement ($r = -0.08$) were more protective (Table 9.4). It is worthwhile to note that according to the above correlations bullying and victimization, and also different scenes of bullying were strongly correlated. It cannot be told from the data which came first: school or online bullying, but those who engaged in the one, became engaged in the other as well at some point. The same correlation can be seen at victimization: those who fell victim at school, very likely became online victims too. Additionally, school victimization was proven to be a predictor (risk factor) of online bullying: those who suffered bullying

Table 9.3 Correlations between cyberbullying and risk factor in Hungary

	1.	2.	3.	4.	5.	6.	7.	8.	9.	10.	11.	12.	13.	14.	15.
1. Cyberbullying	–														
2. Gender (female = 1)	−0.23**	–													
3. Age	0.14**	0.00	–												
4. Presence in social networks profile(s)	0.06	0.08*	0.15**	–											
5. Personally know all friends on social network	−0.09**	−0.004	−0.16**	−0.13**	–										
6. Hours a day online	0.30**	−0.009	0.21**	0.23**	−0.20**	–									
7. Good academic achievement	−0.16**	0.03	−0.07	−0.05	0.13**	−0.15**	–								
8. School bullying	0.57**	−0.18**	0.06†	0.06†	−0.11**	0.21**	−0.08*	–							
9. School victim	0.25**	−0.005	−0.05	0.06†	−0.05	0.08*	−0.04	0.30**	–						
10. Internet addiction	0.28**	0.04	0.13**	0.23**	−0.21**	0.39**	−0.14**	0.16**	0.12**	–					
11. Risk perception	0.47**	−0.19**	0.01	0.02	−0.13*	0.20**	−0.09**	0.44**	0.39**	0.23**	–				
12. Parents talk with kid about Internet Safety	−0.14**	0.21**	−0.15**	−0.02	−0.02	−0.02	0.09**	−0.09**	0.02	−0.12**	−0.08*	–			
13. Parents/significant adult not among kid's online contacts	0.19**	−0.01	0.02	−0.03	−0.02	0.04	−0.09*	0.18**	0.09**	0.03	0.09**	−0.05	–		
14. Perceived popularity among peers	0.18**	−0.12**	−0.03	0.02	0.02	0.15**	0.05	0.12**	−0.006	0.14**	0.13**	0.08*	−0.05*	–	
15. Teachers talk with kid about Internet Safety	−0.13**	0.14**	−0.07*	0.001	0.04	−0.05	0.004	−0.08*	−0.05	−0.03	−0.03	0.27**	−0.08*	0.04	–

Note: †$p < 0.10$; *$p < 0.05$; **$p < 0.01$; ***$p < 0.001$. All variables are standardized

Table 9.4 Correlations between cybervictimization and risk factors in Hungary

	1.	2.	3.	4.	5.	6.	7.	8.	9.	10.	11.	12.	13.	14.	15.
1. Cybervictimization	–														
2. Gender (female = 1)	−0.05	–													
3. Age	0.09**	0.00	–												
4. Presence in social networks profile(s)	0.08*	0.08*	0.15**	–											
5. Personally know all friends on social network	−0.18**	−0.004	−0.16**	−0.13**	–										
6. Hours a day online	0.26**	−0.009	0.21**	0.23**	−0.20**	–									
7. Good academic achievement	−0.08*	0.03	−0.07*	−0.05	0.13**	−0.15**	–								
8. School bullying	0.39**	−0.18**	0.06†	0.06†	−0.11**	0.21**	−0.08*	–							
9. School victimization	0.47**	−0.005	−0.05	0.06†	−0.05	0.08*	−0.04	0.30**	–						
10. Internet addiction	0.26**	0.04	0.13**	0.23**	−0.21**	0.39**	−0.14**	0.16**	0.12**	–					
11. Risk perception	0.45**	−0.19**	0.01	0.02	−0.13**	0.20**	−0.09**	0.44**	0.39**	0.23**	–				
12. Parents talk with kid about Internet Safety	−0.03	0.21**	−0.15**	−0.02	−0.02	−0.02	0.09**	−0.09**	0.02	−0.12**	−0.08*	–			
13. Parents /significant adult not among kid's online contacts	0.08*	−0.01	0.02	−0.03	−0.02	0.04	−0.09**	0.18**	0.09**	0.03	0.09**	−0.05	–		
14. Perceived popularity among peers	0.13**	−0.12**	−0.03	0.02	0.02	0.15**	0.05	0.12**	−0.006	0.14**	0.13**	0.08*	−0.05	–	
15. Teachers talk with kid about Internet Safety	−0.09**	0.14**	−0.07*	0.001	0.04	−0.05	0.004	−0.08*	−0.05	−0.03	−0.03	0.27**	−0.08*	0.04	–

Note: $^†p < 0.10$; $^*p < 0.05$; $^{**}p < 0.01$; $^{***}p < 0.001$. All variables are standardized

offline, had a higher chance to become an online bully than those who have not been school victims.

Logistic regression was then performed to analyse the role that the risk factors that were taken into account could have on students' involvement in cyberbullying and cybervictimization. The same predictors were used for both cyberbullying and cybervictimization (Tables 9.5 and 9.6). This model explains approximately 28% of the variance. According to this model (cyberbullying as a dependent variable) becoming a cyberbully shows very strong significant relation with school bullying (OR = 1.71***), time spent online (OR = 1.39***), being popular among peers (OR = 1.12**) and signs of Internet addiction (OR = 1.09***) (e.g. having difficulties to unplug. searching for excuses to stay online longer etc.). Gender (being a girl: OR = 0.42***) and being familiar with online friends (OR = 0.81*) were again protective. As shown in Table 9.6, fewer variables were

Table 9.5 Logistic regression for cyberbullying in Hungary

Variable	B(SE)	OR	95 C.I. for OR Lower bound	Upper bound
Gender (female = 1)	−0.86 (0.17)	0.42***	0.30	0.59
Age	−0.10 (0.04)	1.11*	1.02	1.21
Presence of social network profile(s)	0.00 (17)	1.00	0.72	1.39
Personally know all friends on social network	−0.21 (0.09)	0.81*	0.67	0.97
Hours a day online	0.33 (0.10)	1.39**	1.13	1.71
Good academic achievement	−0.007 (0.11)	0.99	0.80	1.23
School bullying	0.54 (0.15)	1.71***	1.27	2.30
School victim	−0.009 (0.11)	0.99	0.80	1.23
Internet Addiction	0.09 (0.02)	1.09***	1.06	1.14
Risk perception	0.09 (0.04)	1.09*	1.01	1.18
Parents talk with kid about Internet Safety	−0.07 (0.09)	0.94	0.79	1.11
Parents/significant adult not among kid's online contacts	0.05 (0.38)	1.05	0.50	2.21
Perceived popularity among peers	0.12 (0.04)	1.12**	1.03	1.23
Teachers talk with kid about Internet Safety	−0.14 (0.09)	0.87	0.73	1.03

Note: *$p < 0.05$; **$p < 0.01$; ***$p < 0.000$. R^2: = 0.20 (Cox and Snell). 0.28 (Nagelkerke). $\chi^2(15) = 0.59$***. All variables are standardized
OR odds ratio, C.I. confidence interval, S.E. standard error

Table 9.6 Logistic regression for cybervictimization in Hungary

Variable	B(SE)	OR	95 C.I. for OR Lower bound	Upper bound
Gender (female = 1)	0.20 (0.17)	1.223	0.869	1.721
Age	0.05 (0.04)	1.050	0.962	1.145
Presence of social network profile(s)	0.38 (0.16)	1.467*	1.063	2.025
Personally know all friends on social network	−0.13 (0.09)	0.877	0.734	1.047
Hours a day online	0.17 (0.10)	1.186 †	0.969	1.451
Good academic achievement	0.11 (0.11)	1.122	0.908	1.387
School bullying	0.04 (0.13)	1.042	0.811	1.338
School victim	0.52 (0.11)	1.687***	1.351	2.105
Internet Addiction	0.07 (0.02)	1.073***	1.033	1.115
Risk perception	0.17 (0.04)	1.183***	1.097	1.275
Parents talk with kid about Internet Safety	0.14 (0.08)	1.156 †	0.979	1.366
Parents/significant adult not among kid's online contacts	−0.51 (0.40)	0.602	0.275	1.320
Perceived popularity among peers	0.09 (0.04)	1.102*	1.009	1.202
Teachers talk with kid about Internet Safety	−0.17 (0.09)	0.844 †	0.710	1.003

Note: $^{†}p < 0.10$; $^{*}p < 0.05$; $^{**}p < 0.01$; $^{***}p < 0.000$. R^2: = 0.17 (Cox and Snell).
0.23 (Nagelkerke). $\chi^2(15) = 0.52^{***}$. All variables are standardized
OR odds ratio, *C.I.* confidence interval, *S.E.* standard error

significantly connected with cybervictimization. This regression explains 23% of the variance. School victimization (OR = 1.69***), risk perception (OR = 1.18***) and Internet addiction (OR = 1.073***) were the most likely predictors of cybervictimization. However being a girl had lower risk (OR = 1.22 and not even significant). Being familiar with most of the online friends (OR = 0.88), teachers' talk about Internet safety (OR = 0.84) and parents being an online friend of the student (OR = 0.60) were the most protective in the range of factors.

According to the above analysis of risk and protective factors, we can observe that parents can be successful in protecting their children from online victimization. However when Internet safety becomes a school agenda, it can rather function as a deterrent from committing cyberbullying. This finding underlines other studies' results confirming that teachers who clearly and actively stood for anti-bullying norms are likely to strengthen the normative goal of potential bullies and victims. As an example, at the KiVa anti-bullying programme teachers' efforts cross-sectionally correlated with a higher level of peer-reported bullying in the first year of the evaluation, but over time, they correlated with a drop in peer-reported bullying (Veenstra et al. 2014). In another analysis, KiVa researchers examined the effect of appreciation by the community on popular bullies. The activities of perpetrators of medium and low popularity in intervention schools fell due to the programme, but very popular bullies were not responsive (Garandeau et al. 2014). This result, which is again justified by the Hungarian Tabby as well, is particularly worrying as anti-bullying programmes mostly aimed at victims and communities (e.g. mobilizing bystanders. exercise for supporting victims), but they do not offer alternatives to popular children for maintaining their social position after stopping bullying (Garandeau et al. 2014).

Conclusions and Policy Implications for Hungary

Minors' Legal Responsibility for Cyberbullying and Other Offences

Even though in Hungarian legislation, the terms "bullying" and "cyber-bullying" as such are not used, certain elements of these behaviours are specified in the Criminal Code as actual crimes in themselves. The penalized behaviour with a definition closest to that of bullying in the Hungarian Criminal Code is "zaklatás," which approximately corresponds to stalking or harassment in English. The elements of the definition include making threats of physical harm or intimidation, the deliberate nature of the act and repeated perpetration over a longer period of time, but they do not include a shift in the balance of power.

In addition to the fact that the definition of the crime of "zaklatás" does not contain all the elements of the definition of bullying, legal practice is also inconsistent as regards the interpretation of the individual elements of the definition. So, for example, it is not clear what qualifies as repeated or prolonged harassment or whether certain hierarchic conditions in society correspond to the lack of a balance of power, which is an element of the definition of bullying (Parti 2016, p. 118).

The instrument of bullying may be trespassing interception of online communication, identity theft, unauthorized recording and publication of personal data (photos, videos), online defamation and libel. Since 2013, the new crime of the "making of falsified audio or video recordings suitable for defamation or the publishing of such" has been included in Hungarian legislation. Slut shaming, a widespread behaviour included under the heading of cyberbullying is also covered by this definition. This crime is perpetrated if, for instance, students make videos or GIF images of the teacher during class with the purpose of embarrassing or ridiculing the teacher by posting the recordings online. This behaviour does not constitute bullying in itself, but the flood of rumours and shaming comments on the depicted person may easily lead to the exclusion of the victim.

In another form of slut shaming, youngsters make videos of the victim at house parties or club after lacing the victim's drink with drugs. The victim is no longer in control of him- or herself and is therefore not able to consent to the recordings, which means the recording itself constitutes a crime. It is not the making and sharing of audio or video recordings suitable for defamation, but the more severe crimes of rape, sexual abuse or "child pornography" that are committed when the drugged victim is also undressed and raped. Any person over the age of 14 who participated in the transmission and spreading of the humiliating recording is guilty of the crime of child pornography, independent of whether they (also) appear in the recording or not.

A typical case of bullying by peers may be hazing, which typically occurs between freshmen and students from higher grades. In these cases, the victim is forced to engage in humiliating behaviours and the act is often also recorded on video. This behaviour is the "humiliation of a vulnerable person," which is also punishable under the Criminal Code as a separate crime. If this includes the making of a recording and publishing such to the general public (uploading such to social media websites) the act is more severely punishable.

In many cases, bullying is perpetrated by "defamation" or "libel," if for example humiliating or defaming rumours are spread about the victim online. These acts – which may also be the instruments of (cyber) bullying – are regulated by the Criminal Code independent of whether the act is perpetrated in an offline or online environment.

In the case of online defamation and libel as a precursor or an instrument of bullying, it is very important to identify the severity of the act. An act is reported here, which is only one element of bullying. Yet in such cases, it has to be realized that more severe developments may underlie the act. In such cases, regarding the police's tasks, not only do minutes have to be taken of the reporting, but during the criminal proceedings the school of the students involved needs to be approached to uncover any underlying conflicts, which may potentially affect the whole school community.

However, in the case of offences involving minors or young adults such as bullying or cyberbullying primary prevention and intervention should not be implemented at the level of jurisdiction, but more at school level.

Teachers' Duties

Educators are not only citizens performing a job, their task is far more complex than that: they are care-givers and also perform child-protection and youth-protection work. The duties of educators are laid down in the internal regulations or house rules of the funding authority or organ (foster-home. municipal government. or church) or those of the educational institution. The house rules, for example, also have to stipulate in what cases an educator may decide to confiscate the mobile phones of students for the duration of classes to ensure order in class. The house rules will also have to contain a protocol for bullying among peers. Smaller bullying cases where no crime is committed have to be investigated by the school in disciplinary proceedings.

If, according to the methodology guidelines on preventive child-protection at schools issued by the ministry in charge of the public education system (in Hungary the Ministry of Human Resources), any given case exceeds the school's room for action the class teacher or the child-protection officer reports such to the institution in charge, that is, the guardianship authority or the police. According to the approach of the methodology guidelines, educators perform a so-called explorative activity, which essentially means the close monitoring of children showing signs of vulnerability, who are disadvantaged or are problem cases for educators. By reporting the explored cases, educators perform a secondary crime-prevention activity, which means the prevention of the development of more serious cases, for example, the perpetration of crimes or the involvement of vulnerable children with a group of perpetrators. The educator also performs a primary preventive task, for example, by introducing students to the potential consequences and risks of regular Internet use calls the attention of the students to dangerous situations—well before emergencies occur—and informs students, other educators, and parents about the possibilities of averting emergencies. For example, by informing children and parents where to turn if they find harmful online contents, if they are directly sent such, or if they fall victim to or witness cyberbullying.

In certain European countries, educators are obliged by law to report crimes perpetrated by children at school to the authorities. In Hungary, educators do not have such obligations as they have a position of confidence and mainly perform educational and care activities, in which the emphasis is more on the obligation to prevent crime than on the obligation to respond to it.

Policy Implications and Recommendations

Whereas students mostly talk to their peers about their painful experiments in cyberspace (Davis and Nixon 2014, p. 140), student mentorship training is recommended to be part of cyberbullying prevention and intervention programmes. Peer leaders popular in their schools are recommended to be trained in how to help younger students resolve crucial conflicts in cyberbullying situations. This "high status peer model" programme (Englander et al. 2015) applies to peer mentors speaking to students with little age gap. Student mentors can function best when they collaborate with teachers trained to early detect, resolve and prevent cyberbullying situations. Peer mentors and teachers should act jointly to raise awareness and to lower risk of cyberbullying.

Student mentors have to be trained, however, in how not to abuse their power. In Hungary, some teachers reported that students did not accept student mentors with overly positive manner. If student mentors act "too actively" in preventing cyberbullying, students might suspect they are rather "spies" aiming not to help, but to sneak on those who are involved in cyberbullying as offenders instead. Hence, training student mentors and preparing bystanders has to be extremely sensitive about possible backlash and responsive to children's real needs.

In today's Hungary, there are plenty of small isolated anti-bullying programmes focusing on segments of bullying (e.g. offenders, children with psychological needs, victims etc.) focusing particularly on students in big cities (with excessive technological activities). However, we would need nationally representative researches. Financial support should cover sampling and other aspects of adequate methodology. National representative studies should to be repeated from time to time in order to have longitudinal data following the prevalence and patterns of risk and dangers and their management.

Cyberbullying management must be included in teachers' graduate curriculum. Adults bear a huge gap in digital literacy compared to children so that they have difficulties in understanding younger generations' problems and solutions in cyberspace. Cyberbullying related curricula should not stop at technical knowledge into information technology tools and applications. Teachers should be taught psychological skills to understand and handle cyberbullying.

Cyberbullying management should be taught to teachers and educators not only at the graduate level, but also at the postgraduate level. In Tabby Trip in EU teachers have mostly asked for best practices that can be applied by them in real life situations. Best practices, case studies must be collected and circulated among schools in order to prepare and better manage problematic situations. Recommendations must pay attention to the given county's peculiarities—hence must reflect the socio-economical situations, legal regulations, digital literacy and the digital gap between generations in the current education system).

Teachers and school staff have to be motivated to participate in interventional programmes. The mere fact that a programme is available for free is not enough motivation for teachers overly burdened by fulfilling everyday tasks and being underpaid and underappreciated in their profession. The training material (how to early detect, best handle and prevent cyberbullying) must be offered not only for teachers but also for school professionals – e.g. guidance counsellors, school psychologists and school social workers. Professional assistance, guidance and network have to be provided for teachers encountering cyberbullying situations. As cyberbullying sometimes requires help at a higher level and a deeper level of understanding, mental health school professionals should be trained as well.

Prevention and intervention programmes in cyberbullying have to be harmonized with the locally run Safer Internet Program.[10] Though European Commission's Safer Internet Program (SIP) and its successor, the Better Internet for Kids (BIK), are present in all EU member states teaching safer Internet use is at a different level in member states. Financial and material support must be collected from the industry. Public and Private Partnership must be applied in propelling complex multinational programmes in the future. Not only NGOs, governmental agencies, child-protection and health care agencies, universities and research institutes, but also telecommunication and media industrial bodies might be involved in supplying material and providing continuity for a programme.

Acknowledgements This publication and the study presented has been produced with the financial support of the DAPHNE programme of the European Union. European Daphne III Program (Project JUST/2011/DAP/AG/3259) Tabby in Internet. Threat Assessment of Bullying Behaviour among youngsters. Transferring Internet Preventive procedures in Europe. The contents of this article are the sole responsibility of the authors of the article and can in no way be taken to reflect the views of the European Commission. No conflict of interests present.

Notes

1. Source: Eurostat, Share of households with Internet access in Hungary from 2005 to 2014. Retrieved from www.statista.com/statistics/377743/household-internet-access-in-hungary/; [16-01-2017].

2. Flash Eurobarometer N 248 – Safe Internet for Children. Analytical Report, p. 13.
3. Tabby in the Internet: European Project N. JLS/2009-2010/DAP/AG/1340 AMG.
4. Tabby Trip in EU: European Project N JUST/2011-2012/DAP/AG/3259.
5. The Hungarian partner of the Tabby project was ESZTER Foundation for the Rehabilitation of the Sexually Abused. ESZTER pursues legal advising and ambulant aftercare for sexually abused children and adults and also offers consultation in children's rights and youth crime prevention issues. For details, see: http://eszteralapitvany.hu/.
6. For the details of the cooperation see Telenor's Sustainability Report (in Hungarian) https://www.telenor.hu/upload/pr/telenor_fenntarthatosagijelentes_2013.pdf; [17-01-2017].
7. Schools have joined the Tabby programme from the following counties: Pest county, Szabolcs-Szatmár-Bereg county, Veszprém county, Komárom-Esztergom county.
8. To include the identification number we included 2 questions: "Does your class participate in the TABBY project?" (Yes/No) and if the answerer said yes, we asked "What is your identification code?" The identification code served the aim of being able to separate students in the experimental and in the control group, and also made it possible to match the items between the first and the second (follow up) data collection in order to evaluate the changes in the answerers' risk assessment set after the 4-month experimental period was passed.
9. The students estimated their own risk answering the question "How much chance do you see to be victim of cyberbullying in the following 4 months?".
10. Information on Safer Internet Program (2009-2012) and Better Internet for Kids (2012) available here: https://ec.europa.eu/digital-single-market/en/safer-internet-better-internet-kids; [19-01-2017].

References

Buda, M. (2009). Közérzet és zaklatás az iskolában. *Iskolakultúra, 19*(5–6), 3–15.

Davis, S., & Nixon, C. L. (2014). *The youth voice project: Student insights into bullying and peer mistreatment.* Champaign: Research Press Publishers.

Englander, E., Parti, K., & McCoy, M. (2015). Evaluation of a university-based bullying and cyberbullying prevention program. *Journal of Modern Education Review,* 5(10), 937–950. https://doi.org/10.15341/jmer(2155-7993)/ 11.05.2015

Figula, E. (2004). Az iskolai erőszak jelenségének feltárása. a tanulók érintettségének. szerepviselkedésének elemzése egy vizsgálat tükrében. *Alkalmazott Pszichológia, 4,* 19–35.

Garandeau, C. F., Lee, I. A., & Salmivalli, C. (2014). Differential effects of the KiVa anti-bullying program on popular and unpopular bullies. *Journal of Applied Developmental Psychology, 35,* 44–50. https://doi.org/10.1016/j. appdev.2013.10.004

Gyurkó, Sz., & Virág, Gy. (2009). *Az iskolai erőszak megítélésének különbségei és hasonlóságai a gyermekvédelmi és az oktatási intézményrendszerben. Kutatási zárótanulmány.* Budapest: Országos Kriminológiai Intézet. Available online at the webpage of the Hungarian Institute of Criminology. Retrieved January 15, 2017, from http://www.okri.hu/images/stories/kutatok/ viraggyorgy/isk _eroszak_2009.pdf

Király, O., Zsila, Á., & Demetrovics, Z. (2016). Viselkedési addikciók. In Z. Elekes (Ed.), *Európai iskolavizsgálat az alkohol- és egyéb drogfogyasztási szokásokról (ESPAD) – 2015. Magyarországi eredmények.* Budapest: Budapesti Corvinus Egyetem.

Mayer, J., Nádori, J., & Vígh, S. (2009). *Kis könyv a felelősségről. Adalékok az iskolai agresszió természetrajzához.* Budapest: Mérei Ferenc Pedagógiai és Pályaválasztási Tanácsadó Intézet.

Olweus, D. (1995). Bullying or peer abuse at school: Facts and intervention. *Current Directions in Psychological Science, 4*(6), 196–200. https://doi. org/10.1111/1467-8721.ep10772640

Paksi, B. (2010). Az iskolai agresszió előfordulása. intézményi percepciója. *Új Pedagógiai Szemle* (1–2), 119–134.

Parti, K. (2016). A megfélemlítés (bullying) szabályozása Magyarországon és külföldön. *In Medias Res, 1,* 114–146.

Ságvári, B., & Galácz, A. (2011). *EU Kids Online II. Hungarian report.* Available online at the webpage of the EU Kids Online project. Retrieved from http:// www.lse.ac.uk/media@lse/research/EUKidsOnline/EU%20Kids%20II%20 (2009-11)/National%20reports/ Hungarian%20report.pdf

Simon, D., Zerinváry, B., & Velkey, G. (2012). *Az iskolai bántalmazás megjelenése az 5–8 évfolyamos diákok körében: jelenségek és magyarázatok a normál és az alternatív tantervű iskolákban.* Budapest: Oktatáskutató és Fejlesztő Intézet.

Smith, P. K., Mahdavi, J., Carvalho, M., Fisher, S., Russell, S., & Tippett, N. (2008). Cyberbullying: Its nature and impact in secondary school pupils. *Journal of Child Psychology and Psychiatry, 49*, 376–385. https://doi.org/10.1111/j.1469-7610.2007.01846.x

Várnai, D., & Zsíros, E. (2014). Kortársbántalmazás és verekedés. In Á. Németh & A. Költő (Eds.), *Egészség és egészségmagatartás iskoláskorban.* Budapest: Health Behaviour in School-Aged Children (HBSC): A WHO-collaborative Cross National Study. National Report 2014.

Veenstra, R., Lindenberg, S., Huitsing, G., Sainio, M., & Salmivalli, C. (2014). The role of teachers in bullying: The relation between antibullying attitudes, efficacy, and efforts to reduce bullying. *Journal of Educational Psychology, 106*(4), 1135–1143. https://doi.org/10.1037/a0036110

Virág, G., & Parti, K. (2011). Sweet child in time: Online sexual abuse of children–A research exploration. *The Open Criminology Journal, 4*(1), 71–90. https://doi.org/10.2174/1874917801104010071

10

Cyberbullying in Italy

Anna Sorrentino, Anna Costanza Baldry, and Sonya Cacace

The Prevalence of Cyberbullying and Cybervictimization in Italy

Cyberbullying is well researched in Italy and intervention strategies are disseminated throughout the country. At the central level, the Ministry of Education has implemented guidelines for the prevention and comparing of cyberbullying, and was also an associate partner in this Tabby project. Studies in Italy on the prevalence and nature of cyberbullying are quite extensive, and followed the ones on school bullying (Baldry et al. 2016b; Menesini et al. 2011). Prevalence rates vary depending on age of participants, methods, instruments used, period, and cut-off criteria adopted to measure students' involvement in cyberbullying and cybervictimization.

Since 2007, cyberbullying and cybervictimization prevalence among children and adolescents has become a matter of concern for institutions,

A. Sorrentino (✉) • A. C. Baldry • S. Cacace
Department of Psychology, Universita degli Studi della Campania Luigi Vanvitelli, Caserta, Italy

© The Author(s) 2018   **231**
A. C. Baldry et al. (eds.), *International Perspectives on Cyberbullying*, Palgrave Studies in Cybercrime and Cybersecurity, https://doi.org/10.1007/978-3-319-73263-3_10

schools, teachers, parents, and professionals. The Eighth National report on Childhood and Youth (Eurispes – Telefono Azzurro, 2007) showed that 11.5% of the 1,523 children aged 7–11 years participating in the research admitted they were cybervictimized. Brighi et al. (2012) found, by surveying 2,326 Italian secondary students, that respectively 10.0% and 15.0% of boys and girls were cybervictimized at least once in the previous 2 months.

Menesini et al. (2012) found in their study involving 707 students aged between 11–21 years that the most common cyberbullying behaviours in the previous 2 months were silent phone calls (36.6%) and insults on instant messaging (22.9%). The same pattern was found for cybervictimization incidents: respectively 44.5% and 20.6% of students experienced at least one silent phone call and were insulted on instant messaging.

Vieno et al. (2014) surveyed 24,099 Italian middle school students (M = 13.6, SD = 0.5) about their experiences of cybervictimization in the previous 2 months. Results highlighted that 11.8% of the students declared that they have been cybervictimized (8.7% occasionally and 3.1% frequently). Baldry et al. (2016b) found that 24.0% and 26.2% of participants were involved in cyberbullying and cybervictimization in the study conducted with 2,419 middle and high school students in the previous 6 months. In a further study involving a larger Italian sample of 5,058 students, Baldry et al. (2016a) found that respectively 12.1% and 7.4% of students were involved in both school bullying and cyberbullying and in school victimization and cybervictimization. Palermiti et al. (2017) in their study involving 438 students aged 10–20 years found that 11.0% were involved in cyberbullying (occasional, 9%; severe, 2%), and 15.4% were cybervictims (occasional, 13.1%; severe, 2.3%).

Implementation of the Tabby Project (Threat Assessment of Bullying Behaviour in Youth)

The Tabby programme—aimed to sensitize and increase students and teachers' awareness about the negative consequences of cyberbullying and cybervictimization and risk factors associated with them—was implemented by assigning a random portion of students (classes) to the experimental or control condition, for the total of 7 schools. Four schools (total classes: 14) benefitted from the implementation of the Tabby programme. In order to have enough controls and motivate schools to participate in the data collection, we proposed a waiting list to benefit from the Tabby programme the following year, which we did. Regardless of students' and schools' allocation in the experimental or the control group, all students filled in the online Tabby checklist prior to and 4 months after the intervention (T1 and T2). Only students and teachers in the experimental group benefited from the implementation of the Tabby programme, which consisted of specific training on cyberbullying for teachers and school personnel. Full details of the programme are presented in Chap. 2 of this book. The authors, after having undergone a two-day training by an international expert on the cyberbullying issue, conducted teachers' training, which was scheduled in parallel with the first data collection.

A total of 92 Italian teachers participated in 3 days' training on cyberbullying, its features, types and useful risk recognition and management strategies, and on how to use of the Tabby toolkit (checklist, videos, and booklet) with students. Having completed the training, teachers organized in one or two classes a set of group discussions, consisting of watching Tabby videos and discussing their content. All of the four videos were used as stimuli to make students work in small groups aimed at thinking about the videos' stories, recommendations, and about their risky behaviours on the Internet and how to prevent and stop cyberbullying and cybervictimization. Furthermore, trained teachers worked with their classes in order to create rules on safe Internet use, to make students reflect on their risky online behaviours and on how to help them to prevent their involvement in cyberbullying and cybervictimization. Teachers were trained to recognize risk factors of possible student involvement in cyberbullying and cybervictimization, and on how to manage and resolve these incidents. When teachers identified severe cyberbullying and/or cybervictimization incidents, they were supported and supervised in the management and resolution of the cases by the authors. Four months following the intervention, before the end of the school year, students had to fill in the same online questionnaire, but by referring to the previous 4 months, from the activities undertaken with teachers and seeing the videos.

The Tabby programme had been well received among Italian schools and institutions, which often had difficulties in cyberbullying and cyber-victimization recognition, management and resolution. After the programme implementation, trained teachers continued to work on cyberbullying and cybervictimization prevention, in order to sensitize students on the negative consequences of cyberbullying and cybervictimization and prevention strategies, also including students not involved in the experimental trial. Furthermore, to date, thanks to the national diffusion and dissemination of the Tabby programme, 212 other Italian teachers were trained on Tabby toolkit use and 5,000 students have been involved.

The Present Study

Participants and their Digital Activities

For the Tabby Trip Project, 906 Italian students (50.0% males, 50.0% females), aged 11–19 years (M = 14.83, SD = 2.17), participated in the study in the first wave of data collected. With regard to the use of cyber communication, 56.7% of all respondents reported having at least one profile on a social network. Of these, only 18.2% said that they personally knew all of their contacts on their profile(s). The average number of hours students reported spending online ranged from 0 to 12 per day, with a total of 87.4% saying that they are online between 1 and 4 hours a day. Full details of the whole sample are presented in Table 10.1.

Procedure

Participants were recruited from seven different schools located in two different Italian sites: Milan and surrounding provinces (Northern Italy) and Naples and surrounding provinces (Southern Italy). Of these schools, one was a middle school (11–14-year-old students), three were high schools and three were professional/technical schools (14–18-year-old students). Schools were representative of the types of schools for students aged 11–18 in Italy (middle and high schools) and represented a variety of socio-economic statuses.

Table 10.1 Descriptive statistics for the sample in Italy

	N = 906
Gender (male)	50.0%
Age	M = 14.83(sd = 2.17)
Presence of social network profile(s)	56.7% at least one
Personally know all friends on social network	18.2% everyone
Perceived popularity among peers	8.6% not at all
Parents/significant adult among child's online contacts	19.9% no
Parents talk with child about Internet Safety	10.0% never
Teachers talk with child about Internet Safety	21.2% never
Hours a day online	43.7% 2/4 h
School achievement	8.2% below average
School bullying	85.8% never
	8.7% once or twice
	5.5% > than twice
School victimization	84.9% never
	7.6% once or twice
	7.6% > than twice
Cyberbullying	52.3% never
	34.9% once or twice
	12.8% > than twice
Cybervictimization	3.4% never
	82.8 % once or twice
	13.8% > than twice
Internet addiction	M = 15.23 (sd = 4.68)
Risk perception	M = 2.19 (sd = 2.65)

In order to conduct research with minors, both approval from the Department's Ethical Committee and parental consent were obtained before data collection. Data were gathered via the online procedure Computer Assisted Web Interview (CAWI), and this was scheduled before the winter/Christmas break, during the months of November/December 2014. The first two authors approached students in each school in their own classes, during school time, and then moved into the school computer-technology room to fill in the online questionnaire in groups of 10–20 students, depending on the number of computer stations available. Here, each student sat in front of a PC connected to the *www.tabby.eu* website and was told he/she had to fill in the Tabby Trip anonymous self-report questionnaire dealing with his/her experience with the new communication technologies. Before filling in the questionnaire, the terms 'school bullying' and 'cyberbullying' were explained to the students in order to have a common understanding of what was being investigated. The following definitions were provided:

A student is being bullied or victimized when he or she is exposed, repeatedly and over time, to negative actions on the part of one or more other students. Negative actions can include physical contact, words, making faces or dirty gestures, and intentional exclusion from a group. An additional criterion of bullying is an imbalance in strength: The student who is exposed to the negative actions has difficulty defending himself or herself. (Olweus 1995, p. 197)

Cyberbullying as an aggressive and intentional act, carried out by a group or an individual, using electronic forms of contact, repeatedly over time against a victim who cannot easily defend himself/herself. (Smith et al. 2008, p. 376)

Measures

To measure cyberbullying we refer to the same methodology and instruments adopted for the whole project, and this is explained in the Tabby self-assessment of threats questionnaire.

The scale to measure cyberbullying consisted of 5 items for cyberbullying and 5 items for cybervictimization (total α = 0.79). Students filled in the questionnaire in the presence of one of the researchers and a teacher who monitored the data collection. Students were assured about the confidentiality of the study and the anonymity of the answers provided and were told that no one but the researchers could access the answers, which, once provided, went automatically into a database that analysed them in an aggregated way. Students were given the opportunity to pose questions if they had any. After completing the questionnaire all students returned to their classes, and debriefing was provided if required.

Findings

Prevalence of School Bullying and Cyberbullying

With regard to school bullying, 14.2% of all participating students reported being involved in school bullying at least once or twice, in the previous 4 months, while 15.1% of all participating students reported being involved in school victimization at least once or twice, in the previous 4 months.

With regard to cyberbullying, 34.9% of all participating students reported being involved in cyberbullying at least once or twice, and 12.8% at least sometimes in the previous 4 months. With regard to cybervictimization, 82.8% of all participating students reported being involved in cybervictimization at least once or twice, and 13.8% at least sometimes in the previous 4 months. Overall frequency analysis showed that the most common cyberbullying types in our sample were sending mean, cruel or threatening messages online to someone they know (9.6%) and denigration (8.6%), followed by impersonation (4.9%), exclusion (4.3%), and outing (3.6%).

As for cyberbullying typologies, also with regard to cybervictimization, the most widespread forms in our sample were receiving mean, cruel or threatening messages online (8.8%) and social network profile theft (6.7%), followed by outing (5.1%), exclusion (5.1%), and denigration (4.4%). We then analysed students' involvement in cyberbullying and cybervictimization, also considering gender-significant differences (see Table 10.2). To this aim, we used the categorical classification cut-off 'at least sometimes' for the four possible levels of involvement in cyberbullying and then for cybervictimization to look for gender differences. We used odds ratios (OR) to measure strengths of relationships because (unlike chi-squares) they are not influenced by sample sizes.

Boys were more involved than girls in overall cyberbullying; the odds ratio was 1.87 times greater for boys than for girls. Results underline that boys were involved in all cyberbullying types. In particular, looking also at gender differences, the most frequent forms of cyberbullying in our sample were flaming (12.1% vs. 7.1%) and denigration (11.3% vs. 6.0%); the respective odds ratios were 1.81 and 3.60 greater for boys than for girls.

Girls were more involved than boys in overall cybervictimization; the odds ratio was 0.73 greater for girls than for boys. Flaming (7.9% vs 9.7%) and impersonation (7.1% vs 6.4%) were the most widespread cybervictimization types, among both boys and girls. However, no significant gender differences were found with regard to cybervictimization types.

Table 10.2 Gender differences in cyberbullying and cybervictimization involvement in Italy

		Male	Female
Total cyberbullying			
	N	181	119
	%	40.0	26.3
	OR (C.I.)		1.87*** (1.41–2.47)
Flaming			
	N	55	32
	%	12.1	7.1
	OR (C.I.)		1.81* (1.15–2.87)
Denigration			
	N	51	27
	%	11.3	6.0
	OR (C.I.)		2.00* (1.23–3.25)
Impersonation			
	N	34	10
	%	7.5	2.2
	OR (C.I.)		3.60**(1.75–7.37)
Outing			
	N	27	6
	%	6.0	1.3
	OR (C.I.)		4.72***(1.93–11.55)
Exclusion			
	N	33	9
	%	7.3	2.0
	OR (C.I.)		3.88***(1.83–8.20)
		Male	Female
Total cybervictimization			
	N	332	358
	%	73.3	79.0
	OR (C.I.)		0.73* (.53–99)
Flaming			
	N	36	44
	%	7.9	9.7
	OR (C.I.)		0.80 (.51–1.27)
Denigration			
	N	22	18
	%	4.9	4.0
	OR (C.I.)		1.23 (0.65–2.33)

(continued)

Table 10.2 (continued)

		Male	Female
Impersonation			
	N	32	29
	%	7.1	6.4
	OR (C.I.)		1.11 (0.66–1.87)
Outing			
	N	28	18
	%	6.2	4.0
	OR (C.I.)		1.60 (0.87–2.92)
Exclusion			
	N	24	22
	%	5.3	4.9
	OR (C.I.)		1.09 (0.61–1.98)

Notes: *OR* odds ratio, *C.I.* confidence interval

Risk and Protective Factors

The Tabby instrument consists of several dimensions included as possible different levels of risk factors associated with children's and adolescents' involvement in cyberbullying and cybervictimization.

Tables 10.3 and 10.4 show the relationship between the risk factors and involvement in cyberbullying and cybervictimization. Due to the correlational nature of these data, it is not possible to establish a causal relationship, only the strength of the relationship between proximal and distal risk factors. With regard to cyberbullying, knowing all online contacts personally ($r = -0.11$) and parental education on Internet safety ($r = -0.15$) were negatively related to students' involvement as cyberbullies. Cyberbullying was correlated with spending time online ($r = 0.15$), high levels of Internet addiction ($r = 0.09$), high levels of risk perception ($r = 0.23$) and perception of high popularity among peers ($r = 0.16$). School bullying and cyberbullying were correlated ($r = 0.17$), while no significant associations were found between cyberbullying and school victimization (see Table 10.3). Cybervictimization was related to being female ($r = -0.07$) and was positively associated with knowing all contacts on social networks personally ($r = 0.07$). Cybervictimization was also related to school victimization ($r = 0.07$) and to high levels of risk perception ($r = 0.10$).

Table 10.3 Correlations between cyberbullying and risk factors in Italy

	1.	2.	3.	4.	5.	6.	7.	8.	9.	10.	11.	12.	13.	14.	15.
1. Cyberbullying	–														
2. Gender (male = 1)	0.14**	–													
3. Age	0.17**	0.05	–												
4. Presence of social network profile(s)	0.13**	–0.04	0.23**	–											
5. Personally know all friends on social network	–0.11**	0.06	–0.01	0.06*	–										
6. Hours a day online	0.15**	–0.02	0.21**	0.33**	–0.09**	–									
7. Good academic achievement	–0.03	–0.03	0.01	–0.07*	0.06	–0.09**	–								
8. School bullying	0.17**	0.21**	0.08*	0.06	0.06	0.11**	–0.11**	–							
9. School victim	0.06	0.09**	–0.08*	0.008	0.007	0.02	–0.04	0.28**	–						
10. Internet addiction	0.09**	–0.10**	0.13**	0.32**	–0.05	0.41**	–0.07*	0.02	0.04	–					
11. Risk perception	0.23**	0.13**	0.05	0.07*	–0.06	0.19**	–0.17**	0.35**	0.32**	0.17**	–				
12. Parents talk with child about Internet safety	–0.15**	–0.22**	–0.21**	–0.06	0.11**	–0.06	0.17**	–0.20**	–0.01	–0.05	–0.17**	–			
13. Parents/significant adult not among child's online contacts	–0.04	–0.09**	0.007	0.09**	–0.008	0.02	0.08*	–0.14**	–0.04	–0.04	–0.02	0.14**	–		
14. Perceived popularity among peers	0.16**	0.20**	0.04	0.13**	–0.04	0.13**	0.04	0.17**	–0.01	0.11**	0.07	–0.09**	–0.05	–	
15. Teachers talk with child about Internet safety	–0.06	–0.05	–0.21**	–0.04	0.13**	–0.08*	0.09**	–0.09**	–0.03	–0.05	–0.11**	0.36**	0.04	0.02	–

Note: *$p < 0.05$; **$p < 0.01$; ***$p < 0.000$. All variables are standardized

A logistic regression analysis was then performed to evaluate the role that the risk factors included in our survey could have in students' involvement in cyberbullying and cybervictimization. The same predictors were used for both cyberbullying and cybervictimization. The model under investigation was based on the ecological approach to explain how a set of risk factors related to individual, interpersonal and social levels can influence youth involvement in these phenomena (Baldry et al. 2015).

As shown in Table 10.5, boys were more at risk of being involved in cyberbullying (OR = 1.62); being older and not knowing all online contacts personally (OR = 0.75) were associated with the involvement in cyberbullying. Students reporting high levels of perceived risk and popularity among peers were respectively 1.40 and 1.25 times more at risk of being involved in cyberbullying.

With regard to cybervictimization (see Table 10.6), females and younger students were 0.66 and 0.82 more at risk of being cybervictimized. Students at risk of cybervictimization also showed high levels of risk perception (OR = 1.33).

Conclusions and Policy Implications for Italy

Minors' Legal Responsibility for Cyberbullying and Other Offences

In the Italian legal system, the under-14 minor cannot be impugned (Article 97 of the Criminal Code) and therefore he/she cannot be responsible for his/her actions that may constitute any type of offence, by applying the normal substantive and procedural rules. It is believed that the minor has supposed immaturity arising from his/her young age, and a criminal responsibility exemption takes place. Any 'deviant', 'anti-social' behaviour which could be considered as a criminal offence from 14 onwards (stealing, threats, physical attacks with injuries) cannot be addressed from a criminal point of view.

This is also true for any 'sexual' activity, which could also be related to cyberbullying (cybersexting). Being under 14 implies an age where there is an alleged incapability in the adoption of certain decisions, particularly

Table 10.4 Correlations between cybervictimization and risk factors in Italy

	1.	2.	3.	4.	5.	6.	7.	8.	9.	10.	11.	12.	13.	14.	15.
1. Cybervictimization	1														
2. Gender (male = 1)	-0.07*														
3. Age	-0.06	0.05	–												
4. Presence of social network profile(s)	0.03	-0.04	0.23**	–											
5. Personally know all friends on social network	0.07*	0.06	-0.01	0.06*	–										
6. Number of hours/day online	0.04	-0.02	0.21**	0.33**	-0.09**	–									
7. Good academic achievement	-0.03	-0.03	0.01	-0.07*	0.06	-0.09**	–								
8. School bullying	0.04	0.21**	0.08*	0.06	0.06	0.11**	-0.11**	–							
9. School victim	0.07*	0.09**	-0.08*	0.008	0.007	0.02	-0.04	0.28**	–						
10. Internet addiction	0.04	-0.10**	0.13**	0.32**	-0.005	0.41**	-0.07*	0.02	0.04	–					
11. Risk perception	0.10**	0.13**	0.05	0.07*	-0.06	0.19**	-0.17**	0.35**	0.32**	0.17**	–				
12. Parents talk with child about Internet safety	-0.009	-0.22**	-0.21**	-0.06	0.11**	-0.06	0.17**	-0.20**	-0.01	-0.05	-0.17**	–			
13. Parents/significant adult not among child's online contacts	0.06	-0.09**	0.007	0.09**	-0.008	0.02	0.08*	-0.14**	-0.04	-0.04	-0.02	-0.17**	–		
14. Perceived popularity among peers at school	-0.04	0.20**	0.04	0.13**	-0.04	0.13**	0.04	0.17**	-0.01	0.11**	0.07	-0.09**	0.14**	–	
15. Teachers talk with child about Internet safety	0.02	-0.05	-0.05	-0.04	0.13**	-0.08*	0.09**	-0.09**	-0.03	-0.05	-0.11**	0.36**	0.04	0.02	–

Note: *$p < 0.05$; **$p < 0.01$; ***$p < 0.000$. All variables are standardized

regarding the sexual sphere, so any action against an under-14 boy or girl, regardless of the apparent willingness of the one sharing a sexual image, could be considered a crime for anyone using and sharing this information.

It is classified as sexual violence when, according to art. 609 quarter of the criminal code ("Sexual acts with a minor"), an adult conducts any sexual action with a child under 14, even in the absence of threats and violent acts; if an adult engages in sexual activities with a person who is apparently consenting, it is still considered a crime. With sexting, there is not always direct contact with the victim, so it could fall under the criminal provision of art. 600 *quarter* criminal code (possession of paedopornographic material). These are rules that invoke the principle of under 14 substantial incapacity at the moment of behaviors' perpetration, that cause effects on third parties and society (crime) or on themselves (choices which have implications on personal sphere).

In terms of literature and political debate in general, it is necessary to remember how numerous the appeals are to lower the legal age of consent, and hence of impugnability, on the basis that today's teenagers have developed a greater confidence in their choices, also through the new communication systems.

The law foresees a specific crime, stalking (art. 612 bis, criminal code), as a repeated set of actions such as harassment and threats that cause the victim to reach a state of serious and lasting anxiety and a reasonable state of fear for his/her safety or for the people close to him/her, affecting his/her life. The person found responsible for these criminal acts can be sentenced to a period of imprisonment ranging from 6 months to 4 years. Very few cases of cyberbullying would fall under the category of stalking, but many of the mechanisms taking place in cyberbullying resemble stalking.

The Italian Anti-cyberbullying Law

In Italy a law against cyberbullying was introduced on 3 June 2017 (Law 29 May 2017 n. 71 –"Provisions for the Protection of the Child for the Prevention and Fight Against Cyber Bullying"). The aim of this law is to prevent and compare the diffusion of cyberbullying among minors. The law focuses on prevention, protection and education of minors involved both as cybervictims and cyberbullies, and entrusts a central role to school institutions such as agencies of education and promotion of a healthy web culture (for details see paragraph on Teachers' Duties).

The introduction of the above-cited law constituted a first necessary step in addressing, defining and penalizing cyberbullying behaviours.

For the first time in Italian legislation, cyberbullying has a legal definition: "*any use of the Internet to offend, threaten, abuse, blackmail, denigrate, and steal the identity of minors*". The law also provides some useful direction in preventing and comparing the diffusion of cyberbullying among youth and introduces some important innovations such as the criminalization of the distorted use of the Internet aimed to offend, defame, threaten or steal the identity of a minor. In fact, minors (older than 14 years) who have cyberbullied another minor can be warned by the police commissioner. The warning procedure provides the minor and their parents (or other person exercising parental responsibility) summons from the police commissioner. The effects of the warning procedure cease at the age of majority.

Furthermore, the law allows cybervictims and/or their parents to ask website hosts and social network platforms to remove and block abusive contents within 48 hours.

With regard to the central role recognized to schools and teachers in educating, preventing and comparing cyberbullying among pupils, the law provides clear indications about the need to train school staff, to identify and appoint a teacher to lead initiatives against cyberbullying, and to promote students' active participation in preventing cyberbullying.

Teachers' Duties

Normally teachers are considered as having a public service role because they do not perform merely material jobs, but exercise an activity regulated in the same forms of public functions but characterized by a lack of decision-making proper of this kind of job (Article. 358 pc). As such, under art. 331 of the Code of Criminal Procedure, teachers must report to the

Table 10.5 Logistic regression for cyberbullying in Italy

Variable	B(SE)	OR	95 C.I. for OR Lower bound	Upper bound
Gender (male = 1)	0.48 (0.18)	1.62**	1.15	2.29
Age	0.28 (0.09)	1.32**	1.09	1.59
Presence of social network profile(s)	0.15 (0.12)	1.16	0.92	1.47
Personally know all friends on social network	−0.29 (0.10)	0.75**	0.61	0.91
Hours a day online	0.13 (0.09)	1.14	0.95	1.36
Good academic achievement	0.06 (0.09)	1.07	0.90	1.26
School bullying	0.15 (0.09)	1.16	0.96	1.41
School victim	0.02 (0.09)	1.02	0.85	1.22
Internet addiction	−0.02 (.09)	0.98	0.81	1.19
Risk perception	0.34 (0.09)	1.40***	1.17	1.68
Parents talk with child about Internet safety	−0.11 (0.09)	0.89	0.74	1.08
Parents/significant adult not among child's online contacts	−0.04 (0.08)	0.96	0.81	1.13
Perceived popularity among peers at school	0.22 (0.09)	1.25*	1.05	1.48
Teachers talk with child about Internet safety	0.02 (0.09)	1.02	0.85	1.22

Notes: *$p < 0.05$; **$p < 0.01$; ***$p < 0.000$. $R^2 = 0.12$ (Cox and Snell), 0.17 (Nagelkerke), $\chi2(14) = 97.10$***. All variables are standardized
OR odds ratio, C.I. confidence interval, S.E. standard error

investigative police or to the public prosecutor the news – that is, the existence according to the available elements of which they are aware – of a punishable crime they have known during the exercise or because of their functions. Omission in this case constitutes an offence (Penal Code Section 362).

Teachers are also invested with a particular role that is defined in the court system as "guarantee position" that imposes a series of intervention activities so that the "weak" subjects in their care, that is the pupils during school or extra-curricular activities, are not put in a dangerous situation from which may arise harmful situations. Under the article 40 of the criminal code, who *"does not prevent an event that they have a legal duty to prevent, is equivalent to cause it"*.

Table 10.6 Logistic regression for cybervictimization in Italy

Variable	B(SE)	OR	95 C.I. for OR	
			Lower bound	Upper bound
Gender (male = 1)	−0.41 (0.19)	0.66*	0.46	0.96
Age	−0.20 (0.10)	0.82*	0.67	0.99
Presence of social network profile(s)	0.26 (0.14)	1.30 [†]	0.99	1.70
Personally know all friends on social network	0.15 (0.11)	1.16	0.94	1.44
Hours a day online	0.097 ,104	1.10	0.90	1.35
Good academic achievement	0.05 (0.09)	1.06	0.88	1.27
School bullying	0.06 (0.11)	1.06	0.85	1.32
School victim	0.09 (0.11)	1.10	0.88	1.37
Internet addiction	0.01 (0.10)	1.01	0.83	1.24
Risk perception	0.28 (0.11)	1.33**	1.07	1.65
Parents talk with child about Internet safety	−0.08 (0.10)	0.93	0.76	1.13
Parents/significant adult not among child's online contacts	0.12 (0.09)	1.12	0.95	1.33
Perceived popularity among peers at school	−0.11 (0.09)	0.90	0.75	1.08
Teachers talk with child about Internet safety	0.04 (0.10)	1.04	0.86	1.27

Notes: [†]$p < 0.10$; *$p < 0.05$; **$p < 0.01$; ***$p < 0.000$. $R^2 = 0.044$ (Cox and Snell), 0.07 (Nagelkerke), $\chi 2(14) = 33.57$**. All variables are standardized
OR odds ratio, *C.I.* confidence interval, *S.E.* standard error

It should be remembered as the school personnel's guarantee position to the subjects in their care is configured differently depending first, on age and degree of maturity reached by the students as well as the circumstances of the case and, secondly, by the personnel's specific tasks, but it is in general characterized by the existence of supervision duty of students in order to prevent that the same cause harm to others or themselves, or that they may be exposed to predictable sources of risk or danger.

Policy Recommendation for Italy

From a policy recommendation point of view, we recomand the following steps for Italy:

Raising Public Awareness

a) Disseminate information on the net and Internet Communication Technology (ICT) safe use. Raise people's awareness about cyberbullying, and the negative impact and emotional consequences for both bullies and victims.
b) Promote information, experience and best practices exchange between stakeholders at national and EU levels.

The Role of Teachers and School Staff in Preventing Cyberbullying

a) Train teachers about cyberbullying, prevention, management and resolution. Training teachers could be the first step towards the effective reduction and prevention of the phenomenon.
b) Trained teachers could use their expertise in order to make students think about their risky online behaviours and about their online experiences. Supporting students in debating and exchanging opinions about their online habits could be a great ploy to make them think about the risks and the traps they face in cyberspace.

Improving School Climate

a) Each school should adopt clear policies with regard to the Internet and mobile phone use. With regard to the use of computers, virtual learning environments and access to the Internet, it is necessary for schools to use filter and tracking software on all computers.
b) Each school should have clear and well-known anti-cyberbullying rules. Anti-bullying rules have to be read and discussed with students and their parents. All students must be aware that no incident of cyberbullying will be ignored: victims will be supported and bullies will deal with the consequences of their actions.
c) Increase students' willingness to report cyberbullying to teachers and school administrators. Students have to know that every complaint will be carefully examined by trained teachers.

Promoting Active Participation of Youth in Preventing Cyberbullying

a) Prevent and reduce students' involvement in cyberbullying, it is necessary to involve them in activities aimed at promoting and defining rules for a safer online environment, with the aim of better understanding their views and experiences concerning the use of the communication technologies.
b) Sensitize children to the correct and proper use of social networks and smartphones. It is important to teach adolescents the relevance of protecting their privacy online and strategies to protect themselves while online, as well as how to protect themselves from the most common online traps.

Obtain Financial Support

a) Establish helpdesks (funded at a national and/or at a European level). Promote the existence at a national level of helpdesks aimed to raise people's awareness of cyberbullying and to help and support students, teachers and parents. The helpdesks could also be a reference point for children to report online illegal content and harmful behaviours.
b) Develop a prevention programme in schools to be included in the school curricula.

Acknowledgments This publication and the study presented have been produced with the financial support of the Daphne programme of the European Union. European Daphne III Program (Project JUST/2011/DAP/AG/3259) Tabby Trip. Threat Assessment of Bullying Behaviour in Youth. Transferring Internet Preventive procedures in Europe. The contents of this article are the sole responsibility of the authors and can in no way be taken to reflect the views of the European Commission. No conflict of interest is present.

References

Baldry, A. C., Farrington, D. P., & Sorrentino, A. (2015). "Am I at risk of cyberbullying"? A narrative review and conceptual framework for research on risk of cyberbullying and cybervictimization: The risk and needs assessment approach. *Aggression and Violent Behavior, 23*, 36–51. https://doi.org/10.1016/j.avb.2015.05.014

Baldry, A. C., Farrington, D. P., & Sorrentino, A. (2016a). Cyberbullying in youth: A pattern of disruptive behaviour. *Psicología Educativa, 22*(1), 19–26. https://doi.org/10.1016/j.pse.2016.02.001

Baldry, A. C., Sorrentino, A., & Farrington, D. P. (2016b). Cyberbullying does parental online supervision and youngsters' willingness to report to an adult reduce the risk? In A. Kapardis & D. P. Farrington (Eds.), *The psychology of crime, policing and courts* (pp. 57–74). Oxon: Routledge.

Brighi, A., Guarini, A., Melotti, G., Galli, S., & Genta, M. L. (2012). Predictors of victimisation across direct bullying, indirect bullying and cyberbullying. *Emotional and Behavioural Difficulties, 17*(3–4), 375–388. https://doi.org/10.1080/13632752.2012.704684

Eurispes – Telefono Azzurro. (2007). *8 Rapporto Nazionale sulla Condizione dell'Infanzia e dell'Adolescenza*. Retrieved from http://www.azzurro.it/sites/default/files/Materiali/InfoConsigli/Ricerche%20e%20indagini/sintesirapportoinfanziaadolescenza8.pdf

Menesini, E., Nocentini, A., & Calussi, P. (2011). The measurement of cyberbullying: Dimensional structure and relative item severity and discrimination. *Cyberpsychology, Behavior, and Social Networking, 14*, 267–274. https://doi.org/10.1089/cyber.2010.0002

Menesini, E., Calussi, P., & Nocentini, A. (2012). Cyberbullying and traditional bullying. In Q. Li, D. Cross, & P. K. Smith (Eds.), *Cyberbullying in the global playground: Research from international perspectives* (pp. 245–262). Chichester: Wiley-Blackwell.

Olweus, D. (1995). Bullying or peer abuse at school: Facts and intervention. *Current Directions in Psychological Science, 4*(6), 196–200. https://doi.org/10.1111/1467-8721.ep10772640

Palermiti, A. L., Servidio, R., Bartolo, M. G., & Costabile, A. (2017). Cyberbullying and self-esteem: An Italian study. *Computers in Human Behavior, 69*, 136–141. https://doi.org/10.1016/j.chb.2016.12.026

Smith, P. K., Mahdavi, J., Carvalho, M., Fisher, S., Russell, S., & Tippett, N. (2008). Cyberbullying: Its nature and impact in secondary school pupils. *Journal of Child Psychology and Psychiatry, 49*, 376–385. https://doi.org/10.1111/j.1469-7610.2007.01846.x

Vieno, A., Gini, G., Lenzi, M., Pozzoli, T., Canale, N., & Santinello, M. (2014). Cybervictimization and somatic and psychological symptoms among Italian middle school students. *The European Journal of Public Health, 25*(3), 433–437. https://doi.org/10.1093/eurpub/cku191

11

Cyberbullying in Spain

Juan Calmaestra, Tatiana García-Vélez,
and Antonio Maldonado

The Prevalence of Cyberbullying and Cybervictimization in Spain

Cyberbullying has been a research topic in Spain for approximately 10 years. The first major works on this topic were published by Ombudsman-UNICEF (2007) and Ortega-Ruiz et al. (2008). The first work (Ombudsman-UNICEF 2007) showed a very low incidence rate of cyberbullying – only 0.4% of the respondents could be considered as frequent victims of cyberbullying. Moreover, 5.1% of the sample were regarded to be occasional victims of this problem. The percentage of frequent cyberbullies amounted to 0.6%, while occasional cyberbullies were 4.8%. A year later, the first research work focused on cyberbullying in Spain was published (Ortega-Ruiz et al. 2008), and showed higher

J. Calmaestra (✉)
Department of Psychology, Universidad de Córdoba, Córdoba, Spain

T. García-Vélez • A. Maldonado
Department of Developmental and Educational Psychology, Universidad
Autónoma de Madrid, Madrid, Spain

© The Author(s) 2018   **251**
A. C. Baldry et al. (eds.), *International Perspectives on Cyberbullying*, Palgrave Studies in
Cybercrime and Cybersecurity, https://doi.org/10.1007/978-3-319-73263-3_11

percentages, as follows: frequent cybervictims 1.5%, occasional cybervictims 9.3%; frequent cyberbullies 1.7%; occasional cyberbullies 5.7%; frequent cyberbullies/victims 0.6%; and occasional cyberbullies/victims 7.8%,

In light of these studies, the number of publications in Spain has been increasing almost every year. According to the Scopus database, a total of 132 papers were published by at least one Spanish author from 2008 to 2017 using 'cyberbullying' as a key word (1 in 2008; 2 in 2009; 4 in 2010; 2 in 2011; 17 in 2012; 11 in 2013; 14 in 2014; 31 in 2015; 22 in 2016; and 28 in 2017).

Our second research work (Ortega-Ruiz et al. 2009) had a sample population of 1,671 individuals. The cybervictimization rates using cell phones were 3.7% occasional and 0.5% frequent, while the rates using the Internet were 6.2% occasional and 1.3% frequent.

In 2010, other Spanish research teams began to publish their works on this topic. Therefore, a study with 1,431 participants, carried out by a research team from the University of Deusto (Bilbao), found that 30.1% of the respondents had suffered some type of cyberbullying (Estévez et al. 2010), while 44.1% had displayed cyberbullying behaviors (Calvete et al. 2010). On the other hand, 22.8% of the total sample considered themselves as cybervictims and cyberbullies at the same time (Estévez et al. 2010).

A research team composed of professors at the University of Valencia and University Pablo de Olavide (Seville), in a study with a sample of 2,101 teenagers aged from 11 to 17 years, found an involvement rate as cybervictims of 24.6% via cell phone, and 29% via the Internet (Buelga et al. 2010).

During the same year, a team from the University of Oviedo published a paper based on a research project with a sample of 638 students, highlighting that 35.4% to 51.9% of students had an experience with cyberbullying (Álvarez-García et al. 2011).

The number of publications, as stated above, shows a dramatic increase from 2011. As a summary of all these research efforts, it is advisable to consult the work by Zych et al. (2016), a systematic review of all the Spanish studies up to 2015 which were published in journals included in the prestigious Web of Science or Scopus databases. The data collected in this publication vary from approximately 5% to 25% of frequent cybervictimization. Consequently, this review underlines the diversity of criteria used when studying this topic, which hampers the comparison between different sets of prevalence data. Furthermore, the authors pointed out that prevalence doubled when evaluated with several-item instruments, in contrast with research carried out with single-item instruments.

One of the latest studies published in Spain, based on the largest and most representative sample in this country, is the report by Save the Children (Sastre et al. 2016), with a total of 21.487 participants from all the Autonomous Communities of Spain. This study revealed that 6.9% of the high school population had suffered cybervictimization in the previous two months, while 3.3% admitted they had committed cyberbullying.

The Present Study

Participants and Digital Uses

For the Tabby Trip project, a total of 2,360 Spanish students (males: 52.0%, females: 48.0%), age 9–18 years (M = 13.14, sd = 1.811), participated in the first wave of data collected for the study. Participants were recruited from 15 different schools in Madrid. More specifically, there were 4 primary education schools (10–12 years old), 7 secondary schools (12–16 years old), and 4 primary and secondary schools (10–16 years old). Moreover, 4 of these educational centers were public, while 11 were state schools.

Most of these students (66.5%) had accounts in at least one social network. Over 60% of them had people's contacts in their social networks who they did not know personally. Moreover, 23.5% of the sample felt they were not popular at all among their friends. Just over 15% of the sample had never received any training on Internet security from their parents, and almost the identical percentage had never received any training on Internet security from their teachers. Further details of the whole sample are presented in Table 11.1.

Table 11.1 Descriptive statistics for the sample in Spain

	N = 2360
Gender (males)	52.0%
Age	M = 13.14(sd = 1.81)
Presence of social network profile(s)	66.5% at least one
Personally know all friends on social network	39.2% everyone
Perceived popularity among peers	23.5% not at all
Parents/significant adult among child's online contacts	28.1% no
Parents talk with child about Internet safety	15.9% never
Teachers talk with child about Internet safety	15.8% never
Hours a day online	37.5% 2/4 h
School achievement	10.4% below average
School bullying	83.4% never
	12.0% once or twice
	4.6% > than twice
School victimization	81.0% never
	11.5% once or twice
	7.5% > than twice
Cyberbullying	71.6% never
	12.8% once or twice
	15.6% > than twice
Cybervictimization	69.5% never
	15.0% once or twice
	15.5% > than twice
Internet addiction	M = 14.18 (sd = 5.48)
Risk perception	M = 2.11 (sd = 3.01)

Procedure

The sampling of educational centers was carried out depending on access to schools, but they represented the sociocultural diversity of Madrid. Firstly, e-mails presenting the project were sent to all educational centers in metropolitan Madrid as well as in the Northern Area of the province. Secondly, we scheduled a meeting with the management teams of those centers that showed their interest in participating in the study. Finally, when the permission was obtained from the management teams, parental passive consent was requested so that their children filled the question-naire online.

Most data were collected from November to December 2013, although in some centers the questionnaire was carried out in January 2014 due to organizational issues.

The researchers of the project visited the different educational centers during the data collection period. The students, in classrooms equipped with computers, entered in the website of the project (www.tabby.eu) and filled the questionnaire online. For logistical reasons, paper-based questionnaires had to be conducted in two centers, and later the results were transferred to the website of the project.

The questionnaire included the definitions of 'bullying' and 'cyberbullying' in order to avoid bias in the data collection. The definitions were as follows:

A student is being bullied or victimized when he or she is exposed, repeatedly and over time, to negative actions on the part of one or more other students. Negative actions can include physical contact, words, making faces or dirty gestures, and intentional exclusion from a group. An additional criterion of bullying is an imbalance in strength: The student who is exposed to the negative actions has difficulty defending himself or herself. (Olweus 1995, p. 197)

Cyberbullying is as an aggressive and intentional act, carried out by a group or an individual, using electronic forms of contact, repeatedly over time against a victim who cannot easily defend himself/herself. (Smith et al., 2008, p. 376)

Confidentiality and anonymity of the data collected were ensured. In the same way, students were informed that their participation was voluntary, and they could stop filling the questionnaire if they so wished. Having completed the questionnaire, the results were sent to a database guarded by the Italian research team.

Measures

To measure cyberbullying, we followed the same methodology and instruments adopted for the whole project. The questionnaire used to measure cyberbullying (α_{total} = 0.89) was divided into two scales, a five-item scale for cyberbullying ($\alpha_{cyberbullying}$ = 0.84) and another five-item scale for cybervictimization ($\alpha_{cybervictimization}$ = 0.83).

Findings

Prevalence of School Bullying and Cyberbullying

With regard to school bullying, 16.6% of the sample was involved as aggressors, 12% presenting a frequency of once or twice in the previous 4 months, and 4.6% with a higher frequency. The percentage of bullying victims was higher, as 19% of the sample was involved in the last 4 months (11.5% presenting a frequency of once or twice in the previous 4 months, while 7.5% reported a higher frequency).

On the other hand, with regard to cyberbullying, the percentages were higher. A total of 12.8% of the sample had committed cyberbullying once or twice in the previous 4 months, while 15.6% had done it with a higher frequency. According to our data, 15% of the sample had suffered cybervictimization at least once or twice in the previous 4 months, while 15.5% had experienced cybervictimization with a higher frequency.

The most frequent methods of cyberbullying used by the aggressors were (in this order): flaming (20.6%), exclusion (11.8%), outing (8.1%), and denigration (8.6%). The least used type of cyberbullying was impersonation (3.2%). The victims reported the same order in the frequency of each type of cyberbullying, although the percentages varied slightly (flaming: 15.0%; exclusion: 10.9%; outing: 10.3%; denigration: 8.6%; impersonation: 6.5%). To this aim, we used the categorical classification cut-off 'at least sometimes'.

For this project, we also considered the possible differences among the methods of cybervictimization and cyberbullying between girls and boys (see Table 11.2). We used odds ratios (OR) to measure the strengths of the relationships. In general, boys were more involved than girls as cyberbullies (31.8 boys vs. 24.8 girls). Girls, on the contrary, presented a higher involvement rate as cybervictims when compared to boys, although the differences were not statistically significant (29.4 boys vs. 31.6 girls).

Focusing on the different methods of cyberbullying, boys were involved in a higher rate than girls in all the variations, although differences in 'impersonation' are not statistically significant.

Differences increase in denigration (OR = 0.61), exclusion (OR = 0.62), and outing (OR = 0.62). In all types of cyberbullying, the same

Table 11.2 Gender differences in cyberbullying and cybervictimization involvement in Spain

		Male	Female
Total cyberbullying	N	390	281
	%	31.8	24.8
	OR (C.I.)	0.71*** (0.59–0.85)	
Flaming	N	278	209
	%	22.6	18.5
	OR (C.I.)	0.77*(0.63–0.95)	
Denigration	N	87	50
	%	7.1	4.4
	OR (C.I.)	0.61** (0.42–0.87)	
Impersonation	N	43	33
	%	3.5	2.9
	OR (C.I.)	0.83 (0.52–1.31)	
Outing	N	119	71
	%	9.7	6.3
	OR (C.I.)	0.62**(0.46–0.85)	
Exclusion	N	173	105
	%	14.1	9.3
	OR (C.I.)	0.62*** (0.48–0.81)	
		Male	Female
Total cybervictimization	N	361	358
	%	29.4	31.6
	OR (C.I.)	1.11 (0.93–1.32)	
Flaming	N	159	194
	%	12.9	17.1
	OR (C.I.)	1.39**(1.11–1.75)	
Denigration	N	108	114
	%	8.8	10.1
	OR (C.I.)	1.16 (0.88–1.53)	
Impersonation	N	87	66
	%	7.1	5.8
	OR (C.I.)	0.81 (0.58–1.13)	
Outing	N	136	106
	%	11.1	9.4
	OR (C.I.)	0.83 (0.64–1.08)	
Exclusion	N	160	98
	%	13.0	8.7
	OR (C.I.)	0.63***(0.49–0.83)	

Notes: *OR* odds ratio, *C.I.* confidence interval

order of use was maintained between boys and girls. With regard to cyber-victimization, there was a higher percentage of girls than boys victimized through flaming (OR = 1.39) and denigration (OR = 1.16), although the differences were not statistically significant. Nevertheless, there was a higher number of boys being victims of exclusion (OR = 0.63), imperson-ation (OR = 0.81), and outing (OR = 0.83), although again the differ-ences were not statistically significant. It should be highlighted that the frequency order of victimization for each of the methods changes for boys and girls, and they both only coincide in reporting that the least frequent method of cybervictimization is impersonation. The frequency order of victimization for boys is exclusion, flaming, outing, denigration, and impersonation. For girls, however, the frequency order of victimization is flaming, denigration, outing, exclusion, and impersonation.

Risk and Protective Factors

One of the objectives of the Tabby project consisted of determining the risks and protective factors in cases of cybervictimization and cyberbully-ing. For this purpose, the Tabby Checklist collected very diverse informa-tion from specific variables that could play a key role in cybervictimization and cyberbullying behaviors.

In order to take the first gradualist approach to these realities, we car-ried out a correlation analysis between involvement in cyberbullying and cybervictimization and all the variables collected (see Tables 11.3 and 11.4). It should be noted that correlations do not show causality, but only the relationship between variables – consequently, it is impossible to establish cause-effect relationships between them. However, it is rele-vant to know these relationships to understand which phenomena are produced together and which are not. With regard to cyberbullying, the variable most strongly correlated was being involved as a bully in tradi-tional bullying ($r = 0.44$). This was followed by the perception of the risk of being involved in these problems ($r = 0.39$) and the number of hours connected to the Internet per day ($r = 0.31$). Being a victim of tradi-tional bullying is also an outstanding risk factor ($r = 0.29$), as well as addiction to the Internet ($r = 0.25$). Perceived popularity among peers

Table 11.3 Correlations between cyberbullying and risk factors in Spain

	1.	2.	3.	4.	5.	6.	7.	8.	9.	10.	11.	12.	13.	14.	15.
1. Cyberbullying	–														
2. Gender (female = 1)	-0.07***	–													
3. Age	0.15***	-0.09***	–												
4. Presence of social network profile(s)	0.09***	-0.05*	0.45***	–											
5. Personally know all friends on social network	-0.12***	-0.05*	.28***	-0.10***	–										
6. Hours a day online	0.31***	0.04	0.38***	0.33***	-0.24***	–									
7. Good academic achievement	-0.21***	0.05**	-0.31***	-0.15***	0.18***	-0.27***	–								
8. School bullying	0.44***	-0.08***	-0.03	-0.02	-0.08***	0.15***	-0.15***	–							
9. School victim	0.29***	-0.02	-0.12***	-0.09***	-0.06*	0.09***	-0.07***	0.45***	–						
10. Internet addiction	0.25***	-0.02	0.28**	0.33***	-0.22***	0.44***	-0.23***	0.13***	0.08***	–					
11. Risk perception	0.39***	-0.01	0.05*	0.02	-0.12***	0.15***	-0.19***	0.30***	0.25***	0.23***	–				
12. Parents talk with child about Internet safety	-0.14***	0.16***	-0.17***	-0.09***	0.13***	-0.14***	0.13***	-0.09***	-0.02	-0.10***	-0.04*	–			
13. Parents/significant adult not among child's online contacts	0.09***	-0.06**	0.04†	-0.04†	-0.09**	0.04	-0.07**	0.06**	-0.005	0.06**	0.08**	-0.11***	–		
14. Perceived popularity among peers (both at school and online)	0.22***	-0.16***	0.005	0.08***	-0.02	0.16***	0.04*	0.16***	0.04*	0.12***	0.09***	-0.04†	0.02	–	
15. Teachers talk with child about Internet safety	-0.12***	0.04*	-0.04*	-0.04†	0.09***	-0.11***	0.09***	-0.09***	-0.06**	-0.08***	-0.08***	0.29***	-0.05*	-0.03	–

Note: †p < 0.10; *p < 0.05; **p < 0.01; ***p < 0.000. All variables are standardized

Table 11.4 Correlations between cybervictimization and risk factors in Spain

	1.	2.	3.	4.	5.	6.	7.	8.	9.	10.	11.	12.	13.	14.	15.
1. Cybervictimization	—														
2. Gender (female = 1)	−0.03	—													
3. Age	0.08***	−0.09***	—												
4. Presence of social network profile(s)	0.06**	−0.05*	0.45***	—											
5. Personally know all friends on social network	−0.14***	−0.05*	−0.28***	−0.10***	—										
6. Number of hours/day online	0.27***	0.04	0.38***	0.33***	−0.24***	—									
7. Good academic achievement	−0.18***	0.05**	−0.31***	−0.15***	0.18***	−0.27***	—								
8. School bullying	0.35***	−0.08***	−0.03	−0.02	−0.08***	0.15***	−0.15***	—							
9. School victim	0.48***	−0.02	−0.12***	−0.09***	−0.06*	0.09***	−0.07***	0.45***	—						
10. Internet addiction	0.24***	−0.02	0.28***	0.33***	−0.22***	0.44***	−0.23***	0.13***	0.08***	—					
11. Risk perception	0.39***	−0.01	0.05*	0.02	−0.12***	0.15***	−0.19***	0.30***	0.25***	0.23***	—				
12. Parents talk with child about Internet safety	−0.07***	0.16***	−0.17***	−0.09***	0.13***	−0.14***	0.13***	−0.09***	−0.02	−0.10***	−0.04*	—			
13. Parents/significant adult not among child's online contacts	0.04†	−0.06*	0.04†	−0.04†	−0.09***	0.04	−0.07*	0.06**	−0.005	0.06**	0.08**	−0.11***	—		
14. Perceived popularity among peers at school (both at school and online)	0.13***	−0.16***	0.005	0.08***	−0.02	0.16***	0.04*	0.16***	0.04*	0.12***	0.09***	−0.04†	0.02	—	
15. Teachers talk with child about Internet safety	−0.07***	0.04*	−0.04*	−0.04†	0.09***	−0.11***	0.09***	−0.09***	−0.06**	−0.08***	−0.08***	0.29***	−0.05*	−0.03	—

Note: †$p < 0.10$; *$p < 0.05$; **$p < 0.01$; ***$p < 0.000$. All variables are standardized

(both at school and online) correlates with an intensity similar to the previous variable (r = 0.22). Among the factors that correlated negatively, the following can be highlighted: academic achievement (r = −0.21) and the fact that parents (r = −0.14) or teachers (r = −0.12) talk about Internet safety with minors. Personally know all friends on social network also correlates negatively (r = −0.12).

With regard to cybervictimization, the variables most strongly correlated are the same 5 as in the case of cyberbullying, although they follow a different order. The variable most strongly correlated with cybervictimization is to be a victim of traditional bullying (r = 0.48). A strong relationship is shown again between both types of phenomena − traditional bullying and cyberbullying. The perception of risk (r = 0.39) and being involved as a bully in traditional bullying (r = 0.35) are the other two most related variables, together with the number of hours connected to the Internet per day (r = 0.27) and Internet addiction (r = 0.24). The factors that strongly correlate negatively with cybervictimization are good academic achievement (r = −0.02), personally knowing all their contacts on the Internet (r = −0.14), and again the educational labor on Internet safety carried out by teachers (r = −0.07) and parents (r = −0.07).

In order to improve our understanding of the results, two logistic regressions were carried out by using the 'enter' method, one for cyberbullying and the other for cybervictimization. These regressions allowed us a better understanding of both risk and protection factors in this dynamic (see Tables 11.5 and 11.6).

The same predictors were used for both cyberbullying and cybervictimization. We based our research on the ecological model, which explains the importance of personal and social variables as risk factors involved in this problem (Baldry et al. 2015).

The results of the first regression, whose dependent variable is cyberbullying, show that the model explains approximately 23% of the variance. The biggest risk factor for being a cyberbully is the number of profiles on social networks (OR = 1.54), followed by addiction to the Internet (OR = 1.48), being a bully in traditional bullying (OR = 1.43) and gender (OR = 1.39). The perception of risk (OR = 1.28), the number of hours connected to the Internet (OR = 1.21), being a school victim of bullying (OR = 1.21), and perceived popularity among peers at school

Table 11.5 Logistic regression for cyberbullying in Spain

Variable	B(SE)	OR	95 C.I. for OR Lower bound	95 C.I. for OR Upper bound
Gender (male = 1)	0.33 (0.11)	1.39**	1.11	1.73
Age	0.09 (0.07)	1.09	0.96	1.25
Presence of social network profile(s)	0.43 (0.12)	1.54***	1.22	1.96
Personally know all friends on social network	−0.17 (0.06)	0.84**	0.75	0.94
Hours a day online	0.19 (0.06)	1.21**	1.07	1.36
Good academic achievement	−0.12 (0.06)	0.88*	0.75	0.94
School bullying	0.36 (0.07)	1.43***	1.25	1.63
School victim	0.19 (0.06)	1.21**	1.07	1.36
Internet addiction	0.39 (0.06)	1.48***	1.31	1.68
Risk perception	0.25 (0.06)	1.28***	1.15	1.44
Parents talk with child about Internet safety	−0.07 (.06)	0.94	0.83	1.05
Parents/significant adult not among child's online contacts	0.04 (0.05)	1.05	0.94	1.16
Perceived popularity among peers at school (both at school and online)	0.17 (.06)	1.18**	1.06	1.32
Teachers talk with child about Internet safety	−0.06 (.06)	0.95	0.85	1.06

Notes: $^{t}p < 0.10$; $*p < 0.05$; $**p < 0.01$; $***p < 0.000$. $R^2 = 0.166$ (Cox and Snell), 0.232 (Nagelkerke), $\chi2(15) = 354.197***$. All variables are standardized
OR odds ratio, *C.I.* confidence interval, *S.E.* standard error

(both at school and online) (OR = 1.18) are also noteworthy risk factors. Curiously, being a victim of traditional bullying is another risk factor for being a cyberbully. The most important protection factors, however, are personally knowing all their virtual friends (OR = 0.84) and good academic achievement (OR = 0.88).

Regarding cybervictimization, the regression explains approximately 19% of the variance. Once again, the most outstanding risk factor is being involved in the same role (victim) in traditional bullying (OR = 1.65). The perception of risk (OR = 1.39) and profiles on social networks (OR = 1.35) also arise as relevant risk factors in cybervictimization. As with cyberbullying, addiction to the Internet (OR = 1.34), the number of hours connected to the Internet (OR = 1.15), and being an aggressor in school bullying (OR = 1.14) are three relevant risk factors. Only three

Table 11.6 Logistic regression for cybervictimization in Spain

Variable	B(SE)	OR	95 C.I. for OR Lower bound	Upper bound
Gender (male = 1)	−0.20 (0.11)	0.82[t]	0.66	1.02
Age	−0.05 (.07)	0.95	0.84	1.08
Presence of social network profile(s)	0.30 (0.11)	1.35**	1.08	1.69
Personally know all friends on social network	−0.14 (0.05)	0.87*	0.78	0.97
Hours a day online	0.14 (0.06)	1.15*	1.02	1.29
Good academic achievement	−0.04 (0.06)	0.96	0.86	1.07
School bullying	0.13 (0.06)	1.14*	1.01	1.28
School victim	0.50 (0.07)	1.65***	1.45	1.88
Internet addiction	0.29 (0.06)	1.34***	1.19	1.51
Risk perception	0.33 (0.05)	1.39***	1.25	1.55
Parents talk with child about Internet safety	−0.03 (0.06)	0.97	0.87	1.08
Parents/significant adult not among child's online contacts	−0.12 (.05)	0.89*	0.80	0.99
Perceived popularity among peers at school (both at school and online)	0.05 (0.05)	1.05	0.95	1.17
Teachers talk with child about Internet safety	0.03 (0.05)	1.03	0.93	1.15

Notes: [t]$p < 0.10$; *$p < 0.05$; **$p < 0.01$; ***$p < 0.000$. $R^2 = 0.133$ (Cox and Snell), 0.185 (Nagelkerke), $\chi2(15) = 279.781$***. All variables are standardized
OR odds ratio, *C.I.* confidence interval, *S.E.* standard error

factors have proved to be protectors in the regression: gender (OR = 0.82), personally knowing all their contacts on their social networks (OR = 0.87), and the fact that their parents or other relevant adults are contacts of theirs on their social networks (OR = 0.89).

Conclusions and Policy Implications in Spain

Legal Responsibility of Minors in Cyberbullying and Other Offenses

Cyberbullying as such is not included in the Spanish Criminal Code. In this light, Spanish judges are using the existing criminal code, considering that what happens by using any type of ICT is equal to what happens in physical environments. Although most aggressors in cyberbullying are minors and those younger than 14 cannot be criminally charged, they do have certain responsibilities together with their legal guardians according to the Spanish Organic Law 5/2000, of 12 January, on the Criminal Responsibility of Minors. It is true, moreover, that adolescents aged from 14 to 18 have to comply with judicial measures different from the measures of those of legal age, and all of these are also included in the aforementioned law.

The last reform of the Spanish Criminal Code (in force since 28 October 2015) includes in its Book II several titles referring to crimes that can be committed in cyberbullying situations, as follows:

Crimes against liberty. Among these, the following are highlighted: Threats (Chapter II, Articles 169–71), Constraint (Chapter III, Article 172), and Torture and other crimes against moral integrity (Chapter II, Articles 173–7).

Physical and sexual assault on people under the age of 16; more specifically, Article 183 is focused on punishment and prevention of the phenomenon known as 'grooming'.

Privacy offenses, right of personal portrayal, and inviolability of the home. The crimes refer to discovery, disclosure or dissemination of secrets. Article 197 specifically explains that there may involve imprisonment for those who seize e-mails, images, or private videos (among others) without consent, aiming at further disclosure of their secrets or infringement of their rights to privacy.

Crimes against honor: libel (Chapter I, Articles 205–7) and slander (Chapter II, Articles 208–10).

Falsehoods. These are included in Chapter IV, Article 401, on Usurpation of Civil Status. The term 'civil status' is understood from a legal perspective as the identity of a person. This crime would be closely related to impersonation.

The majority of these offenses require a formal complaint by the victim or their legal guardians to be brought to justice.

Moreover, the Spanish Organic Law 1/1996, of 15 January, on Legal Protection of Minors, partially amending the Civil Code and the Civil Procedure Act (in force since 18 August 2015) gives minors the following rights, among others:

Right to honor, privacy, and personal portrayal, including secrecy of communication.

Right of participation, association, and assembly. Certain types of cyberbullying run against this right (e.g. exclusion).

Right to freedom of expression, within the restrictions of the law in order to ensure the respect of the rights of others.

Right to be heard. Derived from this right, if minors wish to report a cyberbullying offense, adults must hear them and investigate the reported facts.

Moving to a higher-ranking legal document, the Spanish Constitution, in its Article 15, recognizes the right to life, and the right to physical and moral integrity. Furthermore, Article 18 guarantees the right to honor, personal and family privacy, and personal portrayal, as well as secrecy of communication. As can be seen, many of the actions produced in cyberbullying episodes violate the rights included in the Magna Carta.

Teachers' Duties

Teachers have a duty to ensure the integrity of all their students. In Spain, there have been several convictions of educational centers due to 'breach of duty of care' with minors. Court judgments underline the responsibility of the school in terms of custody of their students.

In Andalusia, a region located in southern Spain, as well as in other regions, a bullying intervention protocol has been implemented for alleged acts of school bullying. This protocol has been amended by the Instructions of 11 January 2017 in the cases of cyberbullying and grooming. The document clearly specifies that teachers have a duty to act in cases of cyberbullying, even when the situation has taken place outside the educational center.

Raising Public Awareness

A) Launch of campaigns involving famous and relevant people for youth on the effects of cyberbullying. Recently, there has been an initiative in Spain launched by a rapper with the song 'Se buscan valientes'

('Brave People Wanted') (see: https://youtu.be/omZkxy3wU1c8). These campaigns, however, should be more intense and planned as a global strategy.

Role of Teachers and School Staff in Preventing Cyberbullying

A) Specific training for teachers on cyberbullying (prevention, management, and resolution). Specific tools must be offered, like the Tabby program, of proven efficiency in Spain.
B) Increase the level of authority of teachers, so that cases of cyberbullying can be investigated more frequently and more efficiently.
C) Establish a national protocol so that teachers and school staff know what to do in alleged cases of school bullying and cyberbullying.

Improvement of the School Climate

A) Include in the 'Planes de Convivencia' certain measures to fight against cyberbullying.
B) Involve student helpers and parents, together with teachers, in the prevention of cyberbullying.

Financial Support

A) Establish European research networks on cyberbullying.
B) Fund projects that design and test evidence-based prevention and intervention programs to stop and prevent cyberbullying.

Acknowledgments This publication and the study presented have been produced with the financial support of the Daphne program of the European Union. European Daphne III Program (Project JUST/2011/DAP/AG/3259) Tabby in Internet. Threat Assessment of Bullying Behaviour in Youth. Transferring Internet Preventive procedures in Europe. The contents of this article are the sole responsibility of the authors and can in no way be taken to reflect the views of the European Commission. No conflict of interest is present.

References

Álvarez-García, D., Núñez Pérez, J. C., Álvarez Pérez, L., Dobarro González, A., Rodríguez Pérez, C., & González-Castro, P. (2011). Violencia a través de las tecnologías de la información y la comunicación en estudiantes de secundaria. *Anales de Psicología, 27*(1), 221–230.

Baldry, A. C., Farrington, D. P., & Sorrentino, A. (2015). "Am I at risk of cyberbullying"? A narrative review and conceptual framework for research on risk of cyberbullying and cybervictimization: The risk and needs assessment approach. *Aggression and Violent Behavior, 23*, 36–51. https://doi.org/10.1016/j.avb.2015.05.014

Buelga, S., Cava, M. J., & Musitu, G. (2010). Cyberbullying: Victimización entre adolescentes a través del teléfono móvil y de internet. *Psicothema, 22*(4), 784–789.

Calvete, E., Orue, I., Estévez, A., Villardón, L., & Padilla, P. (2010). Cyberbullying in adolescents: Modalities and aggressors' profile. *Computers in Human Behavior, 26*(5), 1128–1135. https://doi.org/10.1016/j.chb.2010.03.017

Estévez, A., Villardón, L., Calvete, E., Padilla, P., & Orue, I. (2010). Adolescentes víctimas de cyberbullying: prevalencia y características. *Psicología Conductual, 18*(1), 73–89.

Olweus, D. (1995). Bullying or peer abuse at school: Facts and intervention. *Current Directions in Psychological Science, 4*(6), 196–200. https://doi.org/10.1111/1467-8721.ep10772640

Ombudsman-UNICEF. (2007). *Violencia escolar: el maltrato entre iguales en la educación secundaria obligatoria. 1999–2006.* Madrid: Publicaciones de la Oficina del Defensor del Pueblo.

Ortega, R., Elipe, P., Mora-Merchan, J. A., Calmaestra, J., & Vega, E. (2009). The emotional impact on victims of traditional bullying and cyberbullying. A study of Spanish adolescents. *Journal of Psychology, 217*, 197–204. https://doi.org/10.1027/0044-3409.217.4.197

Ortega-Ruiz, R., Calmaestra, J., & Mora-Merchán, J. A. (2008). Cyberbullying. *International Journal of Psychology and Psychological Therapy, 8*(2), 183–192.

Sastre, A., Calmaestra, J., Escorial, A., García, P., Del Moral, C., Perazzo, C., & Ubrich, T. (2016). *Yo a eso no juego: Bullying y Cyberbullying en la infancia.* Madrid: Save The Children.

Smith, P. K., Mahdavi, J., Carvalho, M., Fisher, S., Russell, S., & Tippett, N. (2008). Cyberbullying: Its nature and impact in secondary school pupils.

Journal of Child Psychology and Psychiatry, 49, 376–385. https://doi. org/10.1111/j.1469-7610.2007.01846.x

Zych, I., Ortega-Ruiz, R., & Marín-López, I. (2016). Cyberbullying: A systematic review of research, its prevalence and assessment issues in Spanish studies. *Psicología Educativa, 22*(1), 5–18. https://doi.org/10.1016/j.pse.2016.03.002

Part IV

Conclusions

12

Conclusions and Policy Recommendations

Anna Costanza Baldry, David P. Farrington,
Catherine Blaya, and Anna Sorrentino

Cyberbullying is a serious and rapidly increasing problem in many countries. We hope that this book, which contains information from researchers who were part of the European Union TABBY (*Threat Assessment of Bullying Behaviour in Youth*) project and from world leaders in the field, will help researchers as well as practitioners to increase knowledge and understanding of such a well-known phenomenon which still needs a lot of rigorous and well-planned research.

A. C. Baldry (✉) • A. Sorrentino
Department of Psychology, Università degli Studi della Campania Luigi Vanvitelli, Caserta, Italy

D. P. Farrington
Institute of Criminology, University of Cambridge, Cambridge, UK

C. Blaya
UER Pédagogie Spécialisée - HEP du Canton de Vaud, Lausanne, Switzerland

© The Author(s) 2018
A. C. Baldry et al. (eds.), *International Perspectives on Cyberbullying*, Palgrave Studies in Cybercrime and Cybersecurity, https://doi.org/10.1007/978-3-319-73263-3_12

In this book, we tried to present very useful information about the nature of cyberbullying and about how it is different from traditional school bullying. We also presented a global, comparative perspective on how cyberbullying is defined, its prevalence, and also information about a well-designed and innovative program to try to reduce it.

Out of the research, each participating country in the project also provided a summary of possible recommendations based on empirical data. These address: how to raise public awareness about cyberbullying, the role of teachers and school staff in preventing cyberbullying, how to improve the school climate, how to promote young people's active participation in preventing cyberbullying, the need for parental involvement in preventing cyberbullying, the need for a European strategy in implementing programs to reduce cyberbullying, how to obtain financial support for programs, and legal issues such as whether cyberbullying should be defined as a crime.

In this book, besides providing empirical results, we also wanted to provide very practical advice for teachers, parents, practitioners in general and for young people themselves about how to prevent cyberbullying, what to do if you are victimized, and how to stay out of trouble online either as a victim or as a bully. The TABBY project has produced a useful *checklist* which can be completed online to assess a young person's risk of cyberbullying or cybervictimization and it was used to identify the associated risk factors for cyberbullying by adopting a risk and needs assessment approach.

Based on the findings, and recommendations we also provide at the end in this book, 10 *silver bullet* points about how to reduce the risk of cyberbullying and cybervictimization. These are targeted toward children (e.g. increase their empathy and their likelihood of reporting cyberbullying and intervening to prevent cyberbullying), teachers and school staff (e.g. train them in the understanding and prevention of cyberbullying), the school climate (e.g. promote positive relationships between teachers and students, have explicit anti-bullying policies), parents (e.g. their need to be more knowledgeable about the Internet and to supervise their children's use of the Internet), and public awareness (e.g. publicize the negative effects on children of cybervictimization).

There is a great need for further EU funding of research on cyberbullying. The TABBY project has advanced knowledge greatly, especially in its emphasis on assessing risks and needs in tackling cyberbullying. However, more research is required to establish the key risk factors that encourage cyberbullying and especially the key protective factors that prevent cyberbullying. Information about risk and protective factors should then be used to devise more effective prevention programs that try to reduce risk factors and enhance protective factors. The effectiveness of these programs should be evaluated in high quality experiments in different EU countries.

One could ask at this point whether cyberbullying is all the fault of the web or of the way it is approached and used, or if the problem is much more complex and deserves an array of shared 'holistic', ecological approaches and understandings.

In European countries, the use of the web and of mobile devices such as smartphones constitutes the first way to communicate among young people. This provides many benefits, but it also brings risk especially of cyberbullying. The positive aspect is that research has provided some information about who is at risk and about support and help that can reduce the risk. The TABBY project aimed to increase the awareness of the risk when using the web or any electronic form of communication and to provide information and skills so that young people can protect themselves. The approach used to address cyberbullying in several EU countries and also in the US and Canada is multicomponent and complex. The TABBY model targets a series of individual, interpersonal, social and contextual factors and investigates how they interact, change over time and affect any antisocial behavior. The risk assessment of threats approach is a new approach, commonly and traditionally used in cases of juvenile delinquency, but here it is successfully used to implement the best strategies to address and reduce cyberbullying involvement.

The results, overall, on the risk factors associated with cyberbullying and cybervictimization are quite similar, indicating that no single risk factor explains cyberbullying. An array of individual, interpersonal, social, and community level factors are contributing to its explanation, but no great differences were found between different countries. This indicates, once more, that cyberbullying is a global problem, and that in most industrialized countries where children have access to smartphones, computers and the web communication world, in general they face the same risks.

As a concluding part of this book, all contributing authors from the different countries provided some highlights for recommendations on research and practice that we here present.

Italy: What to Do

Raising Public Awareness

a) Disseminate information on the net and Internet Communication Technology (ICT) safe use. Raise people's awareness about cyberbullying, and the negative impact and the emotional consequences for both bullies and victims.
b) Promote information, experience and best practices exchange between stakeholders at national and EU levels.

Enhance the Role of Teachers and School Staff in Preventing Cyberbullying

a) Train teachers about cyberbullying, prevention, management and resolution. Training teachers could be the first step toward an effective reduction and prevention of cyberbullying.
b) The trained teachers could use their expertise in order to make students think about their risky online behaviors and about their online experiences.
c) Supporting students in debating and exchanging opinions about their online habits could be a great ploy to make them think about the risks and the traps they face in cyberspace.

Improve School Climate

a) Each school should adopt clear policies with regard to the Internet and mobile phone use. With regard to the use of computers, virtual learning environments and access to the internet, it is necessary for schools to use filter and tracking software on all computers.
b) Each school should have clear and well-known anti-cyberbullying rules. Anti-bullying rules should be read and discussed with students and their parents. All students must be aware that no incident of cyberbullying will be ignored: victims will be supported and bullies will deal with the consequences of their actions.

c) Increase students' willingness to report cyberbullying to teachers and school administrators. Students should know that every complaint will be carefully examined by trained teachers.

Promote Youngsters' Active Participation in Preventing Cyberbullying

a) To prevent and reduce students' involvement in cyberbullying it is necessary to involve them in activities aimed at promoting and defining rules for a safer online environment, with the aim of better understanding their views and experiences concerning the use of communication technologies.

b) Sensitize children to the correct and proper use of the social networks and smartphones. It is important to teach adolescents the relevance of protecting their privacy online and strategies to protect themselves while online and how to protect themselves from the most common online traps.

Guarantee Financial Support

a) Establish help desks (funded at a national and/or at a European level). Promote the existence at a national level of help desks aimed to raise people's awareness of cyberbullying and to help and support students, teachers and parents. The help desks could also be a reference point that children can turn to report online illegal content and harmful behaviors.

b) Develop prevention programs in school to be included in the school curricula.

Greece: What to Do

Enhance the Role of Teachers and School Staff Role in Preventing Cyberbullying

a) Involve the entire school staff in anti-violence activities by improving their level of digital literacy.

b) Train teachers in the implementation of such activities.

Improve School Climate

a) Develop and implement specialized activities that promote students' empathy.
b) Develop and implement in-class group activities or interventions aimed at developing a positive, supportive school climate in which there are open discussions about cyberbullying.
c) Incorporate various programs or actions into the school curriculum that address the phenomenon of violence in general.
d) Develop and implement activities aimed at both bullying and cyberbullying prevention.
e) Develop and implement specific school policies and regulations that address specifically the cyberbullying phenomenon.
f) Involve the entire school community in the battle against school violence to develop a school culture that opposes all forms of violence and boosts students' confidence in adults' help.

Promote Youngsters' Active Participation in Preventing Cyberbullying

a) Train students on how to become part of the solution themselves by improving their level of digital literacy and by placing emphasis not only on online risks but on the educational value of the Internet and on its benefits for students' academic and future professional lives.

Involve Parents or Other Significant Adults in Fighting Cyberbullying

a) Develop and implement school activities and provisions that contribute to the improvement of the quality of communication between students and parents/teachers.
b) Involve parents in anti-violence activities by raising their digital literacy level and awareness of safe and risky Internet use so that they can monitor their children's ICT use and its impact on their lives.

Hungary: What to Do

Raise Public Awareness

a) Prevention and intervention programs against cyberbullying have to be harmonized with the locally run Safer Internet Program. The EU's Safer Internet Program (SIP) is present in all EU member states, teaching safer internet use at a different level in member states.

Enhance the Role of Teachers and School Staff in Preventing Cyberbullying

a) Cyberbullying management must be included in teachers' graduate curriculum.
b) Cyberbullying curricula should not stop at technical knowledge about Internet Technology tools and applications.
c) Teachers should acquire psycho-sociological skills to understand and handle cyberbullying.
d) Cyberbullying management should be taught to teachers and educators not only at the graduate but also at the postgraduate level. Best practices and case studies should be collected, published in a textbook, and circulated among schools in order to prepare and better manage problematic situations.
e) Teachers and school staff should be motivated to participate in cyberbullying prevention programs.

Improving School Climate

a) Professional assistance, guidance and networks have to be provided to teachers encountering cyberbullying situations, as cyberbullying sometimes requires a better level of understanding of group dynamics and peers' relations. Teachers should also learn basic knowledge about mental health and school professionals should be trained as well.

b) Student mentors can function best when they collaborate with trained teachers to detect, resolve and prevent cyberbullying situations at an early stage.

c) Student mentors have to be trained, however, not to abuse their power. It is important to train student mentors and prepare constructive and mature bystanders (students from same school but a couple of years older, because they have to be extremely sensitive to possible backlashes and responsive to children's real needs).

Promote Youngsters' Active Participation in Preventing Cyberbullying

a) Student mentorship should be part of the program. As students mostly talk to their peers about their painful experiments in cyberspace, student mentorship training is recommended to be part of cyberbullying intervention programs.

b) Peer leaders who are popular in their schools are recommended to be trained in how to help younger students to resolve crucial conflicts in cyberbullying situations. This "high status peer model" program applies to peer mentors speaking to students a few years younger.

Provide Financial Support

a) Financial and material support must be collected from the private as well as the public sector. A public-private partnership must be applied in propelling a complex multinational program such as TABBY.

b) National financial support is needed on a continuous basis with panel and longitudinal financed studies, to look at the relationship between risk and need factors and their role in the continuation or remission of cyberbullying.

Develop and Implement European Rules for Anti-bullying Programs

a) Even if school systems might vary by member states, we need European rules on the implementation and introduction of anti-bullying programs in schools. This is in order to avoid situations where local or national rules could prevent such programs in schools. Thus, an international program such as TABBY could be promoted in all EU countries given it has been successfully adopted in 8 different EU countries.

France: What to Do

Raise Public Awareness

a) Evidence-based policies should be designed and implemented to focus on the role of parents and also educational staff to inform and educate children on the positive use of the internet.
b) In some ways students have asked for these kinds of initiatives as 47% of the respondents stated that they got little or no information on online safety from their parents and 45% said the same about their teachers.

Enhance the Role of Teachers and School Staff in Preventing Cyberbullying

Initial and continuing training of teachers is necessary. Empowering them to prevent and deal with cyberbullying, so that they become active actors for change, should be made possible through training.

Improve the School Climate

a) In France, 70% of the victims of traditional school violence are also victims of cyber violence, and 67% of school violence perpetrators are authors of cyber violence. This confirms the overlap between the two forms of violence and the need to address both of them to reduce negative online behaviors.
b) It is important to teach young people social skills to enable them to stop negative interactions. Over one child out of 5 reported having been both a victim and a perpetrator during the last 6 months. These findings confirm that there is a strong need to teach children how to protect themselves without adopting the same behavior as their aggressors.
c) Both female and male victim of cyberbullying show low self-esteem.

Promote Youngsters' Active Participation in Preventing Cyberbullying

a) A few basic rules should be taught about positive online behavior such as:

- When online, do not accept invitations from unknown people.
- When interacting, do not provide your personal information.
- A password is like a toothbrush: you do not lend it to anyone.
- When interacting online and in real life, do not use rude words, insults, and racist or hate comments: socializing and having fun does not mean you have to denigrate or insult others.
- Before replying to a rude or nasty message, wait until the following day and think about it carefully. Reactions can sometimes be negative too.

b) Parents should not only teach rules but explain them and provide their own examples.

Involve Parents in Fighting Cyberbullying

a) Parents have an important role in children's technology use. They should supervise their children's online activities and teach them safe ways of interacting and how to screen information when online.

b) Online communication can lead to internet addiction increasing isolation and loss of communication between the child and the parent. Any sign of aggressiveness that is not justified should not be overlooked.

Spain: What to Do

Raise Public Awareness

a) Conduct national advertising campaigns to raise awareness about the risks related to technology misuse.

b) Carry out a national survey in each country to know the real extent of cyberbullying and sexting.

Enhance the Role of Teachers and School Staff in Preventing Cyberbullying

a) Include specific training on cyberbullying prevention and intervention.
b) Permanent Training: Train teachers on the use of Information Communication Technology and cyberbullying prevention, management and resolution.

Improve the School Climate

a) Promote in children and adolescents the safe and positive use of new technologies.
b) Establish a protocol for parents, teachers and principals, containing clear and simple rules about how to deal with cases of cyberbullying.

Involve Parents in Fighting Cyberbullying

a) Offer a workshop to parents to learn to:

  – use new technology and
  – monitor and prepare their children for the virtual world.

b) Make parents accustomed to the internet and familiar with modern devices used by their children.

Develop and Implement European Rules for Anti-bullying Programs

a) Establish at the EU level a strategy for addressing and reducing cyberbullying.
b) In all European countries, develop prevention programs against cyberbullying. The TABBY program based on scientific evidence has proved an interesting and promising application.

Address Legal Aspects

a) Establish measures to avoid the creation of false or fraudulent profiles on the internet, especially in virtual social networks.
b) Enlarge the legal coverage for allegations of cyberbullying, modifying the penal codes of different countries to specifically recognize these crimes.

Cyprus: What to Do

Enhance the Role of Teachers and School Staff in Preventing Cyberbullying

a) Educate teachers on how to use the technology, and incorporate this in the curriculum.
b) Teachers should be taught the tech-language used by students today in order to communicate with them.
c) A group of school teacher 'bully/cyberbully' experts should be in place. These people would be in charge of training and promoting best practices for maintaining and enhancing a good climate inside a school.
d) The Ministry of Education and Culture should train all newly appointed teachers in the field of technology and the use of it as an obligatory course.

Improve the School Climate

a) Schools should provide a direct, online chat service, by a trained professional, available to students, helping them handle issues of cyberbullying.
b) All schools must have an established code of conduct (protocol) to deal with school and cyberbullying.
c) Each school district should form a network of associated schools who will establish good communication with the local community. By doing this, the school, parents and community will promote and sustain best practices in dealing with bullying and cyberbullying.

Involve Parents in Fighting Cyberbullying

a) Parents should be encouraged to take part in school meetings, not just for the School Grades, but making them feel part of the system.
b) Parents should be taught by the school the tech-language used by their children in order to improve communication with them.

Obtain Financial Support

a) School-based programs (interventions) should not be applied only during the time of the project, but ways need to be found in order to sustain these programs within the school.

UK and Ireland: What to Do

Develop and Implement Anti-bullying Programs

a) Because of the overlap between cyberbullying and school bullying, it could be necessary to develop and implement holistic anti-bullying programs.
b) Holistic anti-bullying programs have to be evaluated using high quality methods, in order to reduce cyberbullying and cybervictimization.

Enhance the Role of Teachers and School Staff in Preventing Cyberbullying

a) Teachers could be key players in cyberbullying intervention and prevention. By removing ICTs from a student's possession they are able to physically stop cyberbullying and cybervictimization from taking place in school.
b) Teachers must be trained to prevent and deal with cyberbullying and cybervictimization.

Improve the School Climate

a) Schools must have a clear and defined anti-bullying and anti- cyber-bullying policy.

Address Legal Aspects

a) To date no law in the UK or Ireland criminalizes cyberbullying behaviors. Addressing this legal vacuum through a specific law could reduce cyberbullying and cybervictimization incidence.

Obtain Financial Support

a) Holistic anti-bullying programs should be found in order to assess their effectiveness over time.
b) Financial support may be particularly needed for the implementation of such programs in deprived areas where cyberbullying and cyber-victimization are more prevalent.
c) There is a great need for longitudinal studies to establish cyberbullying and cybervictimization long term negative cognitive and psychological consequences.

Canada: What to Do

Involve Parents and Other Significant Adults

a) Youth involved in cyberbullying were more likely to use the computer for more hours a day and more likely to give their passwords to friends, compared to those who are not involved. Parents play a crucial role in educating their children about cyber safety (e.g., never sharing a password with anyone), as well as in monitoring the type and amount of youths' online activity.
b) Research indicates that people who feel that they can trust people in their family are less likely to be cybervictimized. Prevention programs

to help parents create safe, trusting relationships with their children may prove effective in reducing cyberbullying.

c) Parental involvement in school activities is linked to lower rates of cybervictimization. Parents who are eager to contribute to the prevention of cyberbullying can get involved in their child's school and contribute to a more positive school climate.

d) Emerging research suggests that low self-awareness is associated with a higher level of cybervictimization. Supporting youth to engage in self-reflection may be a useful prevention strategy.

Enhance the Role of Teachers and School Staff in Preventing Cyberbullying

a) Positive student-teacher relationships have been identified as a protective factor against cybervictimization. It is therefore essential to train teachers and other school staff in effective means of creating healthy relationships with students.

b) Research is consistent in revealing a significant overlap between children involved in cyberbullying and cybervictimization. These children are at risk for a range of mental health problems and need support for healthy relationships. It is important to avoid labeling children as "bullies" and instead support them and their classmates in understanding the use of power in relationships and the nature of healthy and unhealthy relationships, as in cyberbullying.

c) Adults in the school can make a difference by modeling inclusive behavior and ensuring that no one is left out during class time (such as when choosing teams or groups). This strategy for creating social groupings has been called social architecture.

Improve School Climate

a) Taking a whole school approach based on values such as respect for differences and inclusion is essential to creating safe spaces and reducing cyberbullying.

b) Given the overlap between cyberbullying and in-person bullying, addressing in-person bullying is an important way to reduce cyberbullying. This can be accomplished by focusing on restorative justice and teaching young people how to repair relationships.

Promote Youths' Active Participation in Preventing Cyberbullying

a) Teach strategies for both online and in-person bystander intervention so that youth can intervene when they witness peers engaging in cyberbullying.
b) Consider youths' voices to identify the kinds of interventions they would find most helpful.
c) According to emerging literature from Canada, youth have expressed a preference for a comprehensive approach to cyberbullying that includes teaching strategies to prevent cyberbullying, encouraging anonymous reporting, and imposing consequences when cyberbullying is detected.

Research, Policies, and Practices to Promote Protective Factors

a) The few studies on protective factors that have been conducted in Canada have highlighted the importance of close relationships with teachers and parents, community-based opportunities for recreation, and the perception of high neighborhood safety, cooperation, and trust. Building on these strengths is one important avenue for preventing cyberbullying and cybervictimization.

USA: What to Do

Involve Parents and Other Significant Adults

a) Inform, sensitize and train parents and other significant adults to address cyberbullying and cyber safety issues.
b) Develop websites, tip sheets and other online resources to inform parents and teachers about how to best protect their children from online risks and cyberbullying.

Develop and Implement Anti-bullying Programs

a) Develop, implement and evaluate the effectiveness of school-based programs against cyberbullying.
b) Efficacious bullying prevention and intervention programs or approaches could be extended to include outcomes focused on cyberbullying and cyber safety.
c) More longitudinal research needs to be conducted to understand the developmental trajectories associated with traditional bullying and cyberbullying, and the risk factors associated with simultaneous change in these behaviors.

Enhance the Role of Teachers and School Staff in Preventing Cyberbullying

a) Improve educators' awareness and perceptions of cyberbullying.
b) More guidance is needed for school practitioners to talk to parents about limiting screen time, monitoring their children's use of the technology, talking to their children about internet safety and privacy, and encouraging open communications when they do experience cyberbullying.
c) Teacher training should focus on identifying warning signs and risk factors for cyberbullying and cybervictimization.

Address Legal Aspects

a) Schools need to be supported to implement anti-cyberbullying programs through stronger legislation that addresses cyberbullying.

Conclusions

Here are tick-off box advice for children and adults on how to stay away from troubles online either as a victim or as a bully.

- Protect your identity on social networks by:
- Checking carefully the privacy settings
- Choose a password that is difficult to guess
- Do not accept the friendship of those you do not know and do not trust appearances that may be deceptive
- Never share personal information and especially do not provide online your cell phone number, address or any other information that can make a person physically traceable
- When you post something on the web, remember that everyone can see it and forward it to others, making it virtually impossible to delete it from the Web
- Think before accepting new people/friendships online that you are not sure about
- Before sharing a friend's information, photos or videos ask them for permission: you may commit a crime, so avoid doing this.
- Everyone is capable of teasing others: to be popular among friends it is better to engage in something positive that harms no one
- Pay attention to your mobile or other personal devices and do not leave them unattended; they contain data and valuable information about you and there might always be someone taking advantage of your vulnerabilities.
- Remember that what may seem like a joke to you can cause pain and discomfort to others
- Talk to an adult you trust if something happens to you that worries you or makes you sick
- Damaging someone's reputation is a crime against the law
- If you are angry with someone, tell him/ her rather than trying to take revenge; this will leave you more satisfied about yourself

We now present a summary of ideas and actions, based on research findings and field empirical experiences.

The 10 silver bullet recommendations for the prevention and reduction of the risk of cyberbullying and cybervictimization:

Overall, the main recommendations can be shared and can be of use for many different countries and for different ages (10–17); they can be summarized in 10 points:

1. *Enhance empathy, moral values and emotional cognitive skills in children.* Children are not evil; they might have characteristics or personalities which exposed them to a higher risk. It is possible to teach them how to understand the consequences of their actions and improve their moral values.
2. *Promote youngsters' active participation in preventing cyberbullying.* Peers, at school and outside school, are key people who can promote a safe internet environment. If they know a friend or a companion is into trouble, they can ask for help or talk to them. Silence and the encouragement of cyberbullying is like cyberbullying itself.
3. *The role of teachers and school staff in preventing cyberbullying.* Adults are key elements. They are not-digital natives and they are often unaware or do not know about the risks. Their role is fundamental in helping children to identify risk and manage a risk situation with no blaming or punishing.
4. *Parents or other care givers' involvement in understanding, preventing and fighting cyberbullying.* Children live, in most cases, with their parents or other significant adults (care givers). These adults buy them the smartphones, and the computer, but they also need to inform children about possible risks in their use, how to recognize risks and how to manage them. Children should not feel intimidated about talking to a parent.
5. *Improve school climate.* At a broader level the school has to have policies about what is and what is not acceptable, not only in regard, to cyberbullying but about accessing the web and mobiles while in class. Having a confidential support group of both adults and peers can be beneficial.
6. *Raise public awareness.* Conferences, media releases, and videos with correct and functional information can be effective. Involve media companies and different levels of institutions alike to share aims and methods.
7. *Disseminate recommendations for children and adults.* On the website *www.tabby.eu* there is material and a handbook available for adults and children. The principles developed from the TABBY trip project are easy: simple steps and cautions can lead to great results.

8. *The need for an European rules in the implementation of effective anti-cyberbullying programs.* There is a paucity of sound research that looks into details on what works in reducing cyberbullying. Information about effective programs would be beneficial for the implementation of measures to implement international campaigns.

9. *Consider crime-related behavior around bullying and cyberbullying.* Cyberbullying can escalate and the behaviors involved be very damaging and serious. Without criminalizing any child involved in cyberbullying, clear rules are needed. Cyberbullying is regulated by laws in some countries especially in the USA and now also in Italy.

10. *Obtain financial support to promote programs and work with vulnerable and high-risk students.* More services and programs are needed. More experimental studies on what works in programs are also needed. These should be coordinated at the national level but tailored at the local level based on the needs of each social and cultural context, within the 1989 New York UN declaration of the rights of children framework.

As a concluding remark, we would like to share this message, which is also in an acronym:

S.T.O.P. C.Y.B.E.R.B.U.L.L.Y.I.N.G.

School efforts directed to the development and implementation of a positive school climate, for positive relationships between school staff members, teachers, parents and students.

Teacher training in cyberbullying for prevention, management and resolution. Trained teachers are a benchmark for both students and parents to facilitate communication with parents and create a positive school climate and positive relationships among students.

Online activities must be guided by netiquette use. Clear rules are needed for youngsters on how to behave in cases of cyberbullying: not to retaliate or reply to cruel or nasty online messages, ignore the cyberbully, save evidence of any misbehavior, and report cyberbullying episodes to someone who can help (teachers and parents).

Parents can prevent cyberbullying by increasing their level of Internet literacy, and supervision, and by sensitizing their children to the correct use of internet and any technological form of communication. Increase awareness of risks with a non-judgmental attitude.

Create programs/activities that address the phenomenon of violence in general.

Young people can be at risk of cyberbullying because of their frequent use of electronic devices. Adults should be open and supportive so that young people can handle violent incidents both offline and online successfully by themselves.

Both traditional bullying and cyberbullying should be addressed by school policies and curricula.

Empathy training is needed to increase understanding of the impact of a person's actions.

Risk and needs assessment of cyberbullying should be promoted among youngsters.

Boost students' confidence in adults' help by involving the entire school community in the battle against violence.

Understand the consequences of cyberbullying.

Lines of communication should be kept open between students and teachers or parents.

Literacy among adults on internet technology should be improved.

Young people should be positive and proactive bystanders.

Investigate those most serious cases, if necessary involving relevant authorities, such as police.

Needs are related to dynamic risk factors; they identify powerful areas for intervention to reduce cyberbullying.

Go and act now; everyone can do something to prevent and stop the vicious cycle of cyberbullying.

References

Aboujaoude, E., Savage, M. W., Starcevic, V., & Salame, W. O. (2015). Cyberbullying: Review of an old problem gone viral. *Journal of Adolescent Health, 57*(1), 10–18. https://doi.org/10.1016/j.jadohealth.2015.04.011

Ackers, M. J. (2012). Cyberbullying: Through the eyes of children and young people. *Educational Psychology in Practice, 28*(2), 141–157. https://doi.org/1 0.1080/02667363.2012.665356.

Agnew, R. (2001). Building on the foundation of general strain theory: Specifying the types of strain most likely to lead to crime and delinquency. *Journal of Research in Crime and Delinquency, 38*(4), 319–361. https://doi. org/10.1177/0022427801038004001.

Ahlfors, R. (2010). Many sources, one theme: Analysis of cyberbullying prevention and intervention websites. *Journal of Social Sciences, 6*(4), 515–522.

Álvarez-García, D., Núñez Pérez, J. C., Álvarez Pérez, L., Dobarro González, A., Rodríguez Pérez, C., & González-Castro, P. (2011). Violencia a través de las tecnologías de la información y la comunicación en estudiantes de secundaria. *Anales de Psicología, 27*(1), 221–230.

Álvarez-García, D., Núñez Pérez, J. C., Dobarro González, A., & Pérez, C. R. (2015). Risk factors associated with cybervictimization in adolescence. *International Journal of Clinical and Health Psychology, 15*(3), 226–235. https://doi.org/10.1016/j.ijchp.2015.03.002

© The Author(s) 2018 **293**
A. C. Baldry et al. (eds.), *International Perspectives on Cyberbullying*, Palgrave Studies in Cybercrime and Cybersecurity, https://doi.org/10.1007/978-3-319-73263-3

Ang, R. P., & Goh, D. H. (2010). Cyberbullying among adolescents: The role of affective and cognitive empathy, and gender. *Child Psychiatry and Human Development, 41*(4), 387–397. https://doi.org/10.1007/s10578-010-0176-3

Ang, R. P., Huan, V. S., & Florell, D. (2013). Understanding the relationship between proactive and reactive aggression, and cyberbullying across United States and Singapore adolescent samples. *Journal of Interpersonal Violence, 29*(2), 237–254. https://doi.org/10.1177/0886260513505149

Antoniadou, N., & Kokkinos, C. M. (2015). A review of research on cyber-bullying in Greece. *International Journal of Adolescence and Youth, 20*(2), 185–201. https://doi.org/10.1080/02673843.2013.778207

Antoniadou, N., Kokkinos, C. M., & Markos, A. (2016). Possible common correlates between bullying and cyber-bullying among adolescents. *Psicología Educativa, 22*(1), 27–38. https://doi.org/10.1016/j.pse.2016.01.003

Aoyama, I., Utsumi, S., & Hasegawa, M. (2012). Cyberbullying in Japan: Cases, government reports, adolescent relational aggression and parental monitoring roles. In Q. Li, D. Cross, & P. K. Smith (Eds.), *Cyberbullying in the global playground: Research from international perspectives* (pp. 183–201). Malden: Blackwell.

Asam, A. E., & Samara, M. (2016). Cyberbullying and the law: A review of psychological and legal challenges. *Computers in Human Behavior, 65*, 127–141. https://doi.org/10.1016/j.chb.2016.08.012

Astor, R. A., & Benbenishty, R. (in press). *Bullying, school violence, and climate in evolving contexts: Culture, organization, and time.* New York: Oxford University Press.

Athanasiades, C., Kamariotis, H., Psalti, A., Baldry, A. C., & Sorrentino, A. (2015). Internet use and cyberbullying among adolescent students in Greece: The "Tabby" project. *Hellenic Journal of Psychology, 12*(1), 14–39.

Baldry, A. C., & Kapardis, A. (2013). The juvenile young violent offender: From bullying to delinquency. In A. C. Baldry & A. Kapardis (Eds.), *Risk-assessment for juvenile violent offenders* (pp. 1–5). London: Routledge.

Baldry, A. C., & Sorrentino, A. (2017). Risk and needs assessment. In C. J. Schreck, M. Leiber, H. L. Miller, & K. Welch (Eds.), *The encyclopedia of juvenile delinquency and justice.* Wiley-Blackwell, https://doi.org/10.1002/978 1118524275.ejdj0110

Baldry, A. C., Farrington, D. P., & Sorrentino, A. (2015). "Am I at risk of cyber-bullying"? A narrative review and conceptual framework for research on risk of cyberbullying and cybervictimization: The risk and needs assessment approach. *Aggression and Violent Behavior, 23*, 36–51. https://doi.org/10.1016/j.avb.2015.05.014

Baldry, A. C., Farrington, D. P., & Sorrentino, A. (2016a). Cyberbullying in youth: A pattern of disruptive behaviour. *Psicología Educativa, 22*(1), 19–26. https://doi.org/10.1016/j.pse.2016.02.001

Baldry, A. C., Sorrentino, A., & Farrington, D. P. (2016b). Cyberbullying does parental online supervision and youngsters' willingness to report to an adult reduce the risk? In A. Kapardis & D. P. Farrington (Eds.), *The psychology of crime, policing and courts* (pp. 57–74). Oxon: Routledge.

Baldry, A. C., Sorrentino, A., & Farrington, D. P. (2017). School bullying and cyberbullying among boys and girls: Roles and overlap. *Journal of Aggression, Maltreatment and Trauma,* 1–15. https://doi.org/10.1080/10926771.2017.1 330793

Bandura, A. (1978). Social learning theory of aggression. *Journal of Communication, 28,* 12–29. https://doi.org/10.1111/j.1460-2466.1978. tb01621.x.

Bandura, A. (1986). *Social foundations of thought and action: A social cognitive theory.* Englewood Cliffs: Prentice-Hall.

Bandura, A. (2001). Social cognitive theory: An agentic perspective. *Annual Review of Psychology, 52*(1), 1–26. https://doi.org/10.1146/annurev. psych.52.1.1.

Barlett, C. P., Gentile, D. A., Anderson, C. A., Suzuki, K., Sakamoto, A., Yamaoka, A., & Katsura, R. (2014). Cross-cultural differences in cyberbullying behavior a short-term longitudinal study. *Journal of Cross-Cultural Psychology, 45*(2), 300–313. https://doi.org/10.1177/0022022113504622

Bauer, N. S., Lozano, P., & Rivara, F. P. (2007). The effectiveness of the Olweus bullying prevention program in public middle schools: A controlled trial. *Journal of Adolescent Health, 40*(3), 266–274. https://doi.org/10.1016/j. jadohealth.2006.10.005

Bauman, S. (2010). Cyberbullying in a rural intermediate school: An exploratory study. *The Journal of Early Adolescence, 30*(6), 803–833. https://doi. org/10.1177/0272431609350927.

Bauman, S. (2013). Cyberbullying: What does research tell us? *Theory Into Practice, 52*(4), 249–256. https://doi.org/10.1080/00405841.2013.829727.

Bauman, S., & Bellmore, A. (2015). New directions in cyberbullying research. *Journal of School Violence, 14*(1), 1–10. https://doi.org/10.1080/15388220.2 014.968281

Bauman, S., Toomey, R. B., & Walker, J. L. (2013). Associations among bullying, cyberbullying, and suicide in high school students. *Journal of Adolescence, 36*(2), 341–350. https://doi.org/10.1016/j.adolescence.2012.12.001

Bayraktar, F., Machackova, H., Dedkova, L., Cerna, A., & Sevcíková, A. (2014). Cyberbullying: The discriminant factors among cyberbullies, cybervictims, and cyberbully-victims in a Czech adolescent sample. *Journal of Interpersonal Violence, 18*, 1–25. https://doi.org/10.1177/0886260514555006

BBC (Producer). (2017). *Love Island's Olivia: I've received death threats.* Retrieved from http://bbcnews.co.uk

BBC News. (2014). *Man charged in Netherlands in Amanda Todd suicide case.* Retrieved from http://www.bbc.com/news/world-europe-27076991

BC Ministry of Education. (2001). *BC performance standards: Social responsibility. A framework.* Retrieved from https://www.bced.gov.bc.ca/perf_stands/sintro.pdf

Beale, A. V., & Hall, K. R. (2007). Cyberbullying: What school administrators (and parents) can do. *The Clearing House: A Journal of Educational Strategies, Issues and Ideas, 81*(1), 8–12. https://doi.org/10.3200/TCHS.81.1.8-12

Berne, S., Frisén, A., Schultze-Krumbholz, A., Scheithauer, H., Naruskov, K., Luik, P., Katzer, C., Erentaite, R., & Zukauskiene, R. (2013). Cyberbullying assessment instruments: A systematic review. *Aggression and Violent Behavior, 18*(2), 320–334. https://doi.org/10.1016/j.avb.2012.11.022

Betts, L. R. (2016). Cyberbullying: Approaches, consequences, and interventions. In J. Binder (Ed.), *Palgrave studies in cyberpsychology*. London: Palgrave Macmillan.

Betts, L. R., & Spenser, K. A. (2017). "People think it's a harmless joke": Young people's understanding of the impact of technology, digital vulnerability and cyberbullying in the United Kingdom. *Journal of Children and Media, 11*(1), 20–35. https://doi.org/10.1080/17482798.2016.1233893

Bevans, K. B., Bradshaw, C. P., & Waasdorp, T. E. (2013). Gender bias in the measurement of peer victimization: An application of item response theory. *Aggressive Behavior, 39*(5), 370–380. https://doi.org/10.1002/ab.21486

Bevilacqua, L., Shackleton, N., Hale, D., Allen, E., Bond, L., Christie, D., Elbourne, D., Fitzgerald-Yau, N., Fletcher, A., Jones, R., Miners, A., Scott, S., Wiggins, M., Bonell, C., & Viner, R. M. (2017). The role of family and school-level factors in bullying and cyberbullying: A cross-sectional study. *BMC Pediatrics, 17*, 160–169. https://doi.org/10.1186/s12887-017-0907-8

Bilsbury, T. (2015). *A systematic review of the prevalence of cyberbullying in Canada* (Master's thesis). Dalhousie University. Retrieved from http://hdl.handle.net/10222/58197

Blaya, C. (2013). *Les ados dans le cyberespace – prises de risqué et cyberviolence.* Bruxelles: De Boeck.

Blaya, C. (2015). (coord.). Cyberviolence et école. *Les Dossiers des Sciences de l'Education, 33*. Presses Université du Mirail.

Blaya, C., & Alava, S. (2012). *Risks and safety for children on the Internet: The FR report. Full findings from the EU Kids Online survey of 9–16 year olds and their parents in France*. Retrieved from www.eukidsonline.net

Blaya, C., & Fartoukh, M. (2015). Digital uses, victimization and online aggression: A comparative study between primary school and lower secondary school students in France. *European Journal on Criminal Policy and Research, 22*(2), 285–300. https://doi.org/10.1007/s10610-015-9293-7

Boak, A., Hamilton, H. A., Adlaf, E. M., Henderson, J. L., & Mann, R. E. (2016). *The mental health and well-being of Ontario students, 1991– 2015: Detailed OSDUHS findings* (CAMH Research Document Series No. 43). Toronto: Centre for Addiction and Mental Health. Retrieved from https://www.camh.ca/en/research/news_and_publications/ontario-student-drug-use-and   healthsurvey/Documents/2015%20OSDUHS%20Documents/2015OSDUHS_ Detailed%20MentalHealthReport.pdf

Bonell, C., Fletcher, A., Fitzgerald-Yau, N., Hale, D., Allen, E., Elbourne, D., Jones, R., Bond, L., Wiggins, M., Miners, A., Legood, R., Scott, S., Christie, D., & Viner, R. (2015). Initiating change locally in bullying and aggression through the school environment (INCLUSIVE): A pilot randomised controlled trial. *Health Technology Assessment, 19*(53), 1–110. https://doi.org/10.3310/hta19530

Borum, R., Fein, R., Vossekuil, B., & Berglund, J. (1999). Threat assessment: Defining an approach for evaluating risk of targeted violence. *Behavioral Sciences & the Law, 17*, 323–337. https://doi.org/10.1002/(SICI)1099-0798(199907/09)17:3<323::AID-BSL349>3.0.CO;2-G

Boulton, M. J., Hardcastle, K., Down, J., Fowles, J., & Simmonds, J. A. (2014). A comparison of preservice teachers' responses to cyber versus traditional bullying scenarios: Similarities and differences and implications for practice. *Journal of Teacher Education, 65*(2), 145–155. https://doi.org/10.1177/0022487113511496

Bowen, G. L., Richman, J. M., Brewster, A., & Bowen, N. (1998). Sense of school coherence, perceptions of danger at school, and teacher support among youth at risk of school failure. *Child and Adolescent Social Work Journal, 15*, 273–286. https://doi.org/10.1023/A:1025159811181

Bowllan, N. M. (2011). Implementation and evaluation of a comprehensive, school-wide bullying prevention program in an urban/suburban middle school. *Journal of School Health, 81*(4), 167–173.

Boxer, P., & Dubow, E. F. (2002). A social-cognitive information-processing model for school-based aggression reduction and prevention programs: Issues for research and practice. *Applied and Preventive Psychology, 10*(3), 177–192. https://doi.org/10.1016/S0962-1849(01)80013-5

Brewer, G., & Kerslake, J. (2015). Cyberbullying, self-esteem, empathy and loneliness. *Computers in Human Behavior, 48*, 255–260. https://doi.org/10.1016/j.chb.2015.01.073

Brighi, A., Guarini, A., Melotti, G., Galli, S., & Genta, M. L. (2012a). Predictors of victimisation across direct bullying, indirect bullying and cyberbullying. *Emotional and Behavioural Difficulties, 17*(3–4), 375–388. https://doi.org/10.1080/13632752.2012.704684

Brighi, A., Ortega, R., Pyzalski, J., Scheithauer, H., Smith, P. K., Tsormpatzoudis, C., & Barkoukis, V., et al. (2012b). *European Cyberbullying Intervention Project Questionnaire (ECIPQ)*. Unpublished Manuscript, University of Bologna. Retrieved from bullyingandcyber.net

Bronfenbrenner, U. (1977). Toward an experimental ecology of human development. *American Psychologist, 32*(7), 513–531. https://doi.org/10.1037/0003-066X.32.7.513

Bronfenbrenner, U. (1979). *Ecology of human development: Experiments by nature and design*. Cambridge, MA: Harvard University Press.

Buckingham, D. (2008). *Youth identity and digital media*. Cambridge, MA: MIT Press.

Buda, M. (2009). Közérzet és zaklatás az iskolában. *Iskolakultúra, 19*(5–6), 3–15.

Buelga, S., Cava, M. J., & Musitu, G. (2010). Cyberbullying: Victimización entre adolescentes a través del teléfono móvil y de internet. *Psicothema, 22*(4), 784–789.

Callaghan, M., Kelly, C., & Molcho, M. (2015). Exploring traditional and cyberbullying among Irish adolescents. *International Journal of Public Health, 60*, 199–206. https://doi.org/10.1007/s00038-014-0638-7

Calvete, E., Orue, I., Estévez, A., Villardón, L., & Padilla, P. (2010). Cyberbullying in adolescents: Modalities and aggressors' profile. *Computers in Human Behavior, 26*(5), 1128–1135. https://doi.org/10.1016/j.chb.2010.03.017

Cappadocia, M. C., Craig, W. M., & Pepler, D. (2013). Cyberbullying prevalence, stability, and risk factors during adolescence. *Canadian Journal of School Psychology, 28*(2), 171–192. https://doi.org/10.1177/0829573513491212

Casas, J. A., Del Rey, R., & Ortega-Ruiz, R. (2013). Bullying and cyberbullying: Convergent and divergent predictor variables. *Computers in Human Behavior, 29*(3), 580–587. https://doi.org/10.1016/j.chb.2012.11.015

Cassidy, W., Brown, K., & Jackson, M. (2012). 'Under the radar': Educators and cyberbullying in schools. *School Psychology International, 33*(5), 520–532. https://doi.org/10.1177/0143034312445245

Cassidy, W., Faucher, C., & Jackson, M. (2013). Cyberbullying among youth: A comprehensive review of current international research and its implications and application to policy and practice. *School Psychology International, 34*(6), 575–612. https://doi.org/10.1177/0143034313479697

Cénat, J. M., Hébert, M., Blais, M., Lavoie, F., Guerrier, M., & Derivois, D. (2014). Cyberbullying, psychological distress and self-esteem among youth in Quebec schools. *Journal of Affective Disorders, 169*, 7–9. https://doi.org/10.1016/j.jad.2014.07.019

Centres for Disease Control and Prevention. (2009a). *Bullying surveillance among youths: Uniform definitions for public health and recommended data elements, Version 1.0.* Atlanta: National Center for Injury Prevention and Control, Centers for Disease Control and Prevention and the United States Department of Education.

Centres for Disease Control and Prevention. (2009b). *Technology and youth: Protecting your child from electronic aggression.* Atlanta: Centres for Disease Control and Prevention.

Chalmers, J. B., & Townsend, M. A. (1990). The effects of training in social perspective taking on socially maladjusted girls. *Child Development, 61*(1), 178–190. https://doi.org/10.1111/j.1467-8624.1990.tb02770.x

Chandler, M. J. (1973). Egocentrism and antisocial behavior: The assessment and training of social perspective-taking skills. *Developmental Psychology, 9*(3), 326. https://doi.org/10.1037/h0034974.

Chen, L., Ho, S. S., & Lwin, M. O. (2017). A meta-analysis of factors predicting cyberbullying perpetration and victimization: From the social cognitive and media effects approach. *New Media & Society, 19*(8), 1194–1213. https://doi.org/10.1177/1461444816634037

Chibnall, S., Wallace, M., Leicht, C., & Lunghofer, L. (2006). *I-safe evaluation. Final report.* Caliber Association, Fairfax. Retrieved from http://www.ncjrs.gov/pdffiles1/nij/grants/213715.pdf

Cohen, L. E., & Felson, M. (1979). Social change and crime rate trends: A routine activity approach. *American Sociological Review, 44*, 588–608.

Committee for Children. (2008). *Second Step: Student success through prevention program.* Seattle: Committee for Children.

Corcoran, L., & Mc Guckin, C. (2014). Addressing bullying problems in Irish schools and in cyberspace: A challenge for school management. *Educational Research, 56*(1), 48–64. https://doi.org/10.1080/00131881.2013.874150

Corcoran, L., Connolly, I., & O'Moore, M. (2012). Cyberbullying in Irish schools: An investigation of personality and self-concept. *Irish Journal of Psychology, 33*(4), 153–165. https://doi.org/10.1080/03033910.2012.677995

Corcoran, L., Mc Guckin, C., & Prentice, G. (2015). Cyberbullying or cyber aggression? A review of existing definitions of cyber-based peer-to-peer aggression. *Societies, 5,* 245–255. https://doi.org/10.3390/soc5020245

Cotter, P., & McGilloway, S. (2011). Living in an 'electronic age': Cyberbullying among Irish adolescents. *The Irish Journal of Education, 39,* 44–56.

Couvillon, M. A., & Ilieva, V. (2011). Recommended practices: A review of schoolwide preventative programs and strategies on cyberbullying. *Preventing School Failure: Alternative Education for Children and Youth, 55*(2), 96–101. https://doi.org/10.1080/1045988X.2011.539461

Craig, W. M., & Pepler, D. J. (2007). Understanding bullying: From research to practice. *Canadian Psychology, 48*(2), 86–93. https://doi.org/10.1037/cp2007010

Craig, W. M., Pepler, D., & Atlas, R. (2000). Observations of bullying in the playground and in the classroom. *School Psychology International, 21*(1), 22–36. https://doi.org/10.1177/0143034300211002

Craig, W., Lambe, L., & McIver, T. (2016). Bullying and fighting. In J.G. Freeman, M. A. King, & W. Pickett (Eds.), *Health Behaviour in School-aged Children (HBSC) in Canada: Focus on relationships* (pp. 167–182). Ottawa: Public Health Agency of Canada. Retrieved from http://healthyca-nadians.gc.ca/publications/science-research-sciences-recherches/health behaviour-children-canada-2015-comportements-sante-jeunes/index-eng.php

Crick, N. R., & Grotpeter, J. K. (1996). Children's treatment by peers: Victims of relational and overt aggression. *Development and Psychopathology, 8,* 367–380. https://doi.org/10.1017/S0954579400007148

Crombie, G., & Trinneer, A. (2003). *Children and internet safety: An evaluation of the missing program. A report to the Research and Evaluation Section of the National Crime Prevention Centre of Justice Canada.* Ottawa: University of Ottawa.

Cross, D., Barnes, A., Papageorgiou, A., Hadwen, K., Hearn, L., & Lester, L. (2015). A social–ecological framework for understanding and reducing cyberbullying behaviours. *Aggression and Violent Behavior, 23,* 109–117. https://doi.org/10.1016/j.avb.2015.05.016

Cunningham, C. E., Vaillancourt, T., Cunningham, L. J., Chen, Y., & Ratcliffe, J. (2011). Modeling the bullying prevention program design recommendations of students from grades 5 to 8: A discrete choice conjoint experiment. *Aggressive Behavior, 37*(6), 521–537. https://doi.org/10.1002/ab.20408

Cunningham, C. E., Chen, Y., Vaillancourt, T., Rimas, H., Deal, K., Cunningham, L. J., & Ratcliffe, J. (2015). Modeling the anti-cyberbullying preferences of university students: Adaptive choice-based conjoint analysis. *Aggressive Behavior, 41*(4), 369–385. https://doi.org/10.1002/ab.21560

Cusson, M. (1983). *Le contrôle social du crime*. Paris: Presses universitaires de France.

Dafoe, T. L. (2016). *The role of social-emotional learning skills in bullying behaviour* (Doctoral dissertation). University of Toronto.

David-Ferdon, C., & Hertz, M. F. (2009). *Electronic media and youth violence: A CDC issue brief for researchers*. Atlanta: Centers for Disease Control and Prevention.

Davis, S., & Nixon, C. L. (2014). *The youth voice project: Student insights into bullying and peer mistreatment*. Champaign: Research Press Publishers.

Dehue, F., Bolman, C., & Völlink, T. (2008). Cyberbullying: Youngsters' experiences and parental perception. *CyberPsychology and Behavior, 11*(2), 217–223. https://doi.org/10.1089/cpb.2007.0008

Dekovic, M. (1999). Risk and protective factors in the development of problem behavior during adolescence. *Journal of Youth and Adolescence, 28*(6), 667–685. https://doi.org/10.1023/A:1021635516758.

Del Rey, R., Elipe, P., & Ortega-Ruiz, R. (2012). Bullying and cyberbullying: Overlapping and predictive value of the co-occurrence. *Psicothema, 24*(4), 608–613.

Del Rey, R., Casas, J. A., Ortega-Ruiz, R., Schultze-Krumbholz, A., Scheithauer, H., Smith, P., Thompson, F., Barkoukis, V., Tsorbatzoudis, H., Brighi, A., Guarini, A., Pyżalski, J., & Plichta, P. (2015). Structural validation and cross-cultural robustness of the European Cyberbullying Intervention Project Questionnaire. *Computers in Human Behavior, 50*, 141–147. https://doi.org/10.1016/j.chb.2015.03.065

Della Cioppa, V., O'Neil, A., & Craig, W. (2015). Learning from traditional bullying interventions: A review of research on cyberbullying and best practice. *Aggression and Violent Behavior, 23*, 61–68. https://doi.org/10.1016/j.avb.2015.05.009

Devine, P., & Lloyd, K. (2012). Internet use and psychological well-being among 10-year-old and 11-year-old children. *Child Care in Practice, 18*(1), 5–22. https://doi.org/10.1080/13575279.2011.621888

Dittrick, C. J., Beran, T. N., Mishna, F., Hetherington, R., & Shariff, S. (2013). Do children who bully their peers also play violent video games? A Canadian national study. *Journal of School Violence, 12*(4), 297–318. https://doi.org/10.1080/15388220.2013.803244

Dodd, V. (2017, August 21). CPS to crack down on social media hate crime, says Alison Saunders. *The Guardian*. Retrieved from http://www.theguardian.com

Dublin, R. (1978). *Theory building*. New York: Free Press.

Education Act, Revised Statutes of Alberta. (2012, Chapter E-0.3). Retrieved from the Province of Alberta website: http://www.qp.alberta.ca/documents/Acts/e00p3.pdf

Eisenberg, N., & Strayer, J. (1987). Critical issues in the study of empathy. In N. Eisenberg & J. Strayer (Eds.), *Empathy and its development: Cambridge studies in social and emotional development* (pp. 3–13). New York: Cambridge University Press.

Ellis, P. L. (1982). Empathy: A factor in antisocial behavior. *Journal of Abnormal Child Psychology, 10*(1), 123–133. https://doi.org/10.1007/BF00915957.

Englander, E., Parti, K., & McCoy, M. (2015). Evaluation of a university-based bullying and cyberbullying prevention program. *Journal of Modern Education Review, 5*(10), 937–950. https://doi.org/10.15341/jmer(2155-7993)/11.05.2015

Erdur-Baker, Ö. (2010). Cyberbullying and its correlation to traditional bullying, gender and frequent and risky usage of internet-mediated communication tools. *New Media & Society, 12*(1), 109–125. https://doi.org/10.1177/1461444809341260

Espelage, D. L. (2012). Bullying prevention: A research dialogue with Dorothy Espelage. *Prevention Researcher, 19*, 17–20.

Espelage, D. L., Rao, M. A., & Craven, R. (2012). Theories of cyberbullying. In S. Bauman, D. Cross, & J. L. Walker (Eds.), *Principles of cyberbullying research: Definitions, measures, and methodology* (pp. 78–97). New York: Routledge.

Espelage, D. L., Low, S., Van Ryzin, M. J., & Polanin, J. R. (2015). Clinical trial of second step middle school program: Impact on bullying, cyberbullying, homophobic teasing, and sexual harassment perpetration. *School Psychology Review, 44*(4), 464–479. https://doi.org/10.17105/spr-15-0052.1

Estévez, A., Villardón, L., Calvete, E., Padilla, P., & Orue, I. (2010). Adolescentes víctimas de cyberbullying: prevalencia y características. *Psicología Conductual, 18*(1), 73–89.

Eurispes – Telefono Azzurro. (2007). *8 Rapporto Nazionale sulla Condizione dell'Infanzia e dell'Adolescenza*. Retrieved from http://www.azzurro.it/sites/default/files/Materiali/InfoConsigli/Ricerche%20e%20indagini/sintesirapportoinfanziaadolescenza8.pdf

Eysenck, H. J., & Eysenck, S. B. G. (1975). *Manual of the Eysenck Personality Questionnaire.* London: Hodder and Stoughton.

Fanti, K. A., Demetriou, A. G., & Hawa, V. V. (2012). A longitudinal study of cyberbullying: Examining risk and protective factors. *European Journal of Developmental Psychology, 9*(2), 168–181. https://doi.org/10.1080/1740562 9.2011.643169

Farrington, D. P., & Ttofi, M. M. (2009). School-based programs to reduce bullying and victimization. *Campbell Systematic Reviews, 2009, 6.*

Fein, R. A., & Vossekuil, B. (1998). *Protective intelligence & threat assessment investigations: A guide for state and local law enforcement officials* (NIROJP/ DOJ Publication No. 170612). Washington, DC: U.S. Department of Justice.

Fein, R. A., & Vossekuil, B. V. (1999). Assassination in the United States: An operational study of recent assassins, attackers, and near-lethal approachers. *Journal of Forensic Sciences, 44*, 321–333.

Fein, R. A., Vossekuil, B., & Holden, G. A. (1995). *Threat assessment: An approach to prevent targeted violence* (Vol. 2). Washington, DC: US Department of Justice, Office of Justice Programs, National Institute of Justice.

Fein, R. A., Vossekuil, B., Pollack, W. S., Borum, R., Modzeleski, W., & Reddy, M. (2002). *Threat assessment in schools. A guide to managing threatening situations and to creating safe school climates.* Washington, DC: United States Secret Service and United States Department of Education.

Feinberg, T., & Robey, N. (2009). Cyberbullying: Intervention and prevention strategies. *National Association of School Psychologists, 38*(4), 22–24.

Felson, M., & Boba, R. (2010). *Crime and everyday life* (4th ed.). Los Angeles: Sage.

Figula, E. (2004). Az iskolai erőszak jelenségének feltárása. a tanulók érintettségének. szerepviselkedésének elemzése egy vizsgálat tükrében. *Alkalmazott Pszichológia, 4*, 19–35.

Fletcher, A., Fitzgerald-Yau, N., Jones, R., Allen, E., Viner, R. M., & Bonell, C. (2014). Brief report: Cyberbullying perpetration and its associations with socio-demographics, aggressive behaviour at school, and mental health outcomes. *Journal of Adolescence, 37*, 1393–1398. https://doi.org/10.1016/j. adolescence.2014.10.005

Floros, G., & Siomos, K. (2013). The relationship between optimal parenting, Internet addiction and motives for social networking in adolescence. *Psychiatry Research, 209*(3), 529–534. https://doi.org/10.1016/j.psychres. 2013.01.010

Foody, M., Samara, M., & O'Higgins Norman, J. (2017). Bullying and cyber-bullying studies in the school-aged population on the island of Ireland: A meta-analysis. *British Journal of Educational Psychology*. https://doi.org/10.1111/bjep.12163

Gámez-Guadix, M., Orue, I., Smith, P. K., & Calvete, E. (2013). Longitudinal and reciprocal relations of cyberbullying with depression, substance use, and problematic internet use among adolescents. *Journal of Adolescent Health, 53*(4), 446–452. https://doi.org/10.1016/j.jadohealth.2013.03.030

Gámez-Guadix, M., Borrajo, E., & Almendros, C. (2016). Risky online behaviors among adolescents: Longitudinal relations among problematic internet use, cyberbullying perpetration, and meeting strangers online. *Journal of Behavioral Addictions, 5*(1), 100–107. https://doi.org/10.1556/2006.5.2016.013

Garandeau, C. F., Lee, I. A., & Salmivalli, C. (2014). Differential effects of the KiVa anti-bullying program on popular and unpopular bullies. *Journal of Applied Developmental Psychology, 35*, 44–50. https://doi.org/10.1016/j.appdev.2013.10.004

Genta, M. L., Smith, P. K., Ortega, R., Brighi, A., Guarini, A., Thompson, F., Tippett, N., Mora-Merchán, J. A., & Calmaestra, J. (2012). Comparative aspects of cyberbullying in Italy, England, and Spain: Findings from a DAPHNE project. In Q. Li, D. Cross, & P. K. Smith (Eds.), *Cyberbullying in the global playground: Research from international perspectives* (pp. 15–31). West Sussex: Wiley-Blackwell.

Gillis, W. (2013, April 12). Rehtaeh Parsons: A family's tragedy and a town's shame. *The Star*. Retrieved from https://www.thestar.com/news/canada/2013/04/12/rehtaeh_parsons_a_ family s_ tragedy_ and_a_towns_shame.html

Goldbaum, S., Craig, W. M., Pepler, D., & Connolly, J. (2003). Developmental trajectories of victimization: Identifying risk and protective factors. *Journal of Applied School Psychology, 19*(2), 139–156. https://doi.org/10.1080/15388220.2013.803244

Goodman, R. (2006). The Strengths and Difficulties Questionnaire: A research note. *Journal of Child Psychology, 38*, 581–586. https://doi.org/10.1111/j.1469-7610.1997.tb01545.x.

Gradinger, P., Strohmeier, D., & Spiel, C. (2009). Traditional bullying and cyberbullying: Identification of risk groups for adjustment problems. *Zeitschrift für Psychologie/Journal of Psychology, 217*(4), 205–213. https://doi.org/10.1027/0044-3409.217.4.205

Gradinger, P., Strohmeier, D., & Spiel, C. (2010). Definition and measurement of cyberbullying. *Cyberpsychology: Journal of Psychosocial Research on Cyberspace*, 4(2), article -1.

Gradinger, P., Strohmeier, D., & Spiel, C. (2011). Motives for bullying others in cyberspace. In Q. Li, D. Cross, & P. K. Smith (Eds.), *Cyberbullying in the global playground: Research from international perspectives* (pp. 263–284). Oxford: Wiley-Blackwell.

Grigg, D. W. (2010). Cyber-aggression: Definition and concept of cyberbullying. *Journal of Psychologists and Counsellors in Schools*, 20(2), 143–156. https://doi.org/10.1375/ajgc.20.2.143

Groff, E. R. (2007). Simulation for theory testing and experimentation: An example using routine activity theory and street robbery. *Journal of Quantitative Criminology*, 23(2), 75–103. https://doi.org/10.1007/s10940-006-9021-z.

Gyurkó, Sz., & Virág, Gy. (2009). *Az iskolai erőszak megítélésének különbségei és hasonlóságai a gyermekvédelmi és az oktatási intézményrendszerben. Kutatási zárótanulmány*. Budapest: Országos Kriminológiai Intézet. Available online at the webpage of the Hungarian Institute of Criminology. Retrieved January 15, 2017, from http://www.okri.hu/images/stories/kutatok/ viraggyorgy/isk_eroszak_2009.pdf

Hasebrink, U., Livingstone, S., & Haddon, L. (2008). *Comparing children's online opportunities and risks across Europe: Cross-national comparisons for EU Kids Online*. London: EU Kids Online. Retrived from http://eprints.lse.ac.uk/21656/1/D3.2_Report-Cross_national_ comparisons.pdf

Hay, C., Meldrum, R., & Mann, K. (2010). Traditional bullying, cyber bullying, and deviance. A general strain theory approach. *Journal of Contemporary Criminal Justice*, 26(2), 130–147. https://doi.org/10.1177/1043986209359557

Hemphill, S. A., & Heerde, J. A. (2014). Adolescent predictors of young adult cyberbullying perpetration and victimization among Australian youth. *Journal of Adolescent Health*, 55(4), 580–587. https://doi.org/10.1016/j.jadohealth.2014.04.014

Hinduja, S., & Patchin, J. W. (2008). Cyberbullying: An exploratory analysis of factors related to offending and victimization. *Deviant Behavior*, 29(2), 129–156. https://doi.org/10.1080/01639620701457816

Hinduja, S., & Patchin, J. W. (2009). *Bullying beyond the schoolyard: Preventing and responding to cyberbullying*. Thousand Oaks: Corwin Press.

Hinduja, S., & Patchin, J. W. (2010a). *Cyberbullying research summary: Cyberbullying and strain.* Retrieved from http://www.cyberbullying.org/cyberbullying_and_strain_research_fact_ sheet.pdf

Hinduja, S., & Patchin, J. W. (2010b). Bullying, cyberbullying and suicide. *Archives of Suicide Research, 14*(3), 206–221. https://doi.org/10.1080/13811 118.2010.494133

Hinduja, S., & Patchin, J. W. (2011). Cyberbullying: A review of the legal issues facing educators. *Preventing School Failure: Alternative Education for Children and Youth, 55*(2), 71–78. https://doi.org/10.1080/1045988X.2011.539433

Hinduja, S., & Patchin, J. (2012a). *School climate 2.0: Preventing cyberbullying and sexting one classroom at a time.* Thousand Oaks: Corwin Press.

Hinduja, S., & Patchin, J. W. (2012b). Cyberbullying: Neither an epidemic nor a rarity. *European Journal of Developmental Psychology, 9*(5), 539–543. https://doi.org/10.1080/17405629.2012.706448

Hinduja, S., & Patchin, J. W. (2013). Social influences on cyberbullying behaviors among middle and high school students. *Journal of Youth and Adolescence, 42*(5), 711–722. https://doi.org/10.1007/s10964-012-9902-4

Hoff, D. L., & Mitchell, S. N. (2009). Cyberbullying: Causes, effects, and remedies. *Journal of Educational Administration, 47*(5), 652–665. https://doi.org/10.1108/09578230910981107

Holfeld, B., & Leadbeater, B. J. (2015). The nature and frequency of cyber bullying behaviors and victimization experiences in young Canadian children. *Canadian Journal of School Psychology, 30*(2), 116–135. https://doi.org/10.1177/0829573514556853

Holladay, J. (2011). Cyberbullying. *Education Digest, 76*(5), 4–9.

Holt, T. J., Fitzgerald, S., Bossler, A. M., Chee, G., & Ng, E. (2014). Assessing the risk factors of cyber and mobile phone bullying victimization in a nationally representative sample of Singapore youth. *International Journal of Offender Therapy and Comparative Criminology,* 1–18. https://doi.org/10.11 77/0306624X14554852

Hong, J. S., & Espelage, D. L. (2012). A review of research on bullying and peer victimization in school: An ecological systems analysis. *Aggression and Violent Behavior, 17,* 311–312. https://doi.org/10.1016/j.avb.2012.03.003

Hong, Y., Li, X., Mao, R., & Stanton, B. (2006). Internet use among Chinese college students: Implications for sex education and HIV prevention. *CyberPsychology and Behavior, 10*(2), 161–169. https://doi.org/10.1089/cpb.2006.9973

Ipsos Insight. (2006). *Mobile phones could soon rival the PC as world's dominant internet platform.* Retrieved from https://www.ipsos.com/en-us/mobile-phones-could-soon-rival-pc-worlds-dominant-internet-platform

Jaghoory, H., Björkqvist, K., & Österman, K. (2015). Cyberbullying among adolescents: A comparison between Iran and Finland. *Journal of Child and Adolescent Behaviour,* 3(6), 265–272. https://doi.org/10.4172/2375-4494.1000265.

Jang, H., Song, J., & Kim, R. (2014). Does the offline bully-victimization influence cyberbullying behavior among youths? Application of general strain theory. *Computers in Human Behavior,* 31, 85–93. https://doi.org/10.1016/j.chb.2013.10.007

Jolliffe, D., & Farrington, D. P. (2006). Development and validation of the Basic Empathy Scale. *Journal of Adolescence,* 29(4), 589–611. https://doi.org/10.1016/j.adolescence.2005.08.010

Juvonen, J., & Gross, E. F. (2008). Extending the school grounds? – Bullying experiences in cyberspace. *Journal of School Health,* 78(9), 496–505. https://doi.org/10.1111/j.1746-1561.2008.00335.x

Kapardis, A. (1985). Lambousa Reform School, Cyprus: A study of its population (1979–1983) and its effectiveness. *Cyprus Law Review,* 4, 1821–1832.

Kapardis, A. (1986). Juvenile delinquency and delinquents in Cyprus. *Cyprus Law Review,* 4, 2371–2379.

Kapardis, A. (2008). Youth delinquency in Cyprus. In M. Steketee, M. Moll, & A. Kapardis (Eds.), *Juvenile delinquency in six new EU member states: Crime, risky behavior and victimization in the capital cities of Cyprus, Czech Republic, Estonia, Lithuania, Poland and Slovenia* (pp. 51–55). Utrecht: Verwey-Jonker Institute.

Kapardis, A. (2013). Delinquency and victimization in Cyprus. *European Journal on Criminal Policy and Research,* 19(2), 171–182. https://doi.org/10.1007/s10610-013-9201-y.

Kapardis, A., & Poyiadjis, G. (2013). The EARN project in Cyprus. In A. C. Baldry & A. Kapardis (Eds.), *Risk-assessment for juvenile violent offenders* (pp. 117–136). London: Routledge.

Kapatzia, K., & Sygkollitou, E. (2008). *Cyberbullying in middle and high schools: Prevalence, gender and age differences* (Unpublished master's thesis). Department of Psychology, Aristotle University, Greece.

Katzer, C., Fetchenhauer, D., & Belschak, F. (2009). Cyberbullying: Who are the victims?: A comparison of victimization in internet chatrooms and victimization in school. *Journal of Media Psychology: Theories, Methods, and Applications,* 21(1), 25–36. https://doi.org/10.1027/1864-1105.21.1.25

Keith, S., & Martin, M. E. (2005). Cyber-bullying: Creating a culture of respect in a cyber world. *Reclaiming Children and Youth,* 13(4), 224–228.

Khurana, A., Bleakley, A., Jordan, A. B., & Romer, D. (2015). The protective effects of parental monitoring and internet restriction on adolescents' risk of online harassment. *Journal of Youth and Adolescence, 44*(5), 1039–1047. https://doi.org/10.1007/s10964-014-0242-4

Király, O., Zsila, Á., & Demetrovics, Z. (2016). Viselkedési addikciók. In Z. Elekes (Ed.), *Európai iskolavizsgálat az alkohol- és egyéb drogfogyasztási szokásokról (ESPAD) – 2015. Magyarországi eredmények.* Budapest: Budapesti Corvinus Egyetem.

Knowler, C., & Frederickson, N. (2013). Effects on an emotional literacy intervention for students identified with bullying behaviour. *Educational Psychology, 33*(7), 862–883. https://doi.org/10.1080/01443410.2013.785052

Kokkinos, C. M., Antoniadou, N., Asdre, A., & Voulgaridou, K. (2016a). Parenting and Internet behavior predictors of cyber-bullying and cyber-victimization among preadolescents. *Deviant Behavior, 37*(4), 439–455. https://doi.org/10.1080/01639625.2015.1060087

Kokkinos, C. M., Baltzidis, E., & Xynogala, D. (2016b). Prevalence and personality correlates of Facebook bullying among university undergraduates. *Computers in Human Behavior, 55*(B), 840–850. https://doi.org/10.1016/j.chb.2015.10.017

Kowalski, R. M., & Limber, S. P. (2013). Psychological, physical, and academic correlates of cyberbullying and traditional bullying. *Journal of Adolescent Health, 53*(1), S13–S20. https://doi.org/10.1016/j.jadohealth.2012.09.018

Kowalski, R. M., Limber, S. P., & Agatston, P. W. (2008). *Cyber bullying: Bullying in the digital age.* Malden: Blackwell Publishing.

Kowalski, R. M., Limber, S. P., Limber, S., & Agatston, P. W. (2012). *Cyberbullying: Bullying in the digital age* (2nd ed.). Chichester: Wiley.

Kowalski, R. M., Giumetti, G. W., Schroeder, A. N., & Lattanner, M. R. (2014). Bullying in the digital age: A critical review and meta-analysis of cyberbullying research among youth. *Psychological Bulletin, 140*(4), 1073–1137. https://doi.org/10.1037/a0035618

Kubiszewski, V., Fontaine, R., Huré, K., & Rusch, E. (2012). Le cyber-bullying à l'adolescence : problèmes psycho-sociaux associés et spécificités par rapport au bullying scolaire. *L'Encéphale, 39*(2), 77–84. https://doi.org/10.1016/j.encep.2012.01.008

Kulig, J. C., Hall, B. L., & Kalischuk, R. G. (2008). Bullying perspectives among rural youth: A mixed methods approach. *Rural and Remote Health, 8*(2), 1–11.

Lane, D. K. (2011). Taking the lead on cyberbullying: Why schools can and should protect students online. *Iowa Law Review, 96*(5), 1791–1811.

Langos, C. (2012). Cyberbullying: The challenge to define. *Cyberpsychology, Behavior, and Social Networking, 15*(6), 285–289. https://doi.org/10.1089/cyber.2011.0588.

Lasher, S., & Baker, C. (2015). *Bullying: Evidence from the longitudinal study of young people in England 2, wave 2* (Research brief). London: Department of Education. Retrieved from www.gov.uk/government/publications

Leadbeater, B., Sukhawathanakul, P., Smith, D., & Bowen, F. (2015). Reciprocal associations between interpersonal and values dimensions of school climate and peer victimization in elementary school children. *Journal of Clinical Child and Adolescent Psychology, 44*(3), 480–493. https://doi.org/10.1080/15374416.2013.873985

Lee, S. H. (2016). Cyberbullying in Eastern countries: Focusing on South Korea and other Eastern cultures. In R. Navarro et al. (Eds.), *Cyberbullying across the globe* (pp. 149–167). Cham: Springer.

Lenhart, A. (2015). *Teens, social media and technology overview 2015*. Washington, DC: Pew Research Center.

Li, Q. (2006). Cyberbullying in schools a research of gender differences. *School Psychology International, 27*(2), 157–170. https://doi.org/10.1177/0143034306064547.

Li, Q. (2007). New bottle but old wine: A research of cyberbullying in schools. *Computer in Human Behavior, 23*(4), 1777–1791. https://doi.org/10.1016/j.chb.2005.10.005

Li, Q. (2008). A cross-cultural comparison of adolescents' experience related to cyberbullying. *Educational Research, 50*(3), 223–234. https://doi.org/10.1080/00131880802309333

Li, J., & Craig, W. (2015). *Young Canadians' experiences with electronic bullying.* Retrieved from http://mediasmarts.ca/sites/mediasmarts/files/publication-report/full/young-canadians-electronic- bullying.pdf

Livingstone, S., & Haddon, L. (2009a). EU Kids Online. *Zeitschrift Für Psychologie/Journal of Psychology, 217*(4), 236–239.

Livingstone, S., & Haddon, L. (2009b). *EU Kids Online: Final report 2009.* London: EU Kids Online, London School of Economics and Political Science. Retrieved from http://eprints.lse.ac.uk

Livingstone, S., & Smith, P. K. (2014). Annual research review: Harms experienced by child users of online and mobile technologies: The nature, prevalence and management of sexual and aggressive risks in the digital age. *Journal of Child Psychology and Psycyhiatry, 55*(6), 635–654. https://doi.org/10.1111/jcpp.12197

Livingstone, S., Haddon, L., Gorzig, A., & Ölafsson, K. (2011a). *Risks and safety on the internet: The perspective of European children. Full findings.* London: EU Kids Online.

Livingstone, S., Haddon, L., Görzig, A., & Ólafsson, K. (2011b). *EU Kids Online: Final report.* London: EU Kids online, London School of Economics and Political Science.

Lobe, B., Livingstone, S., Ólafsson, K., & Vodeb, H. (2011). *Cross-national comparison of risks and safety on the internet: Initial analysis from the EU Kids Online survey of European children.* London: EU Kids Online.

Low, S., & Espelage, D. (2013). Differentiating cyber bullying perpetration from non-physical bullying: Commonalities across race, individual, and family predictors. *Psychology of Violence, 3,* 39–52. https://doi.org/10.1037/a0030308

Luengo, M. A., Carrillo-de-la-Peña, M. T., Otero, J. M., & Romero, E. (1994). A short-term longitudinal study of impulsivity and antisocial behavior. *Journal of Personality and Social Psychology, 66*(3), 542–548. https://doi.org/10.1037/0022-3514.66.3.542

Marcum, C. D., Higgins, G. E., & Ricketts, M. L. (2010). Potential factors of online victimization of youth: An examination of adolescent online behavior utilizing routine activity theory. *Deviant Behavior, 31,* 381–410. https://doi.org/10.1080/01639620903004903

Marczak, M., & Coyne, I. (2010). Cyberbullying at school: Good practice and legal aspects in the United Kingdom. *Australian Journal of Guidance & Counselling, 20*(2), 182–193. https://doi.org/10.1375/ajgc.20.2.182

Marczak, M., & Coyne, I. (2015). A focus on online bullying. In A. Attrill (Ed.), *Cyberpsychology* (pp. 145–163). Oxford: Oxford University Press.

Mascheroni, G., & Cuman, A. (2014). *Net Children Go Mobile: Final report* (with country fact sheets). Deliverables D6.4 and D5.2. Milano: Educatt. Retrieved from netchildrengomobile.eu/ncgm/wp-content/uploads/2013/07/NCGM_FinalReport_Country_DEF.pdf

Mascheroni, G., Micheli, M., & Milesi, D. (2014). *Young children (0–8) and digital technology: A qualitative exploratory study – National report – ITALY.* Retrieved from http://centridiricerca.unicatt.it/osscom_2232.html

Mauss, M. (1950/1997). *Sociologie et anthropologie.* Paris: Presses Universitaires de France.

Mayer, J., Nádori, J., & Vígh, S. (2009). *Kis könyv a felelősségről. Adalékok az iskolai agresszió természetrajzához.* Budapest: Mérei Ferenc Pedagógiai és Pályaválasztási Tanácsadó Intézet.

McAra, L., & McVie, S. (2010). Youth crime and justice: Key messages from the Edinburgh study of youth transitions and crime. *Criminology and Criminal Justice, 10*, 179–209.

McClure Watters. (2011). *The nature and extent of pupil bullying in schools in the North of Ireland* (Research report No. 56). Bangor: Department of Education for Northern Ireland.

McGuckin, C., Cummins, P. K., & Lewis, C. A. (2010). f2f and cyberbullying among children in Northern Ireland: Data from the Kids Life and Times survey. *Psychology, Society, & Education, 2*(2), 83–96.

Melioli, T., Sirou, J., Rodgers, R. F., & Chabrol, H. (2015). Étude du profil des personnes victimes d'intimidation réelle et d'intimidation sur Internet. *Neuropsychiatrie de l'Enfance et de l'Adolescence, 63*(1), 30–35. https://doi.org/10.1016/j.neurenf.2014.07.007

Menesini, E., Nocentini, A., & Calussi, P. (2011). The measurement of cyberbullying: Dimensional structure and relative item severity and discrimination. *Cyberpsychology, Behavior, and Social Networking, 14*, 267–274. https://doi.org/10.1089/cyber.2010.0002

Menesini, E., Calussi, P., & Nocentini, A. (2012a). Cyberbullying and traditional bullying. In Q. Li, D. Cross, & P. K. Smith (Eds.), *Cyberbullying in the global playground: Research from international perspectives* (pp. 245–262). Chichester: Wiley-Blackwell.

Menesini, E., Nocentini, A., & Palladino, B. E. (2012b). Empowering students against bullying and cyberbullying: Evaluation of an Italian peer-led model. *International Journal of Conflict and Violence, 6*(2), 313–320. https://doi.org/10.4119/UNIBI/ijcv.253

Menesini, E., Nocentini, A., Palladino, B. E., Frisén, A., Berne, S., Ortega-Ruiz, R., Calmaestra, J., Scheithauer, H., Schultze-Krumbholz, A., Karin, P. L., Naruskov, K., Blaya, C., Berthaud, J., & Smith, P. K. (2012c). Cyberbullying definition among adolescents: A comparison across six European countries. *Cyberpsychology, Behavior, and Social Networking, 15*(9), 455–463. https://doi.org/10.1089/cyber.2012.0040

MENESR-DEPP. (2014). *Note d'information n 39. Direction de l'Evaluation, de la Prospective et de la Performance.* Paris: Ministère de l'Education Nationale.

Mesch, G. S. (2009). Parental mediation, online activities, and cyberbullying. *CyberPsychology & Behavior, 12*(4), 387–393. https://doi.org/10.1089/cpb.2009.0068

Mishna, F. (2012). *Bullying: A guide to research, intervention, and prevention.* Cary: Oxford University Press.

Mishna, F., Cook, C., Saini, M., Wu, M., & MacFadden, R. (2009a). Interventions for children, youth, and parents to prevent and reduce cyber abuse. *Campbell Systematic Reviews, 2009*, 2.

Mishna, F., Saini, M., & Solomon, S. (2009b). Ongoing and online: Children and youth's perceptions of cyberbullying. *Children and Youth Services Review, 31*, 1222–1228. https://doi.org/10.1016/j.childyouth.2009.05.004

Mishna, F., Cook, C., Gadalla, T., Daciuk, J., & Solomon, S. (2010). Cyber bullying behaviors among middle and high school students. *American Journal of Orthopsychiatry, 80*(3), 362–374. https://doi.org/10.1111/j.1939-0025. 2010.01040.x

Mishna, F., Khoury-Kassabri, M., Gadalla, T., & Daciuk, J. (2012). Risk factors for involvement in cyberbullying: Victims, bullies and bully-victims. *Children &Youth Services Review, 34*(1), 63–70. https://doi.org/10.1016/j. childyouth.2011.08.032

Modecki, K. L., Barber, B. L., & Vernon, L. (2013). Mapping developmental precursors of cyber-aggression: Trajectories of risk predict perpetration and victimization. *Journal of Youth and Adolescence, 42*(5), 651–661. https://doi. org/10.1007/s10964-013-9938-0

Modecki, K. L., Minchin, J., Harbaugh, A. G., Guerra, N. G., & Runions, K. C. (2014). Bullying prevalence across contexts: A meta-analysis measuring cyber and traditional bullying. *Journal of Adolescent Health, 55*(5), 602–611. https://doi.org/10.1016/j.jadohealth.2014.06.007

Monks, C. P., Robinson, S., & Worlidge, P. (2012). The emergence of cyberbullying: A survey of primary school pupils' perceptions and experiences. *School Psychology International, 33*(5), 477–491. https://doi.org/10.1177/ 0143034312445242

Mura, G., Topcu, C., Erdur-Baker, O., & Diamantini, D. (2011). An international study of cyber bullying perception and diffusion among adolescents. *Procedia-Social and Behavioral Sciences, 15*, 3805–3809. https://doi. org/10.1016/j.sbspro.2011.04.377

Myers, C., & Cowie, H. (2016). How can we prevent and reduce bullying amongst university students? *International Journal of Emotional Education, 8*(1), 109–119.

Nansel, T. R., Overpeck, M., Pilla, R. S., Ruan, W. J., Simons-Morton, B., & Scheidt, P. (2001). Bullying behaviors among US youth: Prevalence and association with psychosocial adjustment. *JAMA, 285*(16), 2094–2100. https:// doi.org/10.1001/jama.285.16.2094

National Children's Home. (2005). *Putting U in the picture: Mobile bullying survey*. Retrieved from http://www.nch.org.uk/uploads/documents/Mobile% 20bullying%20report.pdf

National Society for the Prevention of Cruelty to Children. (2015). *What children are telling us about bullying: Childline bullying report 2015/16*. London: Author.

Navarro, J. N., & Jasinski, J. L. (2011). Going cyber: Using routine activities theory to predict cyberbullying experiences. *Sociological Spectrum, 32*, 81–94. https://doi.org/10.1080/02732173.2012.628560

Navarro, J. N., & Jasinski, J. L. (2013). Why girls? Using routine activities theory to predict cyberbullying experiences between girls and boys. *Women and Criminal Justice, 23*(4), 286–303. https://doi.org/10.1080/08974454.2013.784225

Noret, N., & Rivers, I. (2006, April). *The prevalence of bullying by text message or email: Results of a four year study*. Poster Presented at the Annual Conference of the British Psychological Society, Cardiff.

Notar, C. E., Padgett, S., & Roden, J. (2013a). Cyberbullying: A review of the literature. *Universal Journal of Educational Research, 1*(1), 1–9. https://doi.org/10.13189/ujer.2013.010101

Notar, C. E., Padgett, S., & Roden, J. (2013b). Cyberbullying: Resources for intervention and prevention. *Universal Journal of Educational Research, 1*(3), 133–145.

Nuccitelli, M. (2012). Cyber bullying tactics. *Forensic Examiner, 21*(3), 24–27.

O'Higgins Norman, J., O'Moore, M., & McGuire, L. (2016). *Cyberbullying in Ireland: A survey of parents internet usage and knowledge*. Dublin: ABC, National Anti-bullying research and resource centre.

O'Moore, M. (2012). Cyber-bullying: The situation in Ireland. *Pastoral Care in Education, 30*(3), 209–223. https://doi.org/10.1080/02643944.2012.688065

O'Neill, B., & Dinh, T. (2015). Mobile technologies and the incidence of cyberbullying in seven European countries: Findings from Net Children Go Mobile. *Societies, 5*, 384–398. https://doi.org/10.3390/soc5020384

Observatory for School Violence, Ministry of Education and Culture, Republic of Cyprus. (2012). *A Survey of school violence*. Unpublished, in Greek. Retreived from http://www.moec.gov.cy/paratiritirio_via/

Oliver, C., & Candappa, M. (2003). *Tackling bullying: Listening to the views of children and young people* (Research Report RR400). London: Department for Education and Skills.

Olweus, D. (1993). *Bullying at School: What We Know and What We Can Do*. Cambridge, MA: Blackwell Publishers.

Olweus, D. (1995). Bullying or peer abuse at school: Facts and intervention. *Current Directions in Psychological Science, 4*(6), 196–200. https://doi.org/10.1111/1467-8721.ep10772640

Olweus, D. (1996). *The revised bully/victim questionnaire for students.* Bergen: University of Bergen.

Olweus, D. (2012). Cyberbullying: An overrated phenomenon? *European Journal of Developmental Psychology, 9,* 520–538. https://doi.org/10.1080/17 405629.2012.682358

Olweus, D., & Limber, S. P. (2010). Bullying in school: Evaluation and dissemination of the Olweus Bullying Prevention Program. *American Journal of Orthopsychiatry, 80*(1), 124–134. https://doi.org/10.1111/j.1939-0025.2010. 01015.x

Ombudsman-UNICEF. (2007). *Violencia escolar: el maltrato entre iguales en la educación secundaría obligatoria. 1999–2006.* Madrid: Publicaciones de la Oficina del Defensor del Pueblo.

Ortega, R., Elipe, P., Mora-Merchan, J. A., Calmaestra, J., & Vega, E. (2009). The emotional impact on victims of traditional bullying and cyberbullying. A study of Spanish adolescents. *Journal of Psychology, 217,* 197–204. https://doi.org/10.1027/0044-3409.217.4.197

Ortega, R., Elipe, P., Mora-Merchán, J. A., Genta, M. L., Brighi, A., Guarini, A., Smith, P. K., Thompson, F., & Tippett, N. (2012). The emotional impact of bullying and cyberbullying on victims: A European cross-national study. *Aggressive Behavior, 38*(5), 342–356. https://doi.org/10.1002/ab.21440

Ortega-Ruiz, R., & Nùnez, J. C. (2012). Bullying and cyberbullying: Research and intervention at school and social contexts. *Psicothema, 24*(4), 603–607.

Ortega-Ruiz, R., Calmaestra, J., & Mora-Merchán, J. A. (2008). Cyberbullying. *International Journal of Psychology and Psychological Therapy, 8*(2), 183–192.

Ortega-Ruiz, R., Del Rey, R., & Casas, J. A. (2012). Knowing, building and living together on internet and social networks: The ConRed cyberbullying prevention program. *International Journal of Conflict and Violence, 6*(2), 302–312. https://doi.org/10.4119/UNIBI/ijcv.250

Paez, G. R. (2016). Cyberbullying among adolescents: A general strain theory perspective. *Journal of School Violence,* 1–12. https://doi.org/10.1080/15388 220.2016.1220317.

Paksi, B. (2010). Az iskolai agresszió előfordulása. intézményi percepciója. *Új Pedagógiai Szemle* (1–2), 119–134.

Palermiti, A. L., Servidio, R., Bartolo, M. G., & Costabile, A. (2017). Cyberbullying and self-esteem: An Italian study. *Computers in Human Behavior, 69,* 136–141. https://doi.org/10.1016/j.chb.2016.12.026

Palladino, B. E., Nocentini, A., & Menesini, E. (2016). Evidence-based intervention against bullying and cyberbullying: Evaluation of the NoTrap! program in two independent trials. *Aggressive Behavior, 42*(2), 194–206. https://doi.org/10.1002/ab.21636

Parti, K. (2016). A megfélemlítés (bullying) szabályozása Magyarországon és külföldön. *Medias Res, 1*, 114–146.

Patchin, J. W., & Hinduja, S. (2010a). Cyberbullying and self-esteem. *Journal of School Health, 80*(12), 614–624. https://doi.org/10.1111/j.1746-1561.2010.00548.x

Patchin, J. W., & Hinduja, S. (2010b). Traditional and non-traditional bullying among youth: A test of general strain theory. *Youth and Society, 41*, 727–751. https://doi.org/10.1177/0044118X10366951

Patchin, J. W., & Hinduja, S. (2012). *Cyberbullying prevention and response: Expert perspectives.* London: Routledge.

Patchin, J. W., & Hinduja, S. (2015). Measuring cyberbullying: Implications for research. *Aggression and Violent Behavior, 23*, 69–74. https://doi. org/10.1016/j.avb.2015.05.013

Paul, S., Smith, P. K., & Blumberg, H. H. (2010). Addressing cyberbullying in school using the quality circle approach. *Australian Journal of Guidance and Counselling, 20*(2), 157–168. https://doi.org/10.1375/ajgc.20.2.157

Paul, S., Smith, P. K., & Blumberg, H. H. (2012). Revisiting cyberbullying in schools using the quality circle approach. *School Psychology International, 33*(5), 492–504. https://doi.org/10.1177/0143034312445243

Payne, A. A., & Hutzell, K. L. (2017). Old wine, new bottle? Comparing interpersonal bullying and cyberbullying victimization. *Youth & Society, 49*(8), 1149–1178. https://doi.org/10.1177/0044118X15617401

Pearce, N., Cross, D., Monks, H., Waters, S., & Falconer, S. (2011). Current evidence of best practice in whole-school bullying intervention and its potential to inform cyberbullying interventions. *Australian Journal of Guidance and Counselling, 21*(01), 1–21. https://doi.org/10.1375/ajgc.21.1.1

Peluchette, J. V., Karl, K., Wood, C., & Williams, J. (2015). Cyberbullying victimization: Do victims' personality and risky social network behaviors contribute to the problem? *Computers in Human Behavior, 52*, 424–435. https://doi.org/10.1016/j.chb.2015.06.028

Pepler, D. J. (2006). Bullying interventions: A binocular perspective. *Journal of the Canadian Academy of Child and Adolescent Psychiatry, 15*(1), 16–20.

Pergolizzi, F., Pergolizzi, J., Gan, Z., Macario, S., Pergolizzi, J. V., Ewin, T. J., & Gan, T. J. (2011). Bullying in middle school: Results from a 2008 survey. *International Journal of Adolescent Medicine and Health, 23*(1), 11–84. https:// doi.org/10.1515/ijamh.2011.003

Perreault, S. (2011). *Self-reported Internet victimization in Canada, 2009* (Statistics Canada catalogue No. 85-002-X). Retrieved from http://www.statcan.gc.ca/pub/85-002x/2011001/article/11530-eng.htm

Perren, S., & Gutzwiller-Helfenfinger, E. (2012). Cyberbullying and traditional bullying in adolescence: Differential roles of moral disengagement, moral emotions, and moral values. *European Journal of Developmental Psychology, 9*, 195–209. https://doi.org/10.1080/17405629.2011.643168

Piers, E. V., Harris, D. B., & Herzberg, D. S. (2002). *Piers-Harris children's self concept scale* (Rev. ed.). Los Angeles: Western Psychological Services.

Pornari, C. D., & Wood, J. (2010). Peer and cyber aggression in secondary school students: The role of moral disengagement, hostile attribution bias, and outcome expectancies. *Aggressive Behavior, 36*, 81–94. https://doi.org/10.1002/ab.20336

PREVNet. (2015). *For Parents*. Retrieved from http://www.prevnet.ca/resources/policy-and-legislation/ontario/for-parents

Price, M., & Dalgleish, J. (2010). Cyberbullying experiences, impacts and coping strategies as described by Australian young people. *Youth Studies Australia, 29*(2), 51–59.

Purdy, N., & McGuckin, C. (2015). Cyberbullying, schools and the law: A comparative study in Northern Ireland and the Republic of Ireland. *Educational Research, 57*(4), 420–436. https://doi.org/10.1080/00131881.2015.1091203

Purdy, N., & Smith, P. K. (2016). A content analysis of school anti-bullying policies in Northern Ireland. *Educational Psychology in Practice, 32*(3), 281–295. https://doi.org/10.1080/02667363.2016.1161599

Purdy, N., & York, L. (2016). A critical investigation of the nature and extent of cyberbullying in two post-primary schools in Northern Ireland. *Pastoral Care in Education, 34*(1), 13–23. https://doi.org/10.1080/02643944.2015.1127989

Raskauskas, J. (2010). Multiple peer victimization among elementary school students: Relations with social-emotional problems. *Social Psychology of Education, 13*(4), 523–539. https://doi.org/10.1007/s11218-010-9124-0

Raskauskas, J., & Stoltz, A. D. (2007). Involvement in traditional and electronic bullying among adolescents. *Developmental Psychology, 43*(3), 564. https://doi.org/10.1037/0012-1649.43.3.564

Rémond, J. J., Kern, L., & Romo, L. (2015). Etude sur la «cyber-intimidation»: Cyberbullying, comorbidités et mécanismes d'adaptations. *L'Encéphale, 41*(4), 287–294. https://doi.org/10.1016/j.encep.2014.08.003

Renati, R., Berrone, C., & Zanetti, M. A. (2012). Morally disengaged and unempathic: Do cyberbullies fit these definitions? An exploratory study. *Cyberpsychology, Behavior, and Social Networking, 15*(8), 391–398. https://doi.org/10.1089/cyber.2012.0046

Richardson, D. R., Hammock, G. S., Smith, S. M., Gardner, W., & Signo, M. (1994). Empathy as a cognitive inhibitor of interpersonal aggression. *Aggressive Behavior, 20*(4), 275–289. https://doi.org/10.1002/1098-2337(1994)20:4<275::AID-AB2480200402>3.0.CO;2-4

Rivers, I., & Noret, N. (2010). 'I h8 u': Findings from a five-year study of text and email bullying. *British Educational Research Journal, 36*(4), 643–671. https://doi.org/10.1080/01411920903071918

Roberto, A. J., Eden, J., Savage, M. W., Ramos-Salazar, L., & Deiss, D. M. (2014). Outcome evaluation results of school-based cybersafety promotion and cyberbullying prevention intervention for middle school students. *Health Communication, 29*(10), 1029–1042. https://doi.org/10.1080/10410236.2013.831684

Rueckert, L., & Naybar, N. (2008). Gender differences in empathy: The role of the right hemisphere. *Brain and Cognition, 67*(2), 162–167. https://doi.org/10.1016/j.bandc.2008.01.002

Sabella, R. A., Patchin, J. W., & Hinduja, S. (2013). Cyberbullying myths and realities. *Computers in Human Behavior, 29*(6), 2703–2711. https://doi.org/10.1016/j.chb.2013.06.040

Ságvári, B., & Galácz, A. (2011). *EU Kids Online II. Hungarian report*. Available online at the webpage of the EU Kids Online project. Retrieved from http://www.lse.ac.uk/media@lse/research/EUKidsOnline/EU%20Kids%20II%20(2009-11)/National%20reports/ Hungarian%20report.pdf

Salvatore, A. J. (2006). *An anti-bullying strategy: Action research in a 5/6 intermediate school*. Hartford: University of Hartford.

Salvatore, A. J., & Weinholz, D. (2006). *An anti-bullying strategy: Action research in a 5/6 intermediate School* (Dissertation for the degree of Doctor of Education). West Hartford: University of Hartford.

Sampasa-Kanyinga, H., & Hamilton, H. A. (2015). Use of social networking sites and risk of cyberbullying victimization: A population-level study of adolescents. *Cyberpsychology, Behavior, and Social Networking, 18*(12), 704–710. https://doi.org/10.1089/cyber.2015.0145

Sastre, A., Calmaestra, J., Escorial, A., García, P., Del Moral, C., Perazzo, C., & Ubrich, T. (2016). *Yo a eso no juego: Bullying y Cyberbullying en la infancia*. Madrid: Save The Children.

Schneider, S. K., O'Donnell, L., Stueve, A., & Coulter, R. W. S. (2012). Cyberbullying, school bullying, and psychological distress: A regional census of high school students. *American Journal of Public Health, 102*, 171–177. https://doi.org/10.2105/AJPH.2011.300308

Schultze-Krumbholz, A., Göbel, K., Scheithauer, H., Brighi, A., Guarini, A., Tsorbatzoudis, H., Barkoukis, V., Pyżalski, J., Plichta, P., Del Rey, R., Casas, J. A., Thompson, F., & Smith, P. K. (2015). A comparison of classification approaches for cyberbullying and traditional bullying using data from six European countries. *Journal of School Violence, 14*(1), 47–65. https://doi.org /10.1080/15388220.2014.961067

Schumann, L., Craig, W., & Rosu, A. (2014). Power differentials in bullying: Individuals in a community context. *Journal of Interpersonal Violence, 29*(5), 846–865. https://doi.org/10.1177/0886260513505708

Selkie, E. M., Fales, J. L., & Moreno, M. A. (2016). Cyberbullying prevalence among US middle and high school–aged adolescents: A systematic review and quality assessment. *Journal of Adolescent Health, 58*(2), 125–133. https:// doi.org/10.1016/j.jadohealth.2015.09.026

Shariff, S. (2008). *Cyber-bullying: Issues and solutions for the school, the classroom and the home.* New York: Routledge.

Shiakou, M., & Pikkis, L. (in press). *Assessing the role of drama on children's understanding of bullying.*

Shiakou, M., Hatzimicheal, S., Klitou, Ch., & Yerolemou, G. (in press). *Understanding bullying through the eyes of children.*

Simon, D., Zerinváry, B., & Velkey, G. (2012). *Az iskolai bántalmazás megjelenése az 5–8 évfolyamos diákok körében: jelenségek és magyarázatok a normál és az alternatív tantervű iskolákban.* Budapest: Oktatáskutató és Fejlesztő Intézet.

Slonje, R., & Smith, P. K. (2008). Cyberbullying: Another main type of bullying? *Scandinavian Journal of Psychology, 49*, 147–154. https://doi. org/10.1111/j.1467-9450.2007.00611.x

Slonje, R., Smith, P. K., & Frisén, A. (2013). The nature of cyberbullying, and strategies for prevention. *Computers in Human Behavior, 29*(1), 26–32. https://doi.org/10.1016/j.chb.2012.05.024

Smahel, D., & Wright, M. F. (Eds.). (2014). *Meaning of online problematic situations for children. Results of qualitative cross-cultural investigation in nine European countries.* London: EU Kids Online, London School of Economics and Political Science.

Smith, P. K., & Berkkun, F. (2017). How research on cyberbullying has developed. In C. McGuckin & L. Corcoran (Eds.), *Bullying and cyberbullying: Prevalence, psychological impacts and intervention strategies* (pp. 11–27). Hauppauge: Nova Science.

Smith, P. K., Mahdavi, J., Carvalho, M., & Tippett, N. (2006). *An investigation into cyber-bullying, its forms, awareness, and impact, and the relationship between age and gender in cyber-bullying* (Research Brief No. RBX03-06). London: Department for Education and Skills.

Smith, P. K., Mahdavi, J., Carvalho, M., Fisher, S., Russell, S., & Tippett, N. (2008). Cyberbullying: Its nature and impact in secondary school pupils. *Journal of Child Psychology and Psychiatry, 49*, 376–385. https://doi. org/10.1111/j.1469-7610.2007.01846.x

Smith, P. K., del Barrio, C., & Tokunaga, R. S. (2013). Definitions of bullying and cyberbullying: How useful are the terms? In S. Bauman, D. Cross, & J. Walker (Eds.), *Principles of cyberbullying research: Definitions, measures and methodology* (pp. 26–40). New York: Routledge.

Smith, P. K., Kwak, K., & Toda, Y. (Eds.). (2016). *School bullying in different cultures: Eastern and western perspectives.* Cambridge: Cambridge University Press.

Smith, P. K., Sundaram, S., Spears, B., Blaya, C., Schafer, M., & Sandhu, D. (Eds.). (2018). *Bullying, cyberbullying and pupil well-being in schools: Comparing European, Australian and Indian perspectives.* Cambridge: Cambridge University Press.

Smokowski, P. R., Evans, C. B. R., & Cotter, K. L. (2014). The differential impacts of episodic, chronic, and cumulative physical bullying and cyberbullying: The effects of victimization on the school experiences, social support, and mental health of rural adolescents. *Violence and Victims, 29*, 1029–1046. https://doi.org/10.1891/0886-6708.VV-D-13-00076

Snakenborg, J., Van Acker, R., & Gable, R. A. (2011). Cyberbullying: Prevention and intervention to protect our children and youth. *Preventing School Failure: Alternative Education for Children and Youth, 55*(2), 88–95. https://doi.org/1 0.1080/1045988X.2011.539454

Sourander, A., Klomek, A. B., Ikonen, M., Lindroos, J., Luntamo, T., Koskelainen, M., .Ristkari, T., & Helenius, H. (2010). Psychosocial risk factors associated with cyberbullying among adolescents: A population-based study. *Archives of General Psychiatry, 67*(7), 720–728. doi:https://doi.org/10.1001/archgenpsychiatry.2010.79.

Spears, B., Campbell, M., Tangen, D., Slee, P., & Cross, D. (2015). La connaissance et la compréhension des conséquences du cyberharcèlement sur le climatscolaire chez les futurs enseignants en Australie. *Les Dossiers des Sciences de l'Education, 33*, 109–130.

Srabstein, J. C., Berkman, B. E., & Pyntikova, E. (2008). Antibullying legislation: A public health perspective. *Journal of Adolescent Health, 42*(1), 11–20. https://doi.org/10.1016/j.jadohealth.2007.10.007

Steffgen, G., & König, A. (2009). Cyber bullying: The role of traditional bullying and empathy. In B. Sapio, L. Haddon, E. Mante-Meijer, L. Fortunati, T. Turk, & E. Loos (Eds.), *The good, the bad and the challenging. Conference proceedings* (Vol. II, pp. 1041–1047). Brussels: Cost Office.

Steffgen, G., König, A., Pfetsch, J., & Melzer, A. (2011). Are cyberbullies less empathic? Adolescents' cyberbullying behavior and empathic responsiveness. *Cyberpsychology, Behavior, and Social Networking, 14*(11), 643–648. https://doi.org/10.1089/cyber.2010.0445

Sticca, F., Ruggieri, S., Alsaker, F., & Perren, S. (2013). Longitudinal risk factors for cyberbullying in adolescence. *Journal of Community and Applied Social Psychology, 23*(1), 52–67. https://doi.org/10.1002/casp.2136

Subrahmanyam, K., & Greenfield, P. (2008). Online communication and adolescent relationships. *The Future of Children, 18*(1), 119–146. https://doi.org/10.1353/foc.0.0006

Sygkollitou, E., Psalti, A., & Kapatzia, A. (2010). Cyberbullying among Greek adolescents. In J. A. Mora-Merchán & T. Jager (Eds.), *Cyberbullying – A cross-national comparison* (pp. 101–113). Landau: Verlag Empirische Padagogik.

The Guardian. (2016, October 5). Mother of teenager who killed himself appeals for kindness online. Retrieved from https://www.theguardian.com/society/2016/oct/05/felix-alexander-mother-lucy-open-letter-worcester

The Public Schools Act, Revised Statutes of Canada. (2015, C.C.S.M c.P250). Retrieved from the Manitoba Law website: http://web2.gov.mb.ca/laws/statutes/ccsm/_pdf.php?cap=p250

Thompson, F., & Smith, P. K. (2012). Anti-bullying strategies in schools: What is done and what works. *British Journal of Educational Psychology, Monograph Series, 11*(9), 154–173.

Thorton, T. N., Craft, C. A., Dahlberg, L. L., Lynch, B. S., & Baer, K. (2000). *Best practices of youth violence prevention: A sourcebook for community action.* Atlanta: Centers for Disease Control and Prevention.

Tokunaga, R. S. (2010). Following you home from school: A critical review and synthesis of research on cyberbullying victimization. *Computers in Human Behavior, 26*(3), 277–287. https://doi.org/10.1016/j.chb.2009.11.014

Topcu, C., & Erdur-Baker, O. (2010). The Revised Cyberbullying Inventory (RCBI): Validity and reliability studies. *Procedia: Social and Behavioral Sciences, 5*, 660–664. https://doi.org/10.1016/j.sbspro.2010.07.161

Topcu, Ç., & Erdur-Baker, Ö. (2012). Affective and cognitive empathy as mediators of gender differences in cyber and traditional bullying. *School Psychology International, 33*(5), 550–561. https://doi.org/10.1177/0143034312446882

Torney-Purta, J. (2002). The school's role in developing civic engagement: A study of adolescents in twenty-eight countries. *Applied Developmental Science, 6*, 203–212. https://doi.org/10.1207/S1532480XADS0604_7

Torres, F. C., & Vivas, G. M. (2016). Cyberbullying and education: A review of emergent issues in Latin America research. In R. Navarro, S. Yubero, & E. Larranaga (Eds.), *Cyberbullying across the globe* (pp. 131–147). Switzerland: Springer International Publishing.

Touloupis, T., & Athanasiades, C. (2014). The risky use of new technology among elementary school students: Internet addiction and cyberbullying [in Greek]. *Hellenic Journal of Psychology, 11*, 83–110.

Tsitsika, A., Janikian, M., Wójcik, S., Makaruk, K., Tzavela, E., Tzavara, C., Greydanus, D., Merrick, J., & Richardson, C. (2015). Cyberbullying victimization prevalence and associations with internalizing and externalizing problems among adolescents in six European countries. *Computers in Human Behavior, 51*, 1–7. https://doi.org/10.1016/j.chb.2015.04.048

Twyman, K., Saylor, C., Taylor, L. A., & Comeaux, C. (2010). Comparing children and adolescents engaged in cyberbullying to matched peers. *Cyberpsychology, Behavior, and Social Networking, 13*(2), 195–199. https://doi.org/10.1089/cyber.2009.0137

Vaillancourt, T., Trinh, V., McDougall, P., Duku, E., Cunningham, L., Cunningham, C., Hymel, S., & Short, K. (2010). Optimizing population screening of bullying in school-aged children. *Journal of School Violence, 9*(3), 233–250. https://doi.org/10.1080/15388220.2010.483182

Van Cleemput, K., Vandebosch, H., & Pabian, S. (2014). Personal characteristics and contextual factors that determine "helping", "joining in" and "doing nothing" when witnessing cyberbullying. *Aggressive Behavior, 40*(5), 383–396. https://doi.org/10.1002/ab.21534

Van Geel, M., Vedder, P., & Tanilon, J. (2014). Relationship between peer victimization, cyberbullying, and suicide in children and adolescents: A meta-analysis. *JAMA Pediatrics, 168*(5), 435–442. https://doi.org/10.1001/jamapediatrics.2013.4143

Vance, J. W. (2010). *Cyber-harassment in higher education: Online learning environments* (Doctoral dissertation). University of Southern California. Retrieved from http://digitallibrary.usc.edu/cdm/compoundobject/collection/p15799 coll127/id/309077/rec/19

Vandebosch, H., & Van Cleemput, K. (2008). Defining cyberbullying: A qualitative research into the perceptions of youngsters. *Cyberpsychology and Behavior, 11*(4), 1349–1371. https://doi.org/10.1177/1461444809341263

Vandebosch, H., & Van Cleemput, K. (2009). Cyberbullying among youngsters: Profiles of bullies and victims. *New Media & Society, 11*(8), 1349–1371. https://doi.org/10.1177/1461444809341263

Várnai, D., & Zsíros, E. (2014). Kortársbántalmazás és verekedés. In Á. Németh & A. Költő (Eds.), *Egészség és egészségmagatartás iskoláskorban.* Budapest: Health Behaviour in School-Aged Children (HBSC): A WHO-collaborative Cross National Study. National Report 2014.

Veenstra, R., Lindenberg, S., Huitsing, G., Sainio, M., & Salmivalli, C. (2014). The role of teachers in bullying: The relation between antibullying attitudes, efficacy, and efforts to reduce bullying. *Journal of Educational Psychology, 106*(4), 1135–1143. https://doi.org/10.1037/a0036110

Vieno, A., Gini, G., Lenzi, M., Pozzoli, T., Canale, N., & Santinello, M. (2015). Cybervictimization and somatic and psychological symptoms among Italian middle school students. *The European Journal of Public Health, 25*(3), 433–437. https://doi.org/10.1093/eurpub/cku191

Virág, G., & Parti, K. (2011). Sweet child in time: Online sexual abuse of children–A research exploration. *The Open Criminology Journal, 4*(1), 71–90. https://doi.org/10.2174/1874917801104010071

Waasdorp, T. E., Pas, E. T., Zablotsky, B., & Bradshaw, C. P. (2017). Ten-year trends in bullying and related attitudes among 4th- to 12th-graders. *Pediatrics, 139*, e20162615.

Wachs, S. (2012). Moral disengagement and emotional and social difficulties in bullying and cyberbullying: Differences by participant role. *Emotional and Behavioural Difficulties, 17*(3–4), 347–360. https://doi.org/10.1080/136327 52.2012.704318

Wade, A., & Beran, T. (2011). Cyberbullying: The new era of bullying. *Canadian Journal of School Psychology, 26,* 44–61. https://doi.org/10.1177/08295 73510396318

Walrave, M., & Heirman, W. (2011). Cyberbullying: Predicting victimisation and perpetration. *Children & Society, 25*(1), 59–72. https://doi. org/10.1111/j.1099-0860.2009.00260.x

Wang, J., Iannotti, R. J., & Nansel, T. R. (2009). School bullying among adolescents in the United States: Physical, verbal, relational, and cyber. *Journal of Adolescent Health, 45*(4), 368–375. https://doi.org/10.1016/j.jadohealth.2009. 03.021

Wang, W., Vaillancourt, T., Brittain, H. L., McDougall, P., Krygsman, A., Smith, D., Cunningham, C. E., Haltigan, J. D., & Hymel, S. (2014). School climate, peer victimization, and academic achievement: Results from a multi-informant study. *School Psychology Quarterly, 29*(3), 360–377. https://doi. org/10.1037/spq0000084

West, D. (2015). An investigation into the prevalence of cyberbullying among students aged 16–19 in post-compulsory education. *Research in Post-Compulsory Education, 20*(1), 96–112. https://doi.org/10.1080/13596748.2015.993879

Wikstrom, P. O. H. (2009). Routine activity theories. *Oxford Bibliographies.* https://doi.org/10.1093/OBO/9780195396607-0010

Willard, N. E. (2006). *Cyberbullying and Cyberthreats: Responding to the challenge of online social cruelty, threats, and distress.* Centre for Safe and Responsible Internet Use. Available at: https://www.internetsafetyproject.org/wiki/center-safe-and-responsible-internet-use

Willard, N. E. (2007). *Cyberbullying and cyberthreats: Responding to the challenge of online social aggression, threats, and distress.* Champaign: Research Press.

Willard, N. (2011). School response to cyberbullying and sexting: The legal challenge. *Brigham Young University Education & Law Journal, 1*, 75–125.

Williams, K. R., & Guerra, N. G. (2007). Prevalence and predictors of internet bullying. *Journal of Adolescent Health, 41*(6), S14–S21. https://doi.org/10.1016/j.jadohealth.2007.08.018

Williford, A., Elledge, L. C., Boulton, A. J., DePaolis, K. J., Little, T. D., & Salmivalli, C. (2013). Effects of the KiVa antibullying program on cyberbullying and cybervictimization frequency among Finnish youth. *Journal of Clinical Child and Adolescent Psychology, 42*(6), 820–833. https://doi.org/10.1080/15374416.2013.787623

Wilson, E. (2007). As bullies go high-tech, lawmakers say schools should be fighting back. *The Seattle Times.* Retrieved from http://www.seattletimes.com/seattle-news/as-bullies-go-high-tech-lawmakers-say-schools-should-be-fighting-back/

Winkel, F. W., & Baldry, A. C. (1997). An application of the Scared Straight principle in early intervention programming: Three studies on activating the other's perspective in pre-adolescents' perceptions of a stepping-stone behaviour. *Issues in Criminological and Legal Psychology, 26*, 3–15.

Wolke, D., Woods, S., Bloomfield, L., & Karstadt, L. (2000). The association between direct and relational bullying and behaviour problems among primary school children. *Journal of Child Psychology and Psychiatry, 41*(8), 989–1002. https://doi.org/10.1111/1469-7610.00687

Wolke, D., Lee, K., & Guy, A. (2017). Cyberbullying: A storm in a teacup? *European Child and Adolescent Psychiatry, 26*, 899–908. https://doi.org/10.1007/s00787-017-0954-6

Wong-Lo, M. (2009). *Cyberbullying: Responses of adolescents and parents toward digital aggression* (Unpublished Doctoral Dissertation). University of North Texas.

Wright, M. F. (2015). Cyber victimization and adjustment difficulties: The mediation of Chinese and American adolescents' digital technology usage. *Cyberpsychology: Journal of Psychosocial Research on Cyberspace, 9*(1), article 7. https://doi.org/10.5817/CP2015-1-7.

Wright, M. F., & Li, Y. (2013). The association between cyber victimization and subsequent cyber aggression: The moderating effect of peer rejection. *Journal of Youth and Adolescence, 42*(5), 662–674. https://doi.org/10.1007/s10964-012-9903-3

Wright, M. F., Aoyama, I., Kamble, S. V., Li, Z., Soudi, S., Lei, L., & Shu, C. (2015). Peer attachment and cyber aggression involvement among Chinese, Indian, and Japanese adolescents. *Societies, 5*(2), 339–353. https://doi.org/10.3390/soc5020339

Ybarra, M. L., & Mitchell, K. J. (2004). Youth engaging in online harassment: Associations with caregiver-child relationships, Internet use, and personal characteristics. *Journal of Adolescence, 27*, 319–336. https://doi.org/10.1016/j.adolescence.2004.03.007

Ybarra, M. L., Espelage, D. L., & Mitchell, K. J. (2007). The co-occurrence of Internet harassment and unwanted sexual solicitation victimization and perpetration: Associations with psychosocial indicators. *Journal of Adolescent Health, 41*(6), S31–S41. https://doi.org/10.1016/j.jadohealth.2007.09.010

YouGov Plc & Vodafone Plc. (2015). *Cyberbullying-merged unweighted.* Retrieved from https://www.vodafone.com/content/dam/vodafone/parents/assets_2015/pdf/vodafone_%20cyberbullying_survey_results.pdf

Zhang, A., Musu-Gillette, L., & Oudekerk, B. A. (2016). *Indicators of school crime and safety: 2015* (NCES 2016-079/NCJ 249758). Washington, DC: National Center for Education Statistics, U.S. Department of Education, and Bureau of Justice Statistics, U.S. Department of Justice.

Zhou, Z., Tang, H., Tian, Y., Wei, H., Zhang, F., & Morrison, C. M. (2013). Cyberbullying and its risk factors among Chinese high school students. *School Psychology International, 34*(6), 630–647. https://doi.org/10.1177/0143034313479692

Zych, I., Ortega-Ruiz, R., & del Rey, R. (2015). Scientific research on bullying and cyberbullying: Where have we been and where are we going. *Aggression and Violent Behavior, 23*, 1–21.

Zych, I., Ortega-Ruiz, R., & Marín-López, I. (2016). Cyberbullying: A systematic review of research, its prevalence and assessment issues in Spanish studies. *Psicología Educativa, 22*(1), 5–18. https://doi.org/10.1016/j.pse.2016.03.002

Index

© The Author(s) 2018
A. C. Baldry et al. (eds.), *International Perspectives on Cyberbullying*, Palgrave Studies in
Cybercrime and Cybersecurity, https://doi.org/10.1007/978-3-319-73263-3